Classification Algorithms

Classification Algorithms

Mike James

COLLINS
8 Grafton Street, London W1

Collins Professional and Technical Books
William Collins Sons & Co. Ltd
8 Grafton Street, London W1X 3LA

First published in Great Britain by
Collins Professional and Technical Books 1985

Copyright © Mike James 1985

British Library Cataloguing in Publication Data
James, M.
　Classification algorithms.
　1. Classification
　I. Title
　001'.012　　Z696

ISBN 0-00-383054-3

Typeset by V & M Graphics Ltd, Aylesbury, Bucks
Printed and bound in Great Britain by
Mackays of Chatham, Kent

All rights reserved. No part of this publication may
be reproduced, stored in a retrieval system or transmitted,
in any form, or by any means, electronic, mechanical, photocopying,
recording or otherwise, without the prior permission of the
publishers.

Contents

Preface		ix
Notation		xi
1	**Classification**	1
	The range of classification	1
	Discriminant analysis	2
	What classification is not!	3
	Prerequisites	5
	References	6
2	**Classification Rules**	7
	Criterion of classification	7
	Probabilities — some notation	8
	Bayes' rule	9
	A practical rule	11
	Divisions of the sample space — simplicity	12
	Using the Bayes' rule	13
3	**Practical Classification – the Normal Case**	15
	The multivariate normal	15
	The normal form of Bayes' rule	20
	Interpreting the normal Bayes' rule	22
	An example	23
	Equal covariances	25
	Linear discrimination	26
	An example of linear discrimination	27
	The two group case	28
	Summary and discussion	29

4	**Classification in Action**	**30**
	A data entry program	30
	A linear discriminant program	33
	A quadratic discriminant program	43
	A classic data set – Fisher's iris data	52
	References	55
5	**Some Practical Considerations**	**56**
	Some statistical results on the linear discriminant	56
	The bias of the plug in estimator	58
	Linear and quadratic discriminant functions for other distributions	61
	Other criteria of classification	63
	Alternatives to the plug in estimate of a classifier	67
	Probabilities of classification	68
	The reject option	70
	Missing values	72
	References	73
6	**Evaluating Rules – Estimating Error Rates**	**74**
	Statistical estimation of error rates	74
	Theoretical estimates of error	80
	The use of theoretical measures	81
	Confusion matrices	82
	Extending the linear discriminant program	85
	Error rates and practice	92
	References	93
7	**Feature Selection – Canonical Analysis**	**94**
	General formulation of the feature selection problem	94
	The normal or linear discriminant case	96
	Canonical analysis	96
	Multigroup canonical analysis	99
	The geometry of canonical analysis	102
	A canonical analysis program	105

	A canonical analysis of Fisher's iris data	112
	The structure of discrimination	120
	Extending the canonical analysis program	121
	An example of the structure of discrimination	122
	Programs and practice	125
	References	126
8	**Feature Selection – Variable Selection**	**127**
	Variable selection techniques	127
	Measures used in stepwise methods	129
	A typical stepwise procedure	131
	The dangers of stepwise procedures	132
	A stepwise discrimination program	132
	Stepwise analysis of Fisher's iris data	145
	Testing if a subset of the variables is necessary	147
	Overview of feature selection	147
	References	148
9	**Categorical Variables and Non-parametric Methods**	**149**
	Categorical variables	149
	The contingency table	150
	The classification table	152
	Logistic models	157
	Binary variables and linear discrimination	158
	The paradox of the constant Bayes' classifier	159
	Practical categorical classification	160
	Non-parametric methods	161
	K-NN classification rule	167
	A nearest neighbour classification of the iris data	171
	Practical non-parametric classification	171
	References	172
10	**Artificial Intelligence and Pattern Recognition**	**174**
	The data explosion	175
	Simple classification rules	176

viii *Contents*

Fast feature selection	179
The measurement problem	180
The need to reason	182
Presenting results	187
References	188
Appendix One: Matrix Theory for Statistics	189
Appendix Two: A Data Generator	201
Appendix Three: Fisher's Iris Data	206
Index	206

Preface

Classification, the assignment of an object to one of a number of predetermined groups, is of fundamental importance in many areas of science and technology. Its very importance has forced each discipline to develop its own methods and terminology and as a result classification has become a collection of islands with little communication and cross fertilisation. Even the term 'classification' is far from standard and it is not difficult to find disciplines where the terms 'pattern recognition', 'discriminant analysis' and 'supervised learning' are far more common. I have chosen the title 'classification' rather than any of the others because it is the least partisan and the most directly descriptive of the task in hand – I can only hope that specialists in subjects where other terminology reigns will not feel too neglected.

Classification is a subject where intuition can be used to construct practical procedures that work very well and this has sometimes resulted in the loss of a sound theoretical basis for the work. While this may sometimes be unimportant – a classification rule that works is all that can be hoped for – this lack of theory can mean that more difficult problems remain unsolved. Not only can a lack of theory restrict the range of problems that be solved, it can often result in an over-optimistic opinion that a problem has been solved. For example, many methods of classification have been criticised for appearing to work well during the design and testing phase but being inadequate when used 'for real'. In this case the fault usually lies with the inadequate but intuitively obvious test procedures used to estimate the success that the rule will achieve. The theory of classification described in this book is essentially concerned with finding an optimal classification rule, ways of assessing its performance and ways of understanding how it achieves its results. Most of this theory is traditional statistics but much of it comes from the newer areas of pattern recognition and artificial intelligence. So important are these two areas of study that Chapter 10 is devoted to a description of some of their very individual approaches to classification.

Although the theory of classification is explained in the following chapters the practice of classification has not been forgotten! Wherever possible any methods that are described are also accompanied by programs written in BASIC. This not only allows the reader to try the methods, it also clears up any ambiguity about how a method is to be applied. To further enable the reader to become familiar with the methods a data generation program is given in Appendix 2 and this combined with the other programs can be used to explore the ideas and methods before confronting any real data. The analysis programs themselves have been written to be compact so as to make their entry via a keyboard easier but they are suitable for practical application. (Disk versions of these programs are available, see Appendix 2 for details.)

Classification theory still contains many unanswered questions but we are now at a stage where many classification tasks can be automated. Much of the practical work that remains to be done is the application of known methods to create computer programs that are easy to use and fit in with our human ways of working. The future of classification is therefore a joint enterprise in which statisticians, computer scientists and practitioners in many diverse fields all have a contribution to make.

My grateful thanks are due to Bob Mays for the impetus to start writing this book, to Annette Harris and Jane Patience for help in the preparation of the manuscript, to Bernard Watson, Richard Miles and Paul Stringer of Collins Professional and Technical Books for its final production, and also to my wife Sue for her interest and encouragement throughout the project.

Mike James

Notation

$\|\mathbf{A}\|$	Determinant of $\mathbf{A}$.
$d_k(x)$	Quadratic discriminant for group k.
D^2	Sample Mahalanobis distance squared.
e	Total number of cases misclassified.
e_i	Eigenvalue i.
$E(x)$	Mean or average of x.
$E(x\|A)$	Mean or average of x given A.
E_1	Estimate of error rate using independent samples and unknown apriori probabilities.
E_2	Estimate of error rate using independent samples and known apriori probabilities.
E_A	Apparent error rate.
E_L	Leaving-one-out error rate.
E_{ij}	Number of cases from group i classified as group j.
E_i^*	Number of cases misclassified from group i.
f_k	Linear discriminant function for group k.
f_p	Population linear discriminant function.
f_s	Sample linear discriminant function.
G	Number of groups.
ln	Natural log.
M,m	Total sample size.
m_k	Number of cases in group k.
m_{ia}	Number of cases actually in group i.
m_{ic}	Number of cases classified to group i.
N,n	Number of variables.
$P(A)$	Probability of A.
$P(A\|B)$	Probability of A given B.
$SE(x)$	Standard error of x.
S_k	Sample covariance matrix for group k.
s_{ij}^k	Element ij of group k's covariance matrix.
U_i	Unbiased discriminant function.

Notation

VAR(x)	Variance of x.
w(x)	Two group linear discriminant.
w_p	Population two group linear discriminant.
w_s	Sample two group linear discriminant.
x	Vector of measurements.
$\bar{\mathbf{x}}$	Sample mean.
x_i	Variable i.
$\bar{x}_i$	Sample mean of variable i.
x_{ij}	jth measurement on variable i.
δ^2	Population Mahalanobis distance squared.
ϵ	Population error rate.
ϵ_{ij}	Population error rate for group i classified as group j.
λ_i	Eigenvalue i.
$\boldsymbol{\mu}_k$	Population mean vector in group k.
μ_i	Population mean of variable i.
σ^2_{ij}	Population covariance between i and j.
$\boldsymbol{\Sigma}$	Population covariance matrix.
$\sum_i$	Sum over i.
χ^2	Chi squared statistic.

Chapter One
Classification

The need to decide which of a number of possible groups an object belongs to is a surprisingly general problem. For the most part, unless the classification is obvious and trivial we still depend on human expertise to classify on the basis of observations. For example a doctor diagnoses diseases using years of medical training and practice. In a similar way a botanist identifies plant species, a psychologist recognises personality types and so on. As the computer has become more and more accessible so it has become attractive to try and use it either to replace the experts or at the very least to guide and help them.

Even before computer use became common statisticians and others developed fairly simple methods of objective classification based on standard probability theory. However, as the classification problem has proved so important in so many different fields of application it has suffered from being re-solved very many times. Each time a discipline has re-invented the subject of classification it has introduced its own jargon, its own notation and its own favourite methods. For example classification is known as pattern recognition, discriminate analysis, decision theory, assignment analysis etc. Perhaps the most recent and most important re-use of classification analysis is in the area of 'expert systems', programs which seek directly to replace expert reasoning using AI (artifical intelligence) techniques. This proliferation of nomenclature and techniques has caused a great deal of unnecessary confusion in what is both a simple and important subject. The aim of this book is to explain the general theory and specific practice of classification analysis without exclusive reference to any particular field of application. However, to make the subject seem less theoretical, BASIC programs are provided wherever possible so that the reader can explore the methods discussed.

The range of classification

Although classification has a very wide application it is often difficult for a

2   Classification Algorithms

specialist to see that the task in hand is indeed a classification problem. The trouble lies in the application of the idea of assigning an object to a group that it originates from. At its most simple the problem presents itself in terms of objects and groups. For example, if you need to find a way of naming a particular variety of plant then it is obvious that the problem is to find and use a set of measurements that will allow you to assign any specimen to the correct species, i.e. group of plants. In other situations the idea of a group and assignment may be difficult to see. For example, a doctor diagnosing an illness may think of his problem as one of deciding which disease the patient has, but a moment's thought will show that diagnosis is equivalent to assigning the patient to one of a number of possible groups of diseases based on observation of his or her symptoms. In the same way any problem that involves making a decision can be recast as one of assignment to a number of groups – each group representing a possible decision. As an extreme case consider the problem of delivering a judgement of guilt or innocence. This can be considered either as a decision based on the evidence available or as an assignment of the accused into a group of guilty people or a group of innocent people. In other words much that is found in the classical statistical subject of decision theory can be thought of as classification analysis [1].

In the same way predicting which of a number of outcomes will be realised can also be cast as a classification problem. For example the question 'will it rain today?' can either be thought of as prediction or it can be thought of as assigning 'today' to one of the the two possible groups 'rainy' or 'dry'. As prediction of a continuous variable such as temperature is usually associated with regression analysis [2] it will come as no surprise to learn that there are connections between classification and regression. However, it is not profitable to pursue classification as if it were nothing more than a branch of regression analysis because this obscures too much of the simple basis of the subject. It is much better to follow a logical development motivated by the need to classify objects efficiently than to try to find obscure links between classification and other traditional statistical methods.

Discriminant analysis

Many readers will be wondering why the title of this book is not 'Discriminant Analysis' or something similar. If you already know something of the subject of classification then no matter what your specialism you will almost certainly have come across the term 'discriminant analysis'. However, although the term is certainly the one most used to describe any sort of activity connected with the task of classifying unknown objects into groups, its exact meaning depends very much on who is using it!

There are so many different forms of 'discriminant analysis' and so many different usages of the term 'discriminant functions' that it is advisable to steer clear of the term as much as possible. Later chapters will point out which methods are known as discriminant analysis and by whom but it has to be admitted that excessive usage of the term leads to much confusion in practice!

What classification is not!

One of the potential hazards of learning any new approach to a problem is the tendency to see everything in terms of it. This sort of 'blanket application' of a method quickly brings it into disrepute and the inevitable backlash of underuse follows! To avoid this general effect and to avoid the specific misuse of classification analysis it is worth giving instances of its applicability and its non-applicability.

As already stated a number of times, classification analysis addresses itself to the problem of assigning an object to one of a number of possible groups on the basis of observations made on the object. There are ways in which this brief can be elaborated but this is the essence of the problem. Notice that there is nothing said about how we know the existence of the groups to which the object is to be assigned. In classification analysis the existence and structure of the groups themselves is of secondary importance it is the assignment of new cases that concerns us.

There are two main statistical methods that classification analysis is often confused with – 'cluster analysis' and 'analysis of variance'. If you have a mass of currently undifferentiated data and you are curious as to whether or not it has any natural group structure then the method that you should employ is cluster analysis [3]. Cluster analysis attempts to identify any possible tendency for data to 'clump' together to form groups. It is most definitely not concerned with the problem of classifying new objects into existing groups. And to emphasise this point, classification analysis is not concerned with identifying any possible groupings that might be contained within a mass of data.

The second possibility is that you suspect that a particular grouping exists within some data and would like statistical proof of this conjecture. This is the situation most often confused with classification analysis. The reasoning used is that if you can successfully classify new cases to the hypothesised groups with a reasonable accuracy then this is evidence that the groups are more than a figment of the imagination. While this reasoning is true to a certain extent there are more efficient and accurate statistical techniques for testing hypotheses about the existence of differences between groups. These

4   Classification Algorithms

techniques are usually grouped under the heading of analysis of variance or ANOVA and are very well known to most users of statistics [4]. The ideas of ANOVA are in fact often used in classification analysis to determine whether or not the groups involved are sufficiently different to make accurate assignment a possibility and in this connection they are covered in Chapter 7 and 8. However, it is very important not to think of using the efficiency of classification as proof that groups are indeed different in some way.

As an example of the appropriateness of these three different methods of analysis consider the following three situations with respect to the same data. Suppose a psychologist administers a test to a community of patients, then:

(1)   If the aim is to discover if there are a number of different groups of illness then cluster analysis is appropriate. The data would be submitted to a cluster analysis program and the output would be a suggested grouping of the patients according to the test results.

(2)   If the patients are already 'labelled' in some way, i.e. some of them have one form of schizophrenia and the rest have another form, then the objective might be to test the hypothesis that the two groups perform differently on the psychological test. In this case the appropriate analysis would be ANOVA or, more likely, Multivariate ANOVA (MANOVA). Submitting the data, including an indication of which type of schizophrenia each patient had, to a MANOVA program would produce a test statistic and a significance level that would indicate the likelihood that the observed differences in performance of the two groups came about by chance alone. From this information the psychologist could conclude either that there was a real difference between the two groups on test, or there was not.

(3)   Finally, if the objective is, later on, to assign a new patient to one of the two schizophrenia groups, then the appropriate method is classification analysis. In this case the data would be submitted to a classification program, once again along with an indication of the group to which each patient belonged, and this would be used to construct, and possibly test, the performance of a 'classification rule'. This rule would be the main objective of the exercise and if it was effective it would be used subsequently to assign new patients to the correct group of schizophrenics – that is it would be used for diagnosis.

In practice this neat division of methods into cluster analysis to investigate natural groupings, ANOVA to prove that groups are different and classification to assign new objects to the groups is less than clear cut. In particular, classification analysis is often accompanied by a need to discover that characteristics make the groups different. For example if the two groups of schizophrenics do perform differently on the tests the psychologist may want to know the nature of this difference. Finding characteristics that distinguish groups is usually considered to be a branch of classification analysis known as 'feature selection' (see Chapters 7 and 8). However it uses too many of the ideas of ANOVA to be considered as a completely isolated subject. So, as with most statistical techniques, the reason for using classification analysis may be a little more complicated than suggested by the three examples described above but it is important to realise the overall objective of any method and use that which is most appropriate.

Prerequisites

This book is essentially about the application of the theories of probability and statistics to a practical problem. However the emphasis does not fall on theory. It is important to understand how the methods work but this does not entail understanding the formal proofs of a method's correctness or its derivation. Most of the methods can be understood by imagining what is happening in terms of geometry. In subsequent chapters you will find that wherever possible the mathematics is introduced either as a final summary, an additional clarification or as a practice algorithm. In other words mathematics is not relied on to convey an idea without some support! The use of mathematics as the sole explanation of an idea is often adequate but unless it is interpreted and illustrated it is rarely complete. However, to get the most value from this book it would be helpful to know a little probability theory [5], a little statistics [6] and a little matrix algebra [7].

As well as explanations of methods you will also find a number of BASIC programs in the following chapters. Some of these allow you to analyse sample data sets so that you can gain experience with the methods of classification before you approach any real data! Others are straightforward implementations of the methods described and serve both as programs that can be used on real data and to clarify any points of procedure that are difficult to describe in the text. All of the programs are written in a standard form of Microsoft BASIC and they should be easy to convert to any other dialect. (To be exact they are written in Microsoft V5 and will run on almost any CP/M machine.) A particular problem with writing programs that are intended to run on any machine is 'file handling'. Most dialects of BASIC have their own way of opening, reading, writing and closing files but it would be far too restricted to expect data to be input from the keyboard each time for the sake of compatibility! The solution adopted here is to use separate subroutines for each file operation and expect that the reader will

6 *Classification Algorithms*

supply appropriate modifications to make them work on any given machine. As well as the modifications necessary to make the programs work there is also a great deal of scope for adding graphics and for generally improving the output of all of the programs but of course this is an optional extra!

References

1. Ferguson, T.S. (1967) *Mathematical Statistics – A Decision Theoretic Approach*. Academic Press.
2. Draper, N.R. and Smith, H. (1966) *Applied Regression Analysis*. Wiley.
3. Everitt, B.S. (1974) *Cluster Analysis*. Heinemann.
4. Sheffe, H. (1959) *The Analysis of Variance*. Wiley.
5. Meyer, P.L. (1965) *Introductory Probability and Statistical Applications*. Addison-Wesley, Massachusetts.
6. Wetherill, G.B. (1967) *Elementary Statistical Methods*. Methuen.
7. Searle, S.R. (1966) *Matrix Algebra for the Biological Sciences*. Wiley.

Chapter Two
Classification Rules

The problem of classification is to find a way of assigning a new object on the basis of a set of measurements to one of a number of possible groups. Inherent in this statement of the problem is the idea of a 'classification rule' – that is a well defined procedure that can be described and applied without the need for any additional 'subjective' judgements. In this chapter the idea of a classification rule and its desirable properties are explored and one very special rule – the Bayes' rule – is introduced.

Criterion of classification

Obviously it is possible to think up any number of procedures for classifying an object into one of a number of groups, ranging from random allocation to an arbitrary rule using any of the measurements. The problem is to select one of the set of possible classification rules based on its performance. In other words we would like to use the classification rule that was in some sense 'best'. Which rule we choose depends very much on the interpretation given to the word 'best'. At first you might think that there is only one sensible interpretation to give to the best classification rule – it should be the one that makes least classification errors – but, as will be explained in Chapter 5, this is far from true. Even though there are a great many criteria which can be used to select a best classification rule the overwhelming majority of applications make use of the 'obvious' criterion of minimum error and as a result this will be used as the standard criterion. To be precise, unless otherwise stated, the classification rule that we seek is optimum in the sense that minimises the 'total error of classification' or TEC.

Even the apparently straightforward idea of minimising TEC needs a little careful thought. Given a classification rule its TEC is simply the proportion of objects that it misclassifies. This includes all types of misclassification irrespective of the group to which the object is assigned or the group to which it actually belongs. Also notice that the TEC is the

8 Classification Algorithms

performance of the rule in the 'long run' on a random sample of objects. In other words the TEC is a theoretical error rate only obtained when the sample size is effectively infinite. For any sample of a practical size the actual error of classification may be higher or lower than the TEC in the same way the actual number of heads obtained in tossing a fair coin can be more or less than 50% in any given number of throws. To say that the probability of getting heads is 0.5 is a statement about what you would expect in the long run. Thus the TEC should be thought of as the probability that the rule under consideration will misclassify an object.

Probabilities – some notation

Even in the discussion of the TEC it becomes apparent that it is impossible to ignore the subject of probability. It is assumed that the reader is already familiar with the ideas of simple probability theory but it is worth explaining some of the notation that will be used through this book.

The probability of something, an 'event', happening is usually indicated as P(A) which should be read as 'the probability that A will happen'. Thus P(rain) is the probability that it will rain and P(heads) is the probability of getting heads which should be 0.5 for a fair coin. Apart from this simple notation we also need to know something about 'conditional' probabilities. A conditional probability is the probability of an event occurring 'given' the knowledge that another has already occurred. This is usually indicated as P(A|B) which should be read as 'the probability that A will happen *given* that B already has'. You can think of the vertical bar as meaning 'given', as in P(rain|clouds) or 'the probability of rain *given* clouds'.

As an example of conditional probability consider the outcomes of tossing a fair coin. Before tossing any coins the probability of getting two heads in the first two tosses is simply:

$$P(\text{two heads}) = 0.25$$

If the first toss results in a head then the conditional probability of getting two heads is:

$$P(\text{two heads} \mid \text{first toss was heads}) = 0.5$$

Notice that knowing that the first toss came up heads supplied some information which updated the probability of the event. As an extreme case of this consider:

$$P(\text{two heads} \mid \text{first toss was tails})$$

In this case the extra information makes the outcome certain failure! (In other words P(two heads|first toss was tails) is zero.) In this sense you can think of conditional probabilities as ways of using any knowledge we may have of the situation to improve our estimate of the probability of an event occurring. If initially we know that the probability of something is P(A) then this can be regarded as what we know without making any observations. Subsequent observations are then used to update this initial probability to give the conditional probability which reflects our increased knowledge of the situation. For this reason probabilities such as P(A) are usually referred to as 'prior' probabilities and the conditional probabilities after a measurement has been taken into account are known as 'posterior' probabilities.

Obviously when a new piece of information is used to update a prior probability one of three things can happen – the value can increase, decrease or stay the same. For example if you are interested in tossing coins then any observations that you make on the state of the tide are unlikely to effect your state of knowledge of the result. That is:

$$P(\text{two heads}) = P(\text{two heads} \mid \text{local high tide})$$

In general two events A and B are said to be independent if:

$$P(A) = P(A \mid B) \qquad (\text{which implies } P(B) = P(B \mid A))$$

From the point of view of increasing our knowledge of A there is very little point in observing B! What we would really like is that an observation should either increase the probability to as close to one or decrease the probability to as close to zero as possible. The reason for this is simply that in probability terms both one and zero are certainties. For example in the coin tossing example given earlier the information that the first toss resulted in tails changes the prior probability from 0.25 to a conditional probability of 0 and as a result we can be certain that the experiment will fail.

Bayes' rule

As conditional probabilities can be used to summarise any information that we have about an event, it should come as no surprise that they are central to the classification of an object based on any measurements that we have made. For example, suppose that two factories are making the same electronic component using two different production methods and for some reason we need a way of telling which factory made any given component.

10 Classification Algorithms

Obviously if factory A makes 75% of all the components then the probability of any given component coming from factory A is 0.75. That is:

$$P(\text{factory A}) = 0.75$$

and

$$P(\text{factory B}) = 0.25$$

In the absence of any other information it seems reasonable to assign a component of unknown origin to factory A – after all, more components come from factory A! Now suppose, on the basis of a number of measurement (length, weight, materials, purity etc.), it is possible to obtain the probabilities conditional on the set of measurements and for a particular component they are:

$$P(A \mid x) = 0.4$$
$$P(B \mid x) = 0.6$$

Which factory would you allocate the component to? (Notice that x is used to stand for a set of measurements.) It seems reasonable to assume that on the basis of the measurement the component came from factory B. This classification rule:

assign the object to the group with the highest conditional probability

is known as 'Bayes' rule' and it is not difficult to prove that it is the rule which minimises the TEC – that is, it is the optimal rule that we seek.

Put more formally, if there are G groups then Bayes' rule is to assign the object to group i where:

$$P(G_i \mid x) > P(G_j \mid x) \qquad \text{for all } j \neq i$$

If by any chance there is more than one group with the largest conditional probability then the tie can be broken by allocating the object at random to one of the tied groups. If you think about it for a moment, what the success of Bayes' rule is telling us is that all of the information that we have about possible group membership is contained in the set of conditional probabilities.

A practical rule

It looks at this point as if the problem of classification has been entirely solved! All you have to do is apply the Bayes' rule and you will be rewarded with minimum TEC. Of course things are not so simple in practice. In particular how do you go about finding the all important conditional probabilities. Quantities such as $P(G_i|\mathbf{x})$ are very difficult to find by standard methods of estimation; however this is not the case for quantities such as $P(\mathbf{x}|G_i)$. The conditional probability $P(\mathbf{x}|G_i)$, the probability of getting a particular set of measurements $\mathbf{x}$ given that the object comes from group i, is something that can be estimated simply by taking a sample of objects from group i. For example, in the case of the component factories mentioned in the previous section, given a set of measurements consisting of length and weight, it is easy to see how to estimate $P(\mathbf{x}|G_i)$. By taking a sample of components from factory A you could find the number with a particular length and a particular weight, 3 mm and 1 g say, and this would estimate $P(3 \text{ mm and } 1 \text{ g}|\text{factory A})$. You could repeat this for a range of lengths and weights and obtain a table that you could use to look up any $P(\mathbf{x}|\text{factory A})$. Repeating the whole exercise on factory B would yield a similar table of $P(\mathbf{x}|\text{factory B})$.

Now although it is easy 'in principle' to obtain $P(\mathbf{x}|G_i)$ the probability that we are interested in is $P(G_i|\mathbf{x})$. Fortunately there is a connection between the two known as 'Bayes' theorem':

$$P(G_i | \mathbf{x}) = \frac{P(\mathbf{x} | G_i)P(G_i)}{\sum_{\text{all i}} P(\mathbf{x} | G_i)P(G_i)}$$

Notice that all of the items on the right-hand side of the equation can be found by sampling. How to find $P(\mathbf{x}|G_i)$ has already been described and $P(G_i)$ is simply the probability that the object comes from group i in the absence of any information, i.e. it is the proportion of group i in the population.

Now we have a practical optimal rule for classification. Putting Bayes' theorem into Bayes' rule gives:

assign to group i if

$$\frac{P(\mathbf{x} | G_i)P(G_i)}{\sum_{\text{all k}} P(\mathbf{x} | G_k)P(G_k)} > \frac{P(\mathbf{x} | G_j)P(G_j)}{\sum_{\text{all k}} P(\mathbf{x} | G_k)P(G_k)} \qquad \text{for all } j \neq i$$

or, as the bottom lines on both sides of the inequality are the same, they can be cancelled out to give:

12　Classification Algorithms

assign to group i if

$$P(\mathbf{x} \mid G_i)P(G_i) > P(\mathbf{x} \mid G_j)P(G_j) \text{ for all } j \neq i$$

which is the final practical form of Bayes' rule.

Divisions of the sample space – simplicity

It is often helpful to visualise the way that a given classification rule works. For example, in the case of the two factories making the same component if only two measurements are being used – length and weight say – then it is possible to plot a two-dimensional scatter diagram. As every point in this diagram corresponds to a particular pair of values for length and weight, the classification rule can be used to decide if a component with those values should be classified as coming from factory A or factory B. This process can be repeated for every point in the scatter diagram resulting in a 'map' of regions that are assigned to factory A and regions that are assigned to factory B (see Fig. 2.1). Thus a classification rule divides the scatter diagram,

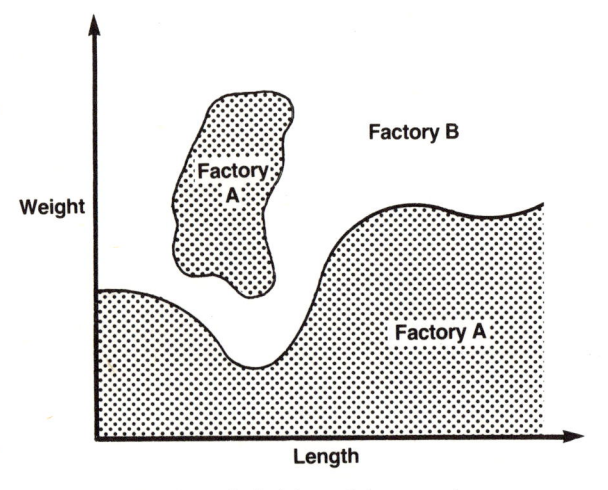

Fig. 2.1　A division of the sample space

or more accurately the sample space, into a number of regions. The way in which the sample space is divided is of great interest because the simplicity and ease of use of a classification rule is directly related to the simplicity of the division of the sample space. In other words, simple divisions give rise to classification rules that are easy to apply. Another reason for being interested in the way the sample space is divided is that very often we have an

Classification Rules

idea that the measurements of the groups 'cluster' together in some way and this suggests that a classification rule ought to divide the sample space simply (see Fig. 2.2). Of course if more than two measurements are involved then it is no longer possible to draw scatter diagrams or imagine the sample space involved. However for the most part these higher dimensional sample spaces can be understood by thinking about what happens in two or at the most three dimensions.

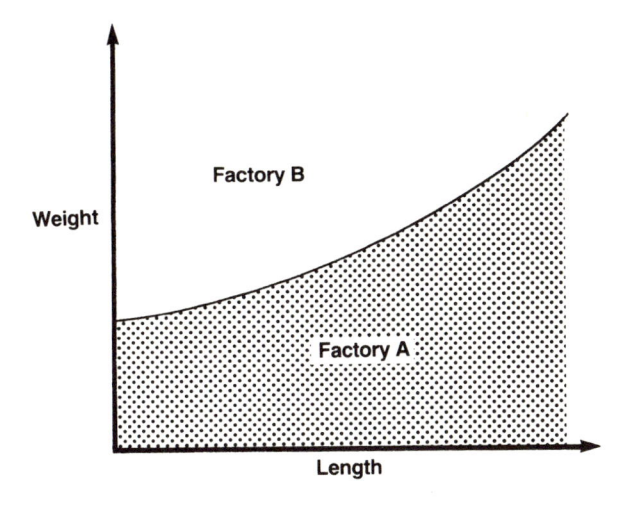

Fig. 2.2 A simple division of the sample space

Using the Bayes' rule

The main problem with the Bayes' rule is that while it solves our problem completely it is almost unusable! The reason for this is the sheer volume of data that has to be collected to estimate $(Px|G_i)$. For example, suppose you are making measurements on five variables each consisting of ten possible categories then even for one group you would be trying to estimate fifty relative frequencies which would require sample sizes in excess of 500. This sampling would of course have to be repeated for each group and the results drawn up into some sort of convenient-to-use table. All in all using Bayes rule in this direct form is fairly impractical (although this method is treated further in Chapter 9).

It is rather frustrating to be in possession of the solution to your problems and not be able to make use of it! However it is not possible to ignore the Bayes' rule – after all it is the best we can hope to achieve – and a great part of classification theory is concerned either with finding practical forms of the

14 Classification Algorithms

rule that are appropriate under special conditions or finding simple approximations to the rule that have acceptably low error rates. Even though for the rest of this book the discussion centres on such practical classification rules it should always be kept in mind that in any situation there is an optimal rule – Bayes' rule – which can outperform the rest!

Chapter Three
Practical Classification – the Normal Case

As explained in the previous chapter the optimal classification rule is the Bayes' rule but its direct use is usually too difficult for most applications. This chapter describes the form of the Bayes' rule when the measurements being used for classification come from a normal distribution. The assumption of normal variables is quite often met either exactly or approximately in practice and so it is pleasing to discover that the resulting classification rule is simple to apply. Before moving on to consider the Bayes' rule in the normal case it is worth describing some of the elementary properties of the multivariate normal distribution.

The multivariate normal

The normal distribution is familiar to anyone who has studied introductory statistics or probability. The normal distribution describes the probability of a single variable and it is specified by two parameters – its mean μ and its standard deviation σ. The well known 'bell' shape of the normal density function can be seen in Fig. 3.1 and this corresponds to the equation:

$$\left(\frac{1}{\sqrt{2\pi\sigma}}\right) \exp[-(x-\mu)^2/2\sigma^2]$$

It is obvious but worth recalling that the mean of the distribution controls the 'location' of the distribution and the standard deviation its 'spread'. Given values for the mean and the standard deviation most people can imagine a rough looking normal distribution centred on the mean and about as wide as two standard deviations. This ability allows a certain amount of reasoning about situations involving the normal distribution without the need to resort to algebra. This is the sort of level of familiarity that is usually absent when it comes to the multivariate normal.

When more than one variable is involved then the multivariate

16 Classification Algorithms

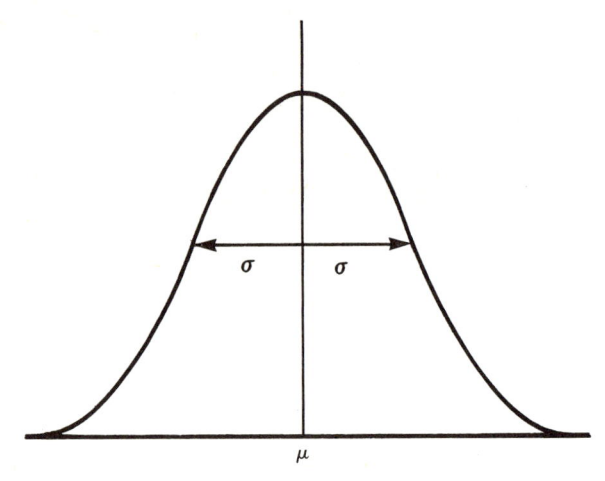

Fig. 3.1 The normal distribution

generalisation of the normal distribution has to be used – the multivariate normal distribution. Instead of a single mean controlling the location of the distribution there is now one mean for each variable making up a 'mean vector'. The description of the way the distribution 'spreads' is also more complicated. The multivariate equivalent of the standard deviation is the 'covariance matrix'. Interpreting the meaning of the covariance matrix is often something that causes problems and for this reason it is worth examining the way it affects the 'shape' of the distribution.

In the case of the multivariate normal for two variables x_1 and x_2, i.e. a bivariate normal, the mean vector and covariance matrix are simply:

$$\text{mean} = \begin{bmatrix} \mu_1 \\ \mu_2 \end{bmatrix} \qquad \text{covariance} = \begin{bmatrix} \sigma_{11} & \sigma_{12} \\ \sigma_{21} & \sigma_{22} \end{bmatrix}$$

where μ_1 and μ_2 are the means of x_1 and x_2 respectively. The diagonal elements of the covariance matrix, that is σ_{11} and σ_{22}, are simply the variances of x_1 and x_2 respectively. From just this information it is possible to draw a rough sketch of the distribution – it is centred on the mean vector and 'spreads' by $2\sqrt{\sigma_{11}}$ in the x_1 direction and $2\sqrt{\sigma_{22}}$ in the x_2 direction (see Fig. 3.2). The off-diagonal terms in the covariance matrix, σ_{12} and σ_{21}, are in fact equal and measure the 'association' between the two variables. In fact the correlation between the two variables is given by:

$$\sigma_{12} = \frac{\sigma_{12}}{\sqrt{\sigma_{11}\sigma_{22}}}$$

and so you can think of σ_{12} as a sort of un-normalised correlation between the two variables. For the moment things are simplified if we assume that σ_{11} and σ_{22} are equal. When σ_{12} is zero then there is no association between the variables and as $\sigma_{11}=\sigma_{22}$ then the spread is circular (see Fig. 3.3). As σ_{12} increases the association between the variables also increases and the spread is 'pulled out' as the variables vary together (see Fig. 3.4). If σ_{12} is negative then the spread is once again 'pulled out' but this time by the tendency of the variables to vary in opposition to one another (see Fig. 3.5). Thus the

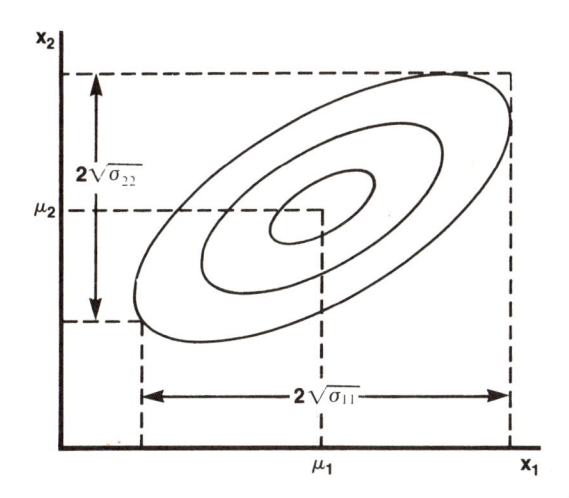

Fig. 3.2 The bivariate normal distribution

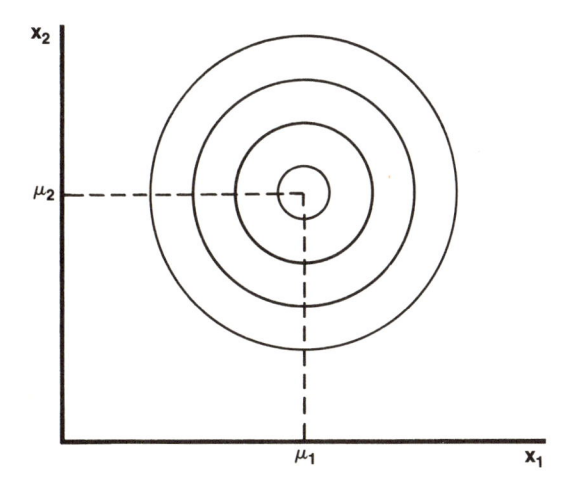

Fig. 3.3 The bivariate normal with $\sigma_{12}=0$

18 *Classification Algorithms*

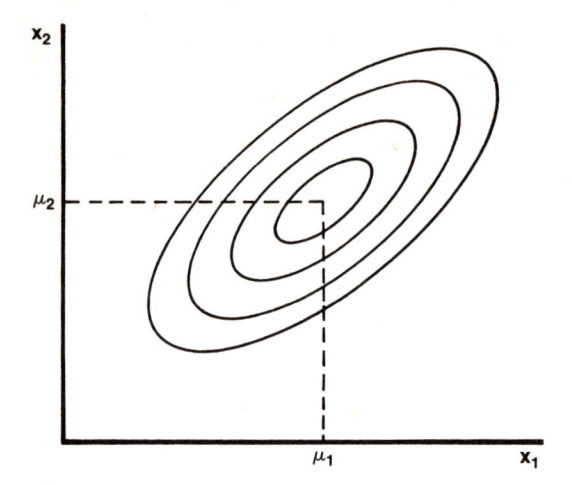

Fig. 3.4 The bivariate normal with $\sigma_{12} > 0$

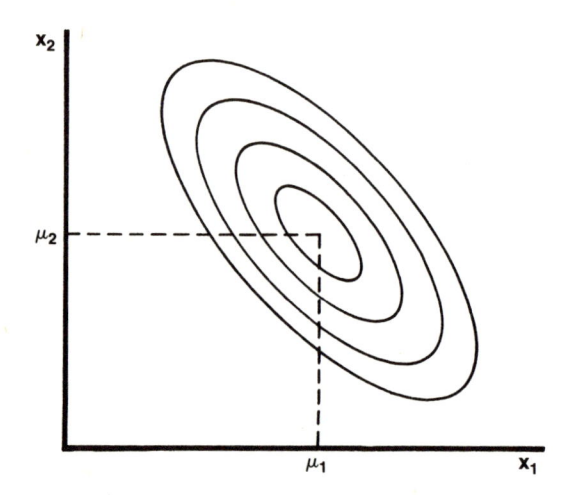

Fig. 3.5 The bivariate normal with $\sigma_{12} < 0$

covariance matrix can be seen to specify the shape of the distribution – the on-diagonal terms affect the spread in the x_1 and x_2 directions and the off-diagonal terms affect the spread between these two directions.

In the bivariate case it is possible to draw a diagram indicating the shape of the distribution but so far what is actually being drawn has not been described. Roughly speaking the bivariate normal distribution gives the probability of any value of x_1 and x_2 occurring. The most obvious way to show the shape of the distribution is to draw lines that connect points which have equal probabilities of occurring. If this is done for the bivariate normal the result is a series of concentric ellipses – see Fig. 3.2. That is, the lines of equal probability for the bivariate normal form a set of ellipses centred on the mean vector. Now it is possible to see in greater detail the effect that the covariance matrix has on the shape of the distribution – σ_{11} and σ_{22} affect the width of the ellipse in the x_1 and x_2 directions and σ_{12} affects the orientation of the major axis of the ellipse.

In moving to more than two variables the usual difficulties of visualising more than two dimensions arise. In three dimensions the lines of equal probability generalise to surfaces of equal probability and the elliptical shapes generalise to ellipsoids. Thus you can imagine a three dimensional multivariate normal as a surface shaped roughly like a rugby ball centred on the mean vector. In this case the covariance matrix is:

$$\begin{bmatrix} \sigma_{11} & \sigma_{12} & \sigma_{13} \\ & \sigma_{22} & \sigma_{23} \\ & & \sigma_{33} \end{bmatrix}$$

(Following the usual practice the elements below the diagonal have been left out as, in general, $\sigma_{ij} = \sigma_{ji}$ i.e. the matrix is symmetrical.) The on-diagonal elements σ_{11}, σ_{22} and σ_{33} affect the spread along the x_1, x_2 and x_3 directions respectively and σ_{12}, σ_{13} and σ_{23} affect the orientation of the ellipsoid. In more than three dimensions there is no way of visualising what the multivariate normal looks like but in general there is no need – two or three dimensions will suffice to imagine anything that can happen in higher dimensions.

The equation for the multivariate normal distribution in matrix form is:

$$\left(\frac{1}{(2\pi)^{n/2}|\Sigma|^{1/2}}\right) \exp[-\tfrac{1}{2}(\mathbf{x} - \boldsymbol{\mu})'\Sigma^{-1}(\mathbf{x} - \boldsymbol{\mu})]$$

(Notice that this equation involves matrix operations, see Appendix 1.)

Finally it is worth saying that in the same way that you would expect a graph of the relative frequency of data from a normal distribution to look roughly bell-shaped so the scatter diagram of data from the bivariate normal should look vaguely elliptical with the density of points increasing toward the mean. In the same way a three dimensional scatter diagram of data from a trivariate normal should cluster in ellipsoidal groups and so on into higher dimensions. Notice that there are statistical tests for normality and multivariate normality and the look of a scatter diagram is not proof that the data is from any particular distribution.

20 Classification Algorithms

The normal form of Bayes' rule

To apply Bayes' rule all we have to know is the value of $P(G_i)$ and $(Px|G_i)$ for each group. As already mentioned, although $P(G_i)$ is easy enough to find $P(x|G_i)$ is something of a problem. However if within each group the variables that make up the measurement vector **x** have a multivariate normal distribution then the form of $(Px|G_i)$ is known. That is:

$$P(x \mid G_i) = \frac{1}{(2\pi)^{n/2}|\Sigma_i|^{1/2}} \exp[-\tfrac{1}{2}(x-\mu_i)'\Sigma_i^{-1}(x-\mu_i)]$$

In this case estimating $P(x|G_i)$ comes down to estimating two parameters for each group, μ_i the group mean vector and Σ_i the group covariance matrix. If there are n measurements in **x** then there are n group means in the mean vector and $n(n+1)/2$ elements in the covariance matrix making a total of $(n^2+3n)/2$ quantities to be estimated for each group but this is considerably fewer than the number required for a direct application of Bayes' rule using estimates of relative frequencies.

Using the normal form of $P(x|G_i)$ in Bayes' rule gives:

assign **x** to G_i if

$$\frac{P(G_i)}{(2\pi)^{n/2}|\Sigma_i|^{1/2}} \exp[-\tfrac{1}{2}(x-\mu_i)'\Sigma_i^{-1}(x-\mu_i)] >$$

$$\frac{P(G_j)}{(2\pi)^{n/2}|\Sigma_j|^{1/2}} \exp\left[-\tfrac{1}{2}(x-\mu_j)'\Sigma_j^{-1}(x-\mu_j)\right]$$

for all $j \neq i$

Taking the natural log (ln) of both sides of the inequality gives:

assign **x** to G_i if

$$-\tfrac{1}{2}n\ln(2\pi) - \tfrac{1}{2}\ln|\Sigma_i| - \tfrac{1}{2}(x-\mu_i)'\Sigma_i^{-1}(x-\mu_i) + \ln(P(G_i)) >$$
$$-\tfrac{1}{2}n\ln(2\pi) - \tfrac{1}{2}\ln|\Sigma_j| - \tfrac{1}{2}(x-\mu_j)'\Sigma_j^{-1}(x-\mu_j) + \ln(P(G_j))$$

for all $j \neq i$

Cancelling all of the terms that are common to both sides gives:

assign **x** to G_i if

$$-\ln|\Sigma_i| - (x - \mu_i)'\Sigma_i^{-1}(x - \mu_i) + \ln(P(G_i)) >$$
$$-\ln|\Sigma_j| - (x - \mu_j)'\Sigma_j^{-1}(x - \mu_j) + \ln(P(G_j))$$
$$\text{for all } j \neq i$$

This expression has one difficulty – cancelling all of the common terms has resulted in a quantity that is negative. This can be corrected by multiplying both sides of the inequality by -1 and changing the greater than sign to a less than sign giving:

assign x to G_i if

$$\ln|\Sigma_i| + (x - \mu_i)'\Sigma_i^{-1}(x - \mu_i) - \ln(P(G_i)) <$$
$$\ln|\Sigma_j| + (x - \mu_j)'\Sigma_j^{-1}(x - \mu_j) - \ln(P(G_j))$$
$$\text{for all } j \neq i$$

Although matrix operations are involved in working out the above expressions the final result is a number for each group which depends on x. That is:

$$\ln|\Sigma_i| + (x - \mu_i)'\Sigma_i^{-1}(x - \mu_i) - \ln(P(G_i))$$

This quantity is often referred to as a 'discriminant score' and

$$d_i(x) = \ln|\Sigma_i| + (x - \mu_i)'\Sigma_i^{-1}(x - \mu_i)$$

as a 'discriminant function'. Notice that although we started from Bayes' rule working in terms of probability and derived $d_i(x)$ using nothing but the assumption of normality and simple algebra, $d_i(x)$ cannot be regarded as a probability. Indeed, as the final form of the classification rule assigns the object to the group with the smallest value of $d_i(x) - \ln(P(G_i))$, we can infer that as $d_i(x)$ gets smaller the evidence for membership of group i increases which is the opposite to the behaviour of $P(G_i|x)$. Even though $d_i(x)$ does not behave like $P(G_i|x)$ it is important to realise that the rule:

assign to group i if

$$d_i(x) - \ln(P(G_i)) < d_j(x) - \ln(P(G_j)) \qquad \text{for all } j \neq i$$

is the Bayes' Rule if x is multivariate normal in each of the groups.

Interpreting the normal Bayes' rule

It is interesting to consider the way that the normal Bayes' rule divides the sample space. Considering a case with only two groups and two measurements simplifies the situation and loses nothing of the principles involved. Obviously the region of the sample space that 'belongs' to group 1 is characterised by values of x_1 and x_2 such that:

$$d_1(x_1, x_2) - \ln(P(G_1)) < d_2(x_1, x_2) - \ln(P(G_2))$$

The dividing line between the region 'belonging' to group 1 and the region 'belonging' to group 2 is given by:

$$d_1(x_1, x_2) - \ln(P(G_1)) = d_2(x_1, x_2) - \ln(P(G_2))$$

It can be shown by matrix algebra or geometry that this dividing line has the form of a quadratic curve. This fact can be seen from an inspection of a diagram of the equal probability contours for the two groups. If the prior probabilities $P(G_1)$ and $P(G_2)$ are assumed to be equal then the classification rule is equivalent to:

$$P(\mathbf{x} \mid G_1) > P(\mathbf{x} \mid G_2)$$

and the dividing line between the two regions is given by:

$$P(\mathbf{x} \mid G_1) = P(\mathbf{x} \mid G_2)$$

In other words the dividing line between the two groups passes through the intersection of the equal probability contours of the two groups. Examples of the shape of the dividing line produced by different group covariance matrices can be seen in Fig 3.6. In each case the curve is a simple quadratic. This is also borne out by the fact that if you expand the matrix operations in $d_i(\mathbf{x})$ (see Appendix 1) the result is a polynomial involving only squares and cross products – i.e. a general quadratic equation. Also notice how the curve takes account of the different elliptical spread of each group determined by the covariance matrices. Thinking about the dividing line between the groups in two dimensions is easy to generalise to higher dimensions where the quadratic dividing line becomes a quadratic dividing surface. It is the quadratic form of the division of the sample space that gives the normal Bayes' classifier its simplicity and its ability to separate groups with very differently shaped spreads. It is the quadratic nature of the separating

Fig. 3.6 Quadratic division of the sample space

surfaces that has resulted in the normal form of Bayes' rule becoming known as the 'quadratic discriminant function'.

There are a number of other interesting properties of the functions $d_i(x)$ that have resulted in a number of alternative names for the normal Bayes' classifier. For example, the fact that $d_i(x)$ decreases as x moves closer to the mean of the group has resulted in the name 'minimum generalised distance classifier'; the fact that $d_i(x)$ is distributed as χ^2 has resulted in the name 'minimum Chi squared classifier', and so on. However none of these names is based on the essential principles that govern the construction of the classifier and so, apart from the confusion they cause, they can be conveniently ignored.

An example

As an example of the practical application of a classification rule, consider the following problem. An electronics engineer notices that the transistors that fail in later use are characterised by a lower gain (amplification factor) and an increased noise rating. In an effort to improve reliability it seems reasonable to try to construct a classification rule that can be used to weed out poor transistors before they are incorporated into equipment. From theoretical considerations and from observations the distribution of gain and noise is known to be multivariate normal. For good transistors there is a positive correlation between gain and noise but for the defective transistors the relationship is negative – that is the lower the gain the higher the noise. This implies that the covariance matrices are different in the two groups and so the quadratic discriminant function is appropriate. From a sample of good and bad transistors the following parameters were estimated:

24 Classification Algorithms

Good transistors

	means	covariance matrix
gain	$\begin{bmatrix} 137.8 \\ 9.2 \end{bmatrix}$	$\begin{bmatrix} 720.8 & 44.5 \\ 44.5 & 9.2 \end{bmatrix}$
noise		

Bad transistors

	means	covariance matrix
gain	$\begin{bmatrix} 96.8 \\ 15.6 \end{bmatrix}$	$\begin{bmatrix} 584.6 & -39.7 \\ -39.7 & 3.6 \end{bmatrix}$
noise		

From these estimates the quadratic discriminant functions for each group can be constructed. The inverse covariance matrices are:

Good transistors

$$\begin{bmatrix} 0.10019 & -0.0096 \\ -0.0096 & 0.1541 \end{bmatrix}$$

Bad transistors

$$\begin{bmatrix} 0.0068 & 0.0758 \\ 0.0758 & 1.1181 \end{bmatrix}$$

(Details of how these were calculated and a program to calculate quadratic discriminant functions are given in the next chapter). The log of the determinants of the two covariance matrices are 8.45 and 6.26 respectively. If the prior probabilities are 0.8 ($\ln(0.8)=-0.223$) for good transistors and 0.2 ($\ln(0.2)=-1.609$) for bad the final discriminant functions can be written:

$$d_1(x) 0 = 0.0019 z_1^2 - 0.0192 z_1 z_2 + 0.1541 z_2^2 + 8.45$$

$$d_2(x) = 0.0068 y_1^2 - 0.1516 y_1 y_2 + 1.1181 y_2^2 + 6.26$$

where

$$z_1 = x_1 - 137.8 = \text{gain} - 137.8$$
$$z_2 = x_2 - 9.2 = \text{noise} - 9.2$$

and

$$y_1 = x_1 - 96.8 = \text{gain} - 96.8$$
$$y_2 = x_2 - 15.6 = \text{noise} - 15.6$$

For example if a transistor has a measured gain of 117.7 and a noise factor of 8 then:

$$z_1 = 117.7 - 137.8 = -20.1$$
$$z_2 = 8 - 9.2 = -1.2$$
$$y_1 = 117.7 - 96.8 = 20.9$$
$$y_2 = 8 - 15.6 = -7.6$$

and

$$d_1(x) - \ln(P(G_1)) = 0.526 + 8.45 + 0.223 = 9.19$$
$$d_2(x) - \ln(P(G_2)) = 43.47 + 6.26 + 1.609 = 51.33$$

As the discriminant score for group 1 is smaller than that for group 2 the transistor would be assigned to the 'good' group. Don't worry too much about the details of the calculation, a complete quadratic discrimination program which eliminates the need for any hand calculation is given in the next chapter!

Equal covariances

Although the normal Bayes' rule is a great simplification over the general case it still involves estimating quite a few parameters to be really convenient. In many cases the correlations between the variables are the same within each group and this can be used to simplify the normal Bayes' classifier yet further. If the correlations are independent of group then all the groups have the same covariance matrix and terms involving this constant can be cancelled from both sides of the inequality giving:

$$d_i(x) = -\mu_i' \Sigma^{-1} x + \tfrac{1}{2} \mu_i' \Sigma^{-1} \mu_i$$

Once again cancelling constants has made the classification function negative and so for convenience it is usual to multiply both sides of the inequality by -1 and define a new function $f_i(x) = -d_i(x)$. That is:

assign to group i if
$$f_i(x) + \ln(P(G_i)) > f_j(x) + \ln(P(G_j)) \qquad \text{for all } j \neq i$$

and

$$f_i(x) = \mu_i' \Sigma^{-1} x - \tfrac{1}{2} \mu_i' \Sigma^{-1} \mu_i$$

The second term in $f_i(x)$ doesn't involve x and so it can be written as a constant for each group - C_{0i}. The matrix multiplication in the first term can

26 Classification Algorithms

also be worked out in advance to give a single vector c_i, that is

$$c'_i = \mu'_i \Sigma^{-1}$$

and

$$f_i(\mathbf{x}) = c'_i \mathbf{x} + C_{0i}$$

Writing this out in full reveals its simplicity:

$$f_i(\mathbf{x}) = \sum_{k=1}^{n} C_{ki} x_k + C_{0i}$$

where the C_{ki} are the elements of the vector c_i. For example in the case of two variables (n=2) $f_i(\mathbf{x})$ becomes:

$$f_i(\mathbf{x}) = C_{1i} x_1 + C_{2i} x_2 + C_{0i}$$

If you are familiar with regression analysis you should recognise $f_i(\mathbf{x})$ as having the same form as a regression equation – that is, it is the sum of a constant times each variable plus a final constant. However notice that there is a different $f_i(\mathbf{x})$ for each group and this means that there are n+1 parameters to estimate per group but this is still a considerable saving over $d_i(\mathbf{x})$.

Linear discrimination

Once again it is worth asking how the sample space is divided by the classification rule. Considering the two group/two variable case for simplicity it is clear that the dividing line between the two areas of the the sample space (one 'belonging' to group 1 and the other 'belonging' to group 2) is given by values of x_1, x_2 satisfying:

$$f_1(x_1, x_2) = f_2(x_1, x_2)$$

(Assuming $P(G_1)=P(G_2)$). A little work soon shows that this division is in fact a straight line. This also fits in with what would be expected from an examination of the way that the equal probability lines of the two distributions intersect (see Fig. 3.7). Thus in general $f_i(\mathbf{x})$ separates groups using flat surfaces or 'hyperplanes'. In two dimensions a hyperplane is a straight line, in three it is the familiar flat plane, and in dimensions higher than three it is not possible to imagine a hyperplane but it possesses many of

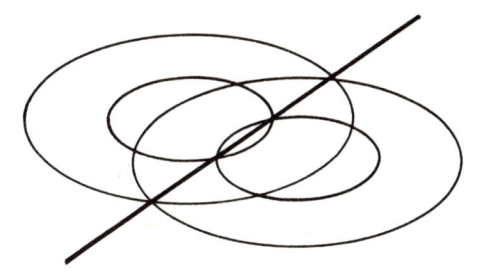

Fig. 3.7 Linear division of the sample space

the properties of the straight line and the plane. The linear form of $f_i(\mathbf{x})$ and the 'straight line' division of the sample space has resulted in $f_i(\mathbf{x})$ being known as a 'linear discriminant' function. However there are many different functions commonly known as linear discriminant functions and the term should be used with care.

The linear discriminant function has a long history of use and a great many desirable properties that make it the general workhorse of classification analysis. However it is important not to forget that it is simply a form of Bayes rule that applies when the measurement vector comes from a multivariate normal distribution *and* all of the groups are assumed to have identical covariance matrices.

An example of linear discrimination

The weights and heights of newborn babies are different for boys and girls. A researcher wishes to classify newborn babies into male or female groups using only this information. After an initial survey it seemed reasonable to conclude that over the restricted range of weights and heights the distribution of both was normal and the correlation between the two was the same in both groups. This suggests the use of the linear discriminant function. From a sample the following were estimated:

girls   girls   boys
height (cm) $\begin{bmatrix} 53.44 \\ 3.16 \end{bmatrix}$ $\begin{bmatrix} 53.64 \\ 3.93 \end{bmatrix}$
weight (kg)

Common covariance matrix

$$\begin{bmatrix} 4.1 & 1.77 \\ 1.77 & 1.07 \end{bmatrix}$$

also

$$P(\text{boy}) = P(\text{girl}) = 0.5$$

Using this information to construct the linear discriminant functions gives:

$f_1(x) + \ln(P(G_1)) = 41.3x_1 - 65.34x_2 - 1000.55 + \ln(0.5)$
$f_2(x) + \ln(P(G_2)) = 40.39x_1 - 63.10x_2 - 959.27 + \ln(0.5)$

Once again there is no need to worry about exactly how these functions were arrived at because a linear discriminant program is given in the next chapter but notice how much simpler the linear discriminant is compared to the quadratic discriminant. If a baby is 53.2 cm tall and weighs 3.7 kg then:

$f_1(x) + \ln(P(G_1)) = 41.3 \times 53.2 - 65.34 \times 3.7 - 1000.55 - 0.693 = 954.66$
$f_2(x) + \ln(PG_2)) = 40.39 \times 53.2 - 63.10 \times 3.7 - 959.27 - 0.693 = 955.31$

As the second discriminant score is larger than the first the baby would be assigned to the female group. You may feel that this example is a little contrived in that there are more direct and simple indicators of sex than $f_1(x)$ and $f_2(x)$ but it is possible that the researcher's interest is in the future progress of the misclassified babies – that is males that have female height/weight characteristics and females that have male height/weight characteristics. This is one of the many indirect uses of classification rules that are encountered in practice.

The two group case

The most often encountered classification problem involves assignment to one of two groups. In the two group case the normal Bayes' rule assuming equal covariance matrices is:

assign to group 1 if

$f_1(x) + \ln(P(G_1)) > f_2(x) + \ln(P(G_2))$

and otherwise to group 2

Taking $f_2(x)$ and $\ln(P(G_1))$ from both sides of the inequality gives:

assign to group 1 if

$f_1(x) - f_2(x) > \ln(P(G_2)) - \ln(P(G_1))$

and otherwise to group 2

The difference between the two linear discriminant functions can be written as a single new function:

$$w(\mathbf{x}) = \mathbf{f}_1(\mathbf{x}) - \mathbf{f}_2(\mathbf{x})$$

In other words, in the two group case only one function is required for classification – values greater than $\ln(P(G_2)/P(G_1))$ implying assignment to group 1 and values less than this implying assignment to group 2. So common is the two group problem that many accounts of classification and many classification programs only consider the function w(**x**) and refer to it as *the* discriminant function. Of course it is simply a special case of the normal Bayes' rule with equal covariance matrices but this fact is difficult to see if you start an account of classification from w(**x**). Also if w(**x**) is the only sort of discriminant function you know, how do you classify objects into more than two groups? A traditional but very inefficient method is to repeatedly apply the two group discriminant function to one group versus the rest until the item is assigned to a single group. As w(**x**) is based on an assumption of normal distributions with equal covariance matrices it is unlikely to work unless the groups are very well separated. In the two group case classification using w(**x**) yields the same result as using $f_i(\mathbf{x})$ but when there are more than two cases the procedure based on $f_i(\mathbf{x})$ described in the last section should be used in preference to any ad hoc procedure based on repeated use of w(**x**) to discriminate between pairs of groups.

Summary and discussion

The assumption of multivariate normality within the groups leads to the quadratic discriminant form of Bayes' rule. Adding the further condition that the covariance matrices are the same for each group leads to the linear discriminant form of Bayes' rule. Notice that if the appropriate assumptions are satisfied *and* the group means and group covariance matrices are *known* then the resulting discriminant functions are the Bayes' rule. On the other hand if the assumptions are only approximately satisfied or if the group means and covariance matrices have to be estimated the discriminant functions are not the Bayes' rule for the data in question. In this case we can be sure that there is a rule that does better than either discriminant function – i.e. the true Bayes' rule for the data. Of course even in situations where neither of the discriminant functions are the true Bayes' rule they may perform well enough for us not to worry about complete optimality. For this reason the properties and practical use of the linear and quadratic discriminant functions form the subject of the next two chapters.

Chapter Four
Classification in Action

In the previous chapter the two most commonly encountered methods of classification, the quadratic and linear discriminant functions, were introduced. In this chapter programs to calculate both forms of discriminant function are described along with a number of examples. The numerical methods used within the programs are also described but these sections (marked **) can be skipped if you are only interested in using the programs and the classification methods. All of the programs in this book can be used for practical data analysis but they should also be used to gain experience of the methods by re-analysing each of the example data sets. (To enable this practical experience to be taken even further a data generation program is given in Appendix 2 which can be used to construct samples from normal populations with known parameters.)

A data entry program

All of the analysis programs in this and the following chapters read their data from disk. This is sensible because it allows the same data to be analysed more than once without having to retype it and it allows data sets larger than can be held in memory to be analysed. However it is necessary first to store the data on disk and to this end the following data entry program is provided:

```
 10 PRINT
 20 PRINT "E N T R Y/E D I T"
 30 GOSUB 1000:REM MENU
 40 IF C=1 THEN GOSUB 2000:REM ENTER DATA
 50 IF C=2 THEN GOSUB 3000:REM LIST DATA
 60 IF C=3 THEN GOSUB 4000:REM SAVE DATA
 70 IF C=4 THEN GOSUB 5000:REM LOAD DATA
 80 IF C=5 THEN GOSUB 6000:REM ALTER DATA
 90 IF C=6 THEN STOP
100 GOTO 10
```

```
1000 PRINT
1010 PRINT "SELECT ONE OF.."
1020 PRINT
1030 PRINT "1..ENTER DATA"
1040 PRINT "2..LIST DATA"
1050 PRINT "3..SAVE DATA"
1060 PRINT "4..LOAD DATA"
1070 PRINT "5..ALTER DATA"
1080 PRINT "6..STOP"
1090 PRINT
1100 INPUT C
1110 RETURN

2000 PRINT
2010 PRINT "NUMBER OF VARIABLES ";
2020 INPUT N
2030 PRINT "NUMBER OF CASES";
2040 INPUT M
2050 DIM D(N,M)
2060 FOR J=1 TO M
2070 FOR I=1 TO N
2080 PRINT "CASE ";J;" VARIABLE ";I;
2090 INPUT D(I,J)
2100 NEXT I
2110 NEXT J
2120 RETURN

3000 PRINT
3010 FOR J=1 TO M
3020 PRINT "CASE ";J
3030 FOR I=1 TO N
3040 PRINT "VARIABLE ";I;"=";D(I,J)
3050 NEXT I
3060 PRINT
3070 NEXT J
3080 RETURN
4000 PRINT
4010 PRINT "FILE NAME ";
4020 INPUT F$
4030 GOSUB 7000:REM OPEN OUTPUT FILE
4040 R=N:GOSUB 7100:REM WRITE R
4050 R=M:GOSUB 7100
4060 FOR J=1 TO M
4070 FOR I=1 TO N
4080 R=D(I,J):GOSUB 7100
4090 NEXT I
4100 NEXT J
4110 GOSUB 7400:REM CLOSE FILE
4120 RETURN

5000 PRINT
5010 PRINT "FILE NAME ";
```

32 Classification Algorithms

```
5020 INPUT F$
5030 GOSUB 7200:REM OPEN INPUT FILE
5040 GOSUB 7300:N=R:REM READ R
5050 GOSUB 7300:M=R
5060 DIM D(N,M)
5070 PRINT "CASES=";M;"VARIABLES=";N
5080 FOR J=1 TO M
5090 FOR I=1 TO N
5100 GOSUB 7300:D(I,J)=R
5110 NEXT I
5120 NEXT J
5130 GOSUB 7400:REM CLOSE FILE
5140 RETURN

6000 PRINT
6010 PRINT "ALTER WHICH CASE ";
6020 INPUT J
6030 PRINT "WHICH VARIABLE ";
6040 INPUT I
6050 PRINT "CURRENT VALUE =";D(I,J)
6060 PRINT "NEW VALUE=";
6070 INPUT D(I,J)
6080 RETURN

7000 OPEN "O",#1,F$
7010 RETURN

7100 PRINT #1,R
7110 RETURN

7200 OPEN "I",#1,F$
7210 RETURN

7300 INPUT#1,R
7310 RETURN

7400 CLOSE #1
7410 RETURN
```

When run this program allows the user to select one of six input and editing options. Option 1 allows new data to be entered, option 2 allows data to be listed, option 3 will save the data on disk. Option 4 will load an existing data set from disk so that it can be listed or altered using option 5. Option 6 stops the program. Although this is a useful utility it has a number of restrictions. It can only be used to edit data sets small enough to be loaded into memory and it cannot be used to extend existing data sets by adding cases or variables. However the program is written in a modular form and it should be relatively easy to add any extra facilities that are required. The purpose of each subroutine is listed in Table 4.1.

Table 4.1 Data entry/edit subroutine use.

Subroutine	Action
10–100	Main program – calls subroutines.
1000	Print menu.
2000	Read in data.
3000	Print variables.
4000	Save data to disk.
5000	Load data from disk.
6000	Alter a value.
7000	Open output file.
7100	Write R to file.
7200	Open input file.
7300	Read R from file.
7400	Close file.

The only subroutines that might need changing if the program is run under another dialect of BASIC are subroutines 7000, to open a file F$ for output; 7100, to write a single variable R to the output file; 7200, to open a file F$ for input; 7300, to read a single variable R from the input file; and subroutine 7400 to close either the input or the output file. The only other information that might be of interest is the format of the data files created by the program. Each file is simply a list of numbers with no special structure. The first number (N) indicates the number of variables and the second (M) the number of cases. Then there are $N \times M$ numbers in case order, that is N numbers that form case 1 followed by N numbers that form case 2 and so on to case M.

A linear discriminant program

Although the quadratic discriminant function should logically come first, as the linear discriminant is just a special case of the more general procedure, it is simpler to describe the linear discriminant program first. The data file that the program reads is assumed to consist of a number of cases from each group in order. Thus a data file consisting of 100 cases might represent twenty cases from the first group followed by thirty from the second and fifty from the third. After asking for the name of the file the program asks for the number of groups, the number of cases from each group and for the prior probability of each group. It then reads the data file and calculates and prints the estimated means and estimated common covariance matrix. It should be noticed that, although the estimates of the group means are based on the number of cases in each group, the common covariance matrix is estimated using all of the data. From these estimates the program then calculates and prints the coefficients of the linear discriminant function for each group. From the point of view of the theory that has been introduced so far, this is all that the program has to do but it would be unsatisfactory not to give some idea of how well the classification rule works. Perhaps the most obvious thing to do is to use the discriminant functions to classify the data that was used to construct them. This is indeed what the program does, it re-reads the data file and works out the value of each discriminant function on each case. The value of the largest discriminant function is printed for each case and a count is kept of how many cases are misclassified in total. As you might expect there are problems with this very simple approach to evaluating how well a classification rule works: in general it tends to overestimate how well the rule does, but it is still a useful guide. (The evaluation of how well a classification rule works is covered in Chapter 6.)

The program given below should be entered and tested using the data presented in the baby weight and height example (see later). If you are using another dialect of BASIC the only subroutines that are likely to need changing are subroutines 7200, open a file F$ for input; 7300, read a single value into R from the input file; and 7400, close the input file.

```
10 GOSUB 1000:REM GET PARAMETERS
20 GOSUB 2000:REM MAKE S AND MEANS
30 GOSUB 3000:REM PRINT STATS
40 GOSUB 4000:REM CALCULATE DISC.
50 GOSUB 5000:REM PRINT RESULTS
60 GOSUB 2500:REM CLASSIFY CASES
70 STOP
1000 PRINT "LINEAR DISCRIMINANT"
1010 PRINT
1020 PRINT "DATA FILE NAME ";
1030 INPUT F$
1040 GOSUB 7200:REM OPEN INPUT FILE
1050 GOSUB 7300:N=R:REM READ R
1060 GOSUB 7300:M=R
1070 PRINT "CASES=";M;"VARIABLES=";N
1080 PRINT "NUMBER OF GROUPS ";
1090 INPUT G
1100 DIM M(G)
1110 FOR I=1 TO G
1120 PRINT "NUMBER OF CASES IN GROUP ";I;
1130 INPUT M(I)
1140 NEXT I
1150 PRINT
1160 DIM S(N,N),X(N),T(N),C(N+1,G),A(N,G),F(G),P(G)
```

```
1170 FOR I=1 TO G
1180 PRINT "PRIOR PROB. FOR GROUP ";I;"=";
1190 INPUT P(I)
1200 NEXT I
1210 RETURN
2000 FOR K=1 TO G
2010 FOR J=1 TO M(K)
2020 FOR I=1 TO N
2030 GOSUB 7300
2040 A(I,K)=A(I,K)+R
2050 X(I)=R
2055 IF K=1 AND J=1 THEN T(I)=R
2060 NEXT I
2070 FOR I=1 TO N
2080 FOR L=1 TO I
2090 S(L,I)=S(L,I)+(X(L)-T(L))*(X(I)-T(I))
2100 NEXT L
2110 NEXT I
2120 NEXT J
2130 NEXT K
2140 FOR K=1 TO G
2150 FOR J=1 TO N
2160 FOR I=1 TO J
2170 S(I,J)=S(I,J)-(A(I,K)-M(K)
*T(I))*(A(J,K)-M(K)*T(J))/M(K)
2180 NEXT I
2190 NEXT J
2200 T=T+M(K)
2210 NEXT K
2230 FOR J=1 TO N
2240 FOR I=1 TO J
2250 S(I,J)=S(I,J)/(T-G)
2260 S(J,I)=S(I,J)
2270 NEXT I
2280 NEXT J
2290 FOR K=1 TO G
2300 FOR I=1 TO N
2310 A(I,K)=A(I,K)/M(K)
2320 NEXT I
2330 NEXT K
2340 RETURN
2500 GOSUB 7400:REM CLOSE FILE
2510 GOSUB 7200:REM OPEN INPUT FILE
2515 GOSUB 7300:GOSUB 7300
2516 E=0
2520 FOR K=1 TO G
2530 PRINT "GROUP ";K
2540 FOR J=1 TO M(K)
2550 FOR I=1 TO N
2560 GOSUB 7300:REM READ R
2570 X(I)=R
2580 NEXT I
```

36 Classification Algorithms

```
2590 GOSUB 2800:REM FIND LARGEST DISCRIMINANT
2600 PRINT "LARGEST IS FUNCTION ";L;"=";F(L)
2605 IF L<>K THEN E=E+1
2610 NEXT J
2620 PRINT:PRINT
2630 NEXT K
2640 PRINT
2650 PRINT E*100/T;"% MISCLASSIFIED"
2660 RETURN

2800 FOR H=1 TO G
2810 F(H)=0
2815 FOR I=1 TO N
2820 F(H)=F(H)+X(I)*C(I,H)
2830 NEXT I
2840 F(H)=F(H)+C(N+1,H)+LOG(P(H))
2850 NEXT H
2860 L=1
2870 P=F(1)
2880 FOR H=2 TO G
2890 IF F(H)>P THEN P=F(H):L=H
2900 NEXT H
2910 RETURN

3000 FOR K=1 TO G
3010 PRINT:PRINT
3020 PRINT "GROUP ";K;" MEANS ON ";M(K);" CASES"
3030 FOR I=1 TO N
3040 PRINT "VARIABLE ";I;"=";A(I,K)
3050 NEXT I
3060 NEXT K
3070 PRINT
3080 PRINT
3085 PRINT "COVARIANCE MATRIX"
3090 FOR I=1 TO N
3100 FOR J=1 TO I
3110 PRINT TAB((J-1)*6);INT(S(I,J)*100)/100;
3120 NEXT J
3130 PRINT
3140 NEXT I
3150 PRINT
3160 RETURN

4000 GOSUB 6000:REM SWEEP ELIMINATION
4010 FOR K=1 TO G
4020 FOR I=1 TO N
4030 C(I,K)=0
4040 FOR J=1 TO N
4050 C(I,K)=C(I,K)-A(J,K)*S(I,J)
4060 NEXT J
4070 NEXT I
4090 FOR I=1 TO N
4100 C(N+1,K)=C(N+1,K)+C(I,K)*A(I,K)
4110 NEXT I
```

```
4120 C(N+1,K)=-C(N+1,K)/2
4130 NEXT K
4140 RETURN

5000 PRINT
5010 PRINT "DISCRIMINANT FUNCTIONS"
5020 PRINT
5030 FOR K=1 TO G
5040 PRINT "GROUP ";K
5050 FOR I=1 TO N
5060 PRINT "C(";I;")=";C(I,K)
5070 NEXT I
5080 PRINT "CONSTANT =";C(N+1,K)
5090 PRINT
5100 NEXT K
5110 RETURN

6000 FOR K=1 TO N
6010 GOSUB 8000:REM MAXIMISE PIVOT
6020 GOSUB 8200:REM PIVOT ON K
6030 NEXT K
6040 RETURN

7200 OPEN "I",#1,F$
7210 RETURN

7300 INPUT#1,R
7310 RETURN

7400 CLOSE #1
7410 RETURN


8000 P=S(K,K)
8010 I=K
8020 FOR J=K TO N
8030 IF ABS(P)>ABS(S(J,K)) THEN GOTO 8060
8040 I=J
8050 P=S(J,K)
8060 NEXT J
8070 IF K=I THEN RETURN
8080 FOR J=1 TO N
8090 P=S(K,J)
8100 S(K,J)=S(I,J)
8110 S(I,J)=P
8120 NEXT J
8130 RETURN
8200 FOR I=1 TO N
8210 IF I=K THEN GOTO 8260
8220 FOR J=1 TO N
8230 IF J=K THEN GOTO 8250
8240 S(I,J)=S(I,J)-S(I,K)*S(K,J)/S(K,K)
8250 NEXT J
```

38 *Classification Algorithms*

```
8260 NEXT I
8270 FOR I=1 TO N
8280 IF I=K THEN GOTO 8310
8290 S(K,I)=S(K,I)/S(K,K)
8300 S(I,K)=S(I,K)/S(K,K)
8310 NEXT I
8320 S(K,K)=-1/S(K,K)
8330 RETURN
```

Details of the linear discriminant program **

The linear discriminant program breaks down into three parts:

(1) The calculation of estimates of the group means and common covariance matrix.
(2) The calculation of the discriminant function coefficients.
(3) The classification of the data set using the discriminant functions.

The calculation of the means and the covariance matrix follows immediately after the parameters of the data set have been obtained by subroutine 1000. Subroutine 1000 also defines a number of arrays that are used later in the program. The purpose of each array can be seen in Table 4.2.

Table 4.2 Array use.

Array	Purpose
S(N,N)	Holds common covariance matrix and is used in computation of inverse covariance matrix.
X(N)	Used to read in each case.
T(N)	Holds first values of first case as 'working mean'.
C(N+1,G)	Stores discriminant function coefficients.
A(N,G)	Holds group means.
F(G)	Used to store values of discriminant functions during classification phase.
P(G)	Prior probabilities of each group.

N is the number of variables and G is the number of groups.

Subroutine 2000 reads the data file and calculates the group means and the covariance matrix. The group means are stored in A(N,G) in such a way that A(I,K) stores the mean of variable I in group K. Calculation of the common covariance matrix is simple enough in theory but in practice care has to be taken to avoid inaccuracy due to the limited precision offered by most versions of BASIC. The common covariance matrix is estimated by first working out an estimate of the covariance matrix within each group:

$$s_{ij}^k = \sum_{P=1}^{m_k} (x_{ip} - \bar{x}_i)(x_{jp} - \bar{x}_j)$$

where s_{ij}^k is the i,jth element of the covariance matrix S_k in group k. Given that each of these covariance matrices is an estimate of the same underlying covariance matrix the obvious thing to do is to average them to give a 'pooled estimated':

$$S = \frac{\sum_k S_k}{\sum_k m_k - G}$$

where m_k is the number of cases in group k and G is the total number of groups. Although this expresses the logic behind the calculation of the estimate of the common covariance matrix it is not the best way of going about the calculation. The usual way of working out a covariance estimate is to use the well known identity:

$$\sum_{P=1}^{m_k} (x_{ip} - \bar{x}_{ip})(x_{jp} - \bar{x}_j) = \sum_{P=1}^{m_k} x_{ip} x_{jp} - \sum_{P=1}^{m_k} x_{ip} \sum_{P=1}^{m_k} x_{jp}/m_k$$

Thus lines 2000 to 2130 calculate the sum of each variable (line 2040) and the sum of the cross products of each variable (line 2090). Then lines 2140 to 2210 correct the cross product sum by subtracting the product of the variable totals (line 2170). Finally the corrected sums-of-products matrix is converted to a covariance matrix by dividing each element by the total number of cases less the number of groups (line 2250). The only complication is that this method of computing covariances is liable to numerical error because the final result depends on the difference between two numbers (the sum of cross products and the cross products of the sums) which tend to be very large. In most computer languages taking the difference between large numbers that are close in value can produce results that are as good as random! One way of avoiding this is to keep the accumulated totals small by subtracting a 'working mean' from all the values. This is in fact what subroutine 2000 does; the elements of the array T(N) hold the values of the first case in the file and as long as these values are reasonably representative of the rest of the cases in the file the calculation of the covariance matrix will be reasonably accurate. (If you would like to know about better methods of calculating covariances then see [1].)

After subroutine 3000 has printed the group means and common covariance matrix, subroutine 4000 begins the work of calculating the discriminant function coefficients. As each set of coefficients is defined as:

$$c_k = \Sigma^{-1} \mu_k$$

where μ_k is the mean vector for the kth group, the first requirement is to find the inverse of the covariance matrix stored in the array S. Subroutine 4000 calls subroutine 6000 which finds the inverse covariance matrix by repeatedly calling subroutines 8000 and 8200. The method used is essentially a modification of Gauss-Jordan elimination [2] that is particularly suited to statistical calculations. Subroutine 8200 performs a 'sweep' operation using S(K,K) as the 'pivot' according to the following equations:

if I≠K and J≠K then

S*(I,J)=S(I,J)−S(I,K)×S(K,J)/S(K,K)

otherwise

S*(K,J)=S(K,J)/S(K,K)
S*(I,K)=S(I,K)/S(K,K)

and

S*(K,K)=−1/S(K,K)

where S* is the value of the covariance matrix after the sweep. By arranging the order of the operations it is possible to carry out a sweep operation on S without using an additional array to store the results – that is, a sweep operation can be seen as simply updating the contents of S. The purpose of defining a sweep operation is that if you perform N sweeps for values of K from 1 to N then the result left in S is −1 times the inverse of the covariance matrix. This is indeed how subroutine 6000 finds the inverse of the covariance matrix – by calling subroutine 8200, which performs a sweep on row and column K, N times. The only complication is that subroutine 8000 is called to swap rows in the array S to produce the largest pivotal element at each sweep. (More information on the use of sweep operations is given in Chapter 8 in connection with stepwise linear discriminant analysis.)

On return from subroutine 6000 all that is left for subroutine 4000 to do is to form the discriminant function coefficients in C(I,G). This is done by a straightforward application of the definition of the discriminant function and the inverse covariance matrix stored in S – lines 4010 to 4070. However to calculate the value of the constant for each function a slightly different method is used. From the definition of the constant:

$$C_{0k} = -\tfrac{1}{2}\mu_k' \Sigma^{-1} \mu_k$$

it is not difficult to see that:

$$C_{0k} = -\tfrac{1}{2}c_k' \mu_k$$

where c_k is the vector of discriminant function coefficients not including the constant. This is the method used by subroutine 4000 (lines 4090 to 4120) and the resulting constant for group K is stored in C(N+1,K).

After subroutine 5000 has printed the discriminant function coefficients subroutine 2500 is called to re-read the data file and classify each case. For each case the value of each discriminant function is calculated by subroutine 2800 and stored in F(G). Subroutine 2800 also finds the largest discriminant function for each case and returns its group number in L. If L isn't equal to the actual group number K then one is added to the error count (line 2605) which is printed as a percentage of the total number of cases after all the cases have been classified.

The purpose and use of all of the subroutines in the linear discriminant program can be seen in Table 4.3.

Table 4.3 Subroutine use.

Subroutine	Action
10–70	Main program.
1000	Get parameters of the problem and define arrays.
2000	Calculate mean and common covariance matrix.
2500	Classify file using discriminant functions.
2800	Calculate discriminant functions.
3000	Print means and covariance matrix.
4000	Calculate discriminant function coefficients.
5000	Print discriminant functions.
6000	Perform N sweeps on S(N,N) to produce inverse.
7200	Open input file F$.
7300	Read single value R from input file.
7400	Close file.
8000	Swap rows of S(N,N) to maximise pivotal element.
8200	Perform sweep on row and column k.

Classification Algorithms

Linear discriminant test data

The test data for the linear discriminant program is in fact the data used in the example of linear discrimination in Chapter 3 (which should be consulted for more information) – the infant height and weight data. There are only ten cases in each group and this makes the job of entering the data, using the program given at the beginning of this chapter, particularly easy.

Infant height and weights.

Girls		Boys	
height (cm)	weight (kg)	height (cm)	weight (kg)
53.1	3.6	52.8	3.5
50.4	2.4	54.2	4.6
52.0	2.5	54.1	4.4
52.8	3.2	54.0	4.0
52.5	2.8	56.9	6.0
54.6	3.5	53.8	4.2
55.7	4.1	49.2	0.9
55.0	3.0	51.9	2.6
56.5	3.3	53.7	4.2
50.8	2.2	54.8	3.9

Assuming the data is stored in a file called BABY the output of the linear discriminant program should be as follows:

```
LINEAR DISCRIMINANT

DATA FILE NAME ?BABY
CASES= 20 VARIABLES= 2
NUMBER OF GROUPS ? 2
NUMBER OF CASES IN GROUP  1?  10
NUMBER OF CASES IN GROUP  2?  10

PRIOR PROB. FOR GROUP   1 = ?.5
PRIOR PROB. FOR GROUP   2 = ?.5

GROUP  1  MEANS ON  10  CASES
VARIABLE  1 = 53.44
VARIABLE  2 = 3.16

GROUP  2  MEANS ON  10  CASES
```

```
VARIABLE  1 = 53.64
VARIABLE  2 = 3.93

COVARIANCE MATRIX
4.1
1.77   1.07

DISCRIMINANT FUNCTIONS

GROUP  1
C( 1 )= 41.328
C( 2 )=-65.3679
CONSTANT =-1001

GROUP  2
C( 1 )= 40.4086
C( 2 )=-63.1318
CONSTANT =-959.704

GROUP  1
LARGEST IS FUNCTION  2 = 955.752
LARGEST IS FUNCTION  2 = 922.407
LARGEST IS FUNCTION  1 = 981.536
LARGEST IS FUNCTION  2 = 968.882
LARGEST IS FUNCTION  1 = 982.59
LARGEST IS FUNCTION  1 = 1023.62
LARGEST IS FUNCTION  1 = 1029.86
LARGEST IS FUNCTION  1 = 1072.84
LARGEST IS FUNCTION  1 = 1115.22
LARGEST IS FUNCTION  1 = 951.553


GROUP  2
LARGEST IS FUNCTION  2 = 949.942
LARGEST IS FUNCTION  2 = 937.069
LARGEST IS FUNCTION  2 = 945.655
LARGEST IS FUNCTION  2 = 966.867
LARGEST IS FUNCTION  2 = 957.788
LARGEST IS FUNCTION  2 = 946.159
LARGEST IS FUNCTION  1 = 970.407
LARGEST IS FUNCTION  1 = 970.867
LARGEST IS FUNCTION  2 = 942.118
LARGEST IS FUNCTION  1 = 1005.74


30 % MISCLASSIFIED
```

A quadratic discriminant program

The quadratic discriminant program is constructed using the linear discriminant program as a starting point. Rather than type the whole quadratic discriminant program in from scratch it is possible to update the linear program in the following way: (The listing of the complete quadratic program is given below.)

44 Classification Algorithms

Change
lines   1000,1160,2090,2170,2590,2600,2820,2840,2890,3110,5010,5060, 5070,5080,5095.

Add
lines   1165,2175,2816,2825,3065,3085,3155,4015,5055,5075
and subroutines   4000,4500 and 4800.

Delete
lines   2230,2240,2250,2260,2270,2280.

The changes to the linear discriminant program are so few that it would be quite possible to combine both programs to produce a single linear/quadratic discriminant program but for the purposes of this book they are better left separate. From the user's point of view the similarity also extends to the questions that the program asks and the information that is printed. After asking for the data file name, the number of groups, the number in each group and the prior probability of each group the program calculates the estimated means and covariance matrix for each group and then prints them. Notice that the only difference in this phase of the program's operation is that a covariance matrix is calculated and printed for each group instead of a single common covariance matrix. The program then calculates and prints the determinant and the inverse covariance matrix for each group. Using this information combined with the group means any new case can be classified using the quadratic discriminant rule. However, as in the case of the linear discriminant program, it is interesting to discover how the classification rule performs on the data used to construct it and so the program re-reads the data file and classifies each case to the group with the smallest quadratic discriminant function.

The complete program is given below and although it can be derived from the linear discriminant program by making a few changes it is worth checking the final program line by line against this listing. The final check is of course that it gives the same results on the quadratic test data given later.

```
10 GOSUB 1000:REM GET PARAMETERS
20 GOSUB 2000:REM MAKE S AND MEANS
30 GOSUB 3000:REM PRINT STATS
40 GOSUB 4000:REM CALCULATE DISC.
50 GOSUB 5000:REM PRINT RESULTS
60 GOSUB 2500:REM CLASSIFY CASES
70 STOP

1000 PRINT "QUADRATIC DISCRIMINANT"
1010 PRINT
1020 PRINT "DATA FILE NAME ";
```

```
1030 INPUT F$
1040 GOSUB 7200:REM OPEN INPUT FILE
1050 GOSUB 7300:N=R:REM READ R
1060 GOSUB 7300:M=R
1070 PRINT "CASES=";M;"VARIABLES=";N
1080 PRINT "NUMBER OF GROUPS ";
1090 INPUT G
1100 DIM M(G)
1110 FOR I=1 TO G
1120 PRINT "NUMBER OF CASES IN GROUP ";I;
1130 INPUT M(I)
1140 NEXT I
1150 PRINT
1160 DIM S(N,N),X(N),T(N),A(N,G),F(G),P(G)
1165 DIM V(N,N*G),D(G)
1170 FOR I=1 TO G
1180 PRINT "PRIOR PROB. FOR GROUP ";I;"=";
1190 INPUT P(I)
1200 NEXT I
1210 RETURN

2000 FOR K=1 TO G
2010 FOR J=1 TO M(K)
2020 FOR I=1 TO N
2030 GOSUB 7300
2040 A(I,K)=A(I,K)+R
2050 X(I)=R
2055 IF K=1 AND J=1 THEN T(I)=R
2060 NEXT I
2070 FOR I=1 TO N
2080 FOR L=1 TO I
2090 V(L,I+N*(K-1))=V(L,I+N*(K-1))+
     (X(L)-T(L))*(X(I)-T(I))
2100 NEXT L
2110 NEXT I
2120 NEXT J
2130 NEXT K
2140 FOR K=1 TO G
2150 FOR J=1 TO N
2160 FOR I=1 TO J
2170 V(I,J+N*(K-1))=(V(I,J+N*(K-1))-
     (A(I,K)-M(K)*T(I))*(A(J,K)-M(K)*T(J))/
     (M(K)-1)
2175 V(J,I+N*(K-1))=V(I,J+N*(K-1))
2180 NEXT I
2190 NEXT J
2200 T=T+M(K)
2210 NEXT K
2290 FOR K=1 TO G
2300 FOR I=1 TO N
2310 A(I,K)=A(I,K)/M(K)
2320 NEXT I
2330 NEXT K
```

46 Classification Algorithms

```
2340 RETURN

2500 GOSUB 7400:REM CLOSE FILE
2510 GOSUB 7200:REM OPEN INPUT FILE
2515 GOSUB 7300:GOSUB 7300
2516 E=0
2520 FOR K=1 TO G
2530 PRINT "GROUP ";K
2540 FOR J=1 TO M(K)
2550 FOR I=1 TO N
2560 GOSUB 7300:REM READ R
2570 X(I)=R
2580 NEXT I
2590 GOSUB 2800:REM FIND SMALLEST DISCRIMINANT
2600 PRINT "SMALLEST IS FUNCTION ";L;"=";F(L)
2605 IF L<>K THEN E=E+1
2610 NEXT J
2620 PRINT:PRINT
2630 NEXT K
2640 PRINT
2650 PRINT E*100/T;"% MISCLASSIFIED"
2660 RETURN

2800 FOR H=1 TO G
2810 F(H)=0
2815 FOR I=1 TO N
2816 FOR L=1 TO N
2820 F(H)=F(H)+V(I,L+N*(H-1))*(X(I)-A(I,H))*
     (X(L)-A(L,H))
2825 NEXT L
2830 NEXT I
2840 F(H)=F(H)-LOG(P(H))+LOG(D(H))
2850 NEXT H
2860 L=1
2870 P=F(1)
2880 FOR H=2 TO G
2890 IF F(H)<P THEN P=F(H):L=H
2900 NEXT H
2910 RETURN

3000 FOR K=1 TO G
3010 PRINT:PRINT
3020 PRINT "GROUP ";K;" MEANS ON ";M(K);
     " CASES"
3030 FOR I=1 TO N
3040 PRINT "VARIABLE ";I;"=";A(I,K)
3050 NEXT I
3060 NEXT K
3065 FOR K=1 TO G
3070 PRINT
3080 PRINT
3085 PRINT "COVARIANCE MATRIX FOR GROUP ";K
3090 FOR I=1 TO N
```

```
3100 FOR J=1 TO I
3110 PRINT TAB((J-1)*6);INT(V(I,J+N*(K-1))
     *100)/100;
3120 NEXT J
3130 PRINT
3140 NEXT I
3150 PRINT
3155 NEXT K
3160 RETURN

4000 FOR L=1 TO G
4010 GOSUB 4500:REM SET UP S FOR GROUP L
4015 D(L)=1
4020 GOSUB 6000:REM GAUSS ELIMINATION
4030 GOSUB 4800:REM STORE INVERSE IN V
4040 NEXT L
4050 RETURN

4500 FOR I=1 TO N
4510 FOR J=1 TO N
4520 S(I,J)=V(I,J+N*(L-1))
4550 NEXT J
4560 NEXT I
4570 RETURN


4800 FOR I=1 TO N
4810 FOR J=1 TO N
4820 V(I,J+N*(L-1))=-S(I,J)
4830 NEXT J
4840 NEXT I
4850 RETURN

5000 PRINT
5010 PRINT "INVERSE COVARIANCE MATRICES"
5020 PRINT
5030 FOR K=1 TO G
5040 PRINT "GROUP ";K
5050 FOR I=1 TO N
5055 FOR J=1 TO N
5060 PRINT TAB(6*(J-1));INT(V(I,J+N*(K-1))
     *10000)/10000;
5070 NEXT J
5075 PRINT
5080 NEXT I
5090 PRINT
5095 PRINT "DET OF COVARIANCE MATRIX =";D(K)
5100 NEXT K
5110 RETURN

6000 FOR K=1 TO N
6010 GOSUB 8000:REM MAXIMISE PIVOT
6015 D(L)=D(L)*S(K,K)
6020 GOSUB 8200:REM SWEEP ON K
```

```
6030 NEXT K
6040 RETURN

7200 OPEN "I",#1,F$
7210 RETURN

7300 INPUT#1,R
7310 RETURN

7400 CLOSE #1
7410 RETURN

8000 P=S(K,K)
8010 I=K
8020 FOR J=K TO N
8030 IF ABS(P)>ABS(S(J,K)) THEN GOTO 8060
8040 I=J
8050 P=S(J,K)
8060 NEXT J
8070 IF K=I THEN RETURN
8080 FOR J=1 TO N
8090 P=S(K,J)
8100 S(K,J)=S(I,J)
8110 S(I,J)=P
8120 NEXT J
8130 RETURN

8200 FOR I=1 TO N
8210 IF I=K THEN GOTO 8260
8220 FOR J=1 TO N
8230 IF J=K THEN GOTO 8250
8240 S(I,J)=S(I,J)-S(I,K)*S(K,J)/S(K,K)
8250 NEXT J
8260 NEXT I
8270 FOR I=1 TO N
8280 IF I=K THEN GOTO 8310
8290 S(K,I)=S(K,I)/S(K,K)
8300 S(I,K)=S(I,K)/S(K,K)
8310 NEXT I
8320 S(K,K)=-1/S(K,K)
8330 RETURN
```

Details of the quadratic discriminant program **

The action of each subroutine within the quadratic discriminant program can be seen in Table 4.4.

Once again the program follows the three stages of:

(1) Estimating means and covariance matrices.

(2) Working out the discriminant functions.

(3) Classifying each case using the functions worked out in stage 2.

Table 4.4 Subroutine use.

Subroutine	Action
10–70	Main program.
1000	Get parameters of the problem and define arrays.
2000	Calculate means and covariance matrices.
2500	Classify file using discriminant functions.
2800	Calculate discriminant functions.
3000	Print means and covariance matrices.
4000	Calculate inverse and determinant.
4500	Set up array S for inversion of group L covariance matrix.
4800	Store result back in array V.
5000	Print inverse matrices and determinants.
6000	Perform N sweeps on S(N,N).
7200	Open input file F$.
7300	Read single value R from input file.
7400	Close file.
8000	Swap rows of S(N,N) to maximise pivotal element.
8200	Perform sweep on row and column K.

Stage one is essentially the same as for the linear discriminant program. The only real difference is that now a separate covariance matrix has to be estimated for each group. Rather than use a three dimensional array V(N,N,G) which some versions of BASIC do not support it is preferable to use different areas of a two dimensional array to store each of the covariance matrices. Line 1165 sets up an array V(N,N*G) and the first N columns are used to store the covariance matrix of the first group, the next N are used for the covariance matrix of the second group and so on. Thus the I,Jth element of the covariance matrix belonging to the Kth group is stored in V(I,J+N*(K−1)). Using this information you should be able to see how the individual covariance matrices are built up by subroutine 2000 using the same sums of products and products of sums methods described for the linear discriminant program. This is the method used by subroutine 4000 to find the inverse of each of the covariance matrices in turn. Subroutine 4500 transfers the covariance matrix for group L into the array S. Subroutine 6000 then finds the inverse covariance matrix using the sweep operations described in connection with the linear discriminant program. The result is left in the array S. Finally subroutine 4800 is called to store the inverse

50 Classification Algorithms

matrix back into the same area (in the array V) that the covariance matrix occupied.

The only other modification to the Gauss elimination stage of the program is due to the need to calculate the determinant of each covariance matrix. Fortunately this is an easy modification because it is not difficult to show that the determinant of the matrix is equal to the product of the pivots used at each stage of sweeping. Thus the determinant can be calculated by adding line 6∅15 which stores the results in the array D(G).

The classification stage proceeds in exactly the same way as for the linear discriminant program apart from the changes in subroutine 28∅∅ to calculate the quadratic function and to select the smallest rather than the largest function.

Quadratic discriminant test data

The quadratic discriminant test data is based on the 'good' and 'bad' transistor example in Chapter 3 which should be consulted if more information is required. The number of cases in each group is kept to ten to make entering and testing faster:

Transistor data.

Good transistors		Bad transistors	
gain	noise	gain	noise
117.6	7.9	71.8	15.5
116.2	5.8	131.0	12.3
139.4	4.2	69.5	18.4
127.2	9.4	96.7	15.9
117.7	11.0	107.6	15.0
112.1	7.9	71.5	17.5
186.2	10.4	82.1	15.4
153.0	9.2	122.1	14.8
127.6	9.6	128.8	12.9
179.7	15.4	87.6	16.9

If the above data is stored in a file called TRAN then the output of the quadratic discriminant program (if the analysis of Chapter 3 is performed) should be:

```
QUADRATIC DISCRIMINANT

DATA FILE NAME ?TRAN
CASES= 20 VARIABLES= 2
NUMBER OF GROUPS ? 2
NUMBER OF CASES IN GROUP  1 ? 10
NUMBER OF CASES IN GROUP  2 ? 10

PRIOR PROB. FOR GROUP  1 =?  .8
PRIOR PROB. FOR GROUP  2 =?  .2


GROUP  1   MEANS ON  10   CASES
VARIABLE  1 = 137.77
VARIABLE  2 = 9.18


GROUP  2   MEANS ON  10   CASES
VARIABLE  1 = 96.97
VARIABLE  2 = 15.56


COVARIANCE MATRIX FOR GROUP   1
 720.78
  44.49   9.23



COVARIANCE MATRIX FOR GROUP   2
 584.6
 -39.67   3.58


INVERSE COVARIANCE MATRICES

GROUP  1
 .0019  -.0096
-.0096   .1541

DET OF COVARIANCE MATRIX = 4676.97
GROUP  2
 .0068   .0758
 .0758  1.1181

DET OF COVARIANCE MATRIX = 522.811
GROUP  1
SMALLEST IS FUNCTION   1 = 9.23292
SMALLEST IS FUNCTION   1 = 9.90192
SMALLEST IS FUNCTION   1 = 12.5102
SMALLEST IS FUNCTION   1 = 8.96953
SMALLEST IS FUNCTION   1 = 10.7587
SMALLEST IS FUNCTION   1 = 9.6051
SMALLEST IS FUNCTION   1 = 12.3737
SMALLEST IS FUNCTION   1 = 9.10482
SMALLEST IS FUNCTION   1 = 9.01509
SMALLEST IS FUNCTION   1 = 13.2635


GROUP  2
SMALLEST IS FUNCTION   2 = 12.0279
SMALLEST IS FUNCTION   2 = 10.6588
SMALLEST IS FUNCTION   2 = 10.462
SMALLEST IS FUNCTION   2 = 8.07399
SMALLEST IS FUNCTION   2 = 8.14587
```

```
SMALLEST IS FUNCTION  2 = 9.08333
SMALLEST IS FUNCTION  2 = 9.50301
SMALLEST IS FUNCTION  2 = 10.1942
SMALLEST IS FUNCTION  2 = 9.78605
SMALLEST IS FUNCTION  2 = 8.75132


0 % MISCLASSIFIED
```

A classic data set — Fisher's iris data

The set of measurements that can be seen in Appendix 3 relate to three species of iris. Measurements of sepal and petal length and width were made on fifty plants from each of iris setosa, iris versicolor and iris virginica for the purpose of constructing a classification rule. In fact this data set has been used many times as an example for a wide range of analysis techniques. It was the data that originally motivated Fisher [3] to derive the linear discriminant function and so it is appropriate that it should be re-analysed here. It is worth entering the data in Appendix 3 because it is used to demonstrate other methods introduced in later chapters.

If you use the quadratic discriminant program to analyse the iris data the results are very good – an error rate of only 2%. An examination of the covariance matrices suggests that although groups 2 and 3 are similiar, group 1's covariance matrix is fairly different. Even so if the same data is submitted to the linear discriminant program the same successful error rate of 2% is achieved. It is interesting to note that both the linear and quadratic discriminant functions misclassify the same cases. The reason for the good performance of both methods is simply due to the three groups being well separated – in this case there is no reason not to use the simpler linear discriminant classifier even though the population covariance matrices are unlikely to be the same. The output of both the quadratic and linear discriminant programs can be seen below:

Quadratic discriminant analysis of the iris data

```
QUADRATIC DISCRIMINANT

DATA FILE NAME ?IRIS
CASES= 150 VARIABLES= 4
NUMBER OF GROUPS ? 3
NUMBER OF CASES IN GROUP 1 ? 50
NUMBER OF CASES IN GROUP 2 ? 50
NUMBER OF CASES IN GROUP 3 ? 50

PRIOR PROB. FOR GROUP 1 =? 0.333
PRIOR PROB. FOR GROUP 2 =? 0.333
PRIOR PROB. FOR GROUP 3 =? 0.333
```

Classification in Action 53

```
GROUP   1    MEANS ON   50   CASES
VARIABLE   1 = 5.006
VARIABLE   2 = 3.428
VARIABLE   3 = 1.462
VARIABLE   4 = 0.246


GROUP   2    MEANS ON   50   CASES
VARIABLE   1 = 5.936
VARIABLE   2 = 2.77
VARIABLE   3 = 4.26
VARIABLE   4 = 1.326


GROUP   3    MEANS ON   50   CASES
VARIABLE   1 = 6.588
VARIABLE   2 = 2.974
VARIABLE   3 = 5.552
VARIABLE   4 = 2.026


COVARIANCE MATRIX FOR GROUP   1
 0.12
 0.09   0.14
 0.01   0.01   0.03
 0.01   0.00   0.00   0.01



COVARIANCE MATRIX FOR GROUP   2
 0.26
 0.08   0.09
 0.18   0.08   0.22
 0.05   0.04   0.07   0.03



COVARIANCE MATRIX FOR GROUP   3
 0.4
 0.09   0.1
 0.3    0.07   0.3
 0.04   0.04   0.04   0.07


INVERSE COVARIANCE MATRICES

GROUP   1
  18.9434  -12.4049   -4.5003  -4.7762
 -12.4049   15.5705    1.111   -2.1041
  -4.5003    1.111    38.776  -17.9351
  -4.7762   -2.104   -17.935  106.046

DET OF COVARIANCE MATRIX = 2.11308E-06

GROUP   2
   9.8511  -3.7212   -9.15      6.9263
  -3.7212  19.7127    2.1526  -19.4757
  -9.15     2.1526   20.3669  -27.1841
   6.926  -19.4757  -27.1841   86.8878

DET OF COVARIANCE MATRIX = 1.84142E-05


GROUP   3
```

```
    10.534    -3.4795   -9.9604    1.7877
    -3.479    15.8755    1.1024   -8.4731
    -9.9604    1.1024   13.406    -2.8904
     1.7877   -8.4731   -2.8904   19.3144

DET OF COVARIANCE MATRIX = 1.32742E-04
GROUP   1
SMALLEST IS FUNCTION   1 =-11.5186
SMALLEST IS FUNCTION   1 = -9.88665
       .         .         .
       .         .         .
GROUP   2
SMALLEST IS FUNCTION   2 =-3.66325
SMALLEST IS FUNCTION   2 =-7.37802
       .         .         .
       .         .         .
GROUP   3
SMALLEST IS FUNCTION   3 =-3.28204
SMALLEST IS FUNCTION   3 =-3.81981
       .         .         .
       .         .         .


      2 % MISCLASSIFIED
```

Linear discriminant analysis of the iris data

```
LINEAR DISCRIMINANT

DATA FILE NAME IRIS
CASES= 150 VARIABLES= 4
NUMBER OF GROUPS  3
NUMBER OF CASES IN GROUP  1 ? 50
NUMBER OF CASES IN GROUP  2 ? 50
NUMBER OF CASES IN GROUP  3 ? 50

PRIOR PROB. FOR GROUP   1 =? 0.333
PRIOR PROB. FOR GROUP   2 =? 0.333
PRIOR PROB. FOR GROUP   3 =? 0.333


GROUP  1   MEANS ON   50   CASES
VARIABLE   1 = 5.006
VARIABLE   2 = 3.428
VARIABLE   3 = 1.462
VARIABLE   4 = 0.246


GROUP  2   MEANS ON   50   CASES
VARIABLE   1 = 5.936
VARIABLE   2 = 2.77
VARIABLE   3 = 4.26
VARIABLE   4 = 1.326


GROUP  3   MEANS ON   50   CASES
VARIABLE   1 = 6.588
VARIABLE   2 = 2.974
VARIABLE   3 = 5.552
VARIABLE   4 = 2.026
```

```
COVARIANCE MATRIX
0.26
0.09  0.11
0.16  0.05  0.18
0.03  0.03  0.04  0.04

DISCRIMINANT FUNCTIONS

GROUP  1
C( 1 )= 23.8563
C( 2 )= 23.4916
C( 3 )=-16.8361
C( 4 )=-17.2237
CONSTANT =-85.5512

GROUP  2
C( 1 )= 15.7664
C( 2 )=  7.05326
C( 3 )=  5.06666
C( 4 )=  6.54266
CONSTANT =-71.6933

GROUP  3
C( 1 )= 12.423
C( 2 )=  3.69468
C( 3 )= 12.7225
C( 4 )= 21.1587
CONSTANT =-103.167

GROUP  1
LARGEST IS FUNCTION  1 = 90.2216
   .        .        .      .
   .        .        .

GROUP  2
LARGEST IS FUNCTION  2 = 93.1156
   .        .        .      .
   .        .        .

GROUP  3
LARGEST IS FUNCTION  3 = 115.423
   .        .        .
   .        .        .


   2 % MISCLASSIFIED
```

References

1. Welford, B.P. (1962) 'Note on a method for calculating corrected sums of squares and products', *Technometrics*, **4**, 419–20.
2. Wait, R. (1979) *The Numerical Solution of Algebraic Equations*: Wiley.
3. Fisher, R.A. (1936) 'The use of multiple measurements in taxonomic problems', *Ann. Eugenics*, **7**, 179–88.

Chapter Five
Some Practical Considerations

So far the only classification rules that we have considered minimise the total error of classification (TEC) if and only if the groups are multivariate normal. Not only this but up to this point we have supposed that the population parameters, the mean and the covariance matrices, have been known exactly. It is true that in the last chapter sample estimates of both the mean and the covariance matrices were used to compute discriminant functions but, while this may seem like a reasonable thing to do, it deserves closer examination. In practice it is rare that we can be sure that data has a normal distribution and it is clearly important to consider both the effect that this has on the quadratic and linear discriminant functions and investigate alternative classification procedures. This chapter is a discussion of some of the ideas and problems that occur in the application of classification methods to real data.

Some statistical results on the linear discriminant

Before going on to consider the problems of using estimates of the linear discriminant function it is worth examining the characteristics of the exact population discriminant function. For simplicity only the two group case is considered but the extension to the many group case is straightforward. If we know the values of the discriminant coefficients (or equivalently the population means and common covariance matrix) we are not working with an estimate of the discriminant function but the true or *population* discriminant function $w_p(\mathbf{x})$. (Recall that $w(\mathbf{x}) = f_1(\mathbf{x}) - f_2(\mathbf{x})$.) In this case it is easy to show that the mean of w_p in group 1 is:

$$E(w_p \mid G_1) = \tfrac{1}{2}(\boldsymbol{\mu}_1 - \boldsymbol{\mu}_2)'\boldsymbol{\Sigma}^{-1}(\boldsymbol{\mu}_1 - \boldsymbol{\mu}_2)$$
$$= \tfrac{1}{2}\delta^2$$

and in group 2 it is:

$$E(w_p \mid G_2) = -\tfrac{1}{2}\delta^2$$

where the notation E( ) is used to indicate the mean or expected value of the quantity between the brackets.

The quantity δ^2 is known as the Mahalanobis distance squared and it is a measure of how far apart or how separable the two groups are. Note that it is a population quantity; its sample estimate is:

$$D^2 = (\bar{x}_1 - \bar{x}_2)'S^{-1}(\bar{x}_1 - \bar{x}_2)$$

The variance of w_p in either population is:

$$VAR(w_p) = \delta^2$$

These results hold even if the two groups are not multivariate normal. If they are multivariate normal then w_p has a normal distribution within each group. Thus the distribution of w_p can be imagined as shown in Fig. 5.1. In the next chapter we will return to the subject of how the Mahalanobis distance affects the accuracy of classification.

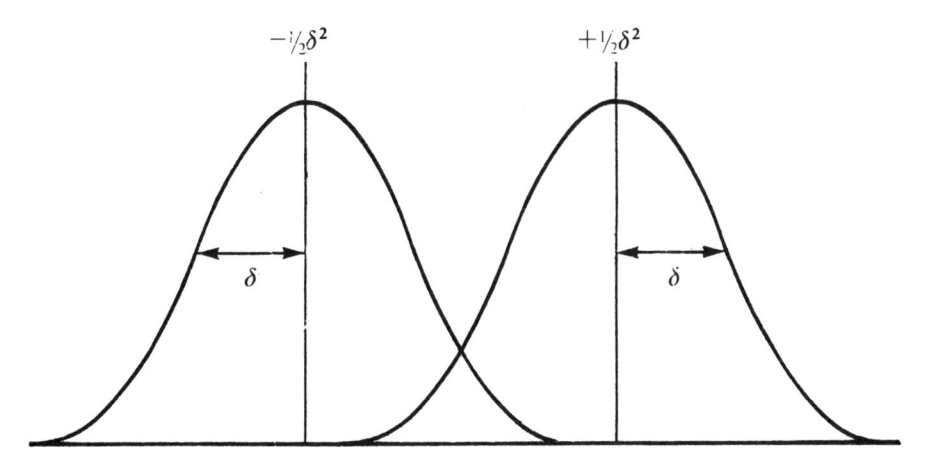

Fig. 5.1 Distribution of f_p

The standard situation is not to know the mean and covariance matrix of the groups and hence for the discriminant functions to be unknown. The obvious method of estimating the discriminant functions is to use sample estimates of the means and covariance matrix in the equations that define the discriminant functions – the so called 'plug in estimator'. In this case the discriminant function coefficients are themselves random variables. (That is, the value of the discriminant function coefficients would change with each sample that was used to estimate them even though the true discriminant functions remained constant.) In this case it would be interesting to know the distribution of the sample discriminant function w_s for repeated sampling; however this is a very difficult problem. A simpler question relates to the distribution of w_s when calculated from a single sample. That is, if we take a single sample and estimate the mean and covariance matrix, what is the distribution of the resulting values of w_s in future samples? In this case the means and variance can be shown to be:

$$E(w_s \mid G_1) = [\mu_1 - \tfrac{1}{2}(\bar{x}_1 - \bar{x}_2)]'S^{-1}(\bar{x}_1 - \bar{x}_2)$$

$$E(w_s \mid G_2) = [\mu_2 - \tfrac{1}{2}(\bar{x}_1 - \bar{x}_2)]'S^{-1}(\bar{x}_1 - \bar{x}_2)$$

$$\mathrm{VAR}(w_s) = (\bar{x}_1 - \bar{x}_2)'S^{-1}\Sigma S^{-1}(\bar{x}_1 - \bar{x}_2)$$

If in these quantities we replace the (unknown) population quantities by their usual sample estimates we obtain $D^2/2$, $-D^2/2$ and D^2 for the means and variance, where D^2 is the sample estimate of σ^2. (In other words, D is the sample Mahalanobis distance.) We can thus use D as an estimate of the standard error of w_s in either population. It should be noted that these are estimates of the means and variance of a discriminant function obtained from a single sample. If the underlying populations are normal then so is w_s.

The bias of the plug in estimator

The use of the plug in estimate, that is, the substitution of sample estimates for parameters in the equation for the population discriminant function, seems simple and direct but there is no particular justification for using it in preference to any other estimate. It is clearly worth investigating its behaviour to see if there are any improvements that can be made. For any estimator there are two important questions concerning its behaviour – is it biased? (that is, does it show any tendency to be consistently higher or lower than the true value?) and how far away from the true value does it tend to be? If there was a free choice there is no doubt that we would all prefer to use an estimate that was unbiased and as close to the true value as possible! All of the questions that are relevant to an estimator can be answered by reference to its distribution but, as already stated, the distribution of the plug in estimate of

Some Practical Considerations

the linear discriminant function is very complicated. However it is possible to derive some useful results concerning the bias of the plug in estimate without knowing its distribution.

The bias of an estimator is usually taken to refer to the behaviour of its expected value or mean. An estimate, ê, of a population parameter e is said to be unbiased if its expected value is the same as the parameter, that is:

$$E(ê) = e$$

and biased otherwise. If an estimator is biased and its expectation can be expressed as:

$$E(ê) = ae + b$$

(and as long as a and b are not functions of any of the quantities we are trying to estimate) we can form a new estimator (ê−b)/a that is unbiased:

$$E((ê - b)/a) = e$$

so there is a possibility of improving an estimator once the bias has been found.

The first important observation is that any bias present in the plug in estimator will reduce as the sample size increases. As $f_s(x)$, the sample linear discriminant function, is given by:

$$f_{s_i}(x) = \bar{x}_i' S^{-1} x - \tfrac{1}{2} \bar{x}_i' S^{-1} \bar{x}_i$$

and as $\bar{x}_i$ and S, on average, become closer to their true population values as the sample size increases so we can expect f_{s_i} to tend to f_{p_i} as the sample size increases. From this very rough and ready argument we can say that any bias in f_s is likely to be important only for small samples.

Using standard results on the expectation of the sample covariance matrix and the sample means, the expectation of f_s can be shown to be:

$$E(f_{s_i}(x)) = \frac{(M - G)}{(M - G - n - 1)} \left[f_{p_i}(x) - \frac{1}{2} \frac{n}{m_i} \right]$$

where M is the total sample size, m_i is the number in the sample from group i (thus $M = \Sigma m_i$), G is the number of groups and n is the number of variables. (The expectation is conditional on x and is more correctly written $E(f_{s_i}(x)|x)$ but its meaning seems clear in its present form.) Examining this expression bears out the prediction that the bias decreases as the sample size increases. For large values of M and m_i the quantity $(M-G)/(M-G-n-1)$ tends to 1 and n/m_i tends to 0 and so $E(f_{s_i}(x))$ tends to $f_{p_i}(x)$ and the plug in estimator is unbiased. A more subtle point is that if the same number of cases are sampled from each group (i.e. $m_i = M/G$) then the bias makes no difference to how cases are assigned because it is the same for each discriminant function and doesn't alter which is the largest.

These facts can be seen more clearly from the unbiased version of the plug in estimator:

$$U_i(x) = \frac{(M-G-n-1)}{(M-G)} f_{s_i}(x) + \frac{1}{2}\frac{n}{m_i}$$

If $U_i(x)$ is used for classification when $m_i = N/G$ then it produces exactly the same results as $f_{s_i}(x)$, the usual linear discriminant function. In most practical applications it is not worth going to the trouble of using $U_i(x)$ because M−G will be much larger than n+1. For example, for a sample of 100 from two groups involving ten variables the correction factor by which $f_{s_i}(x)$ should be multiplied is 97/98 or 0.99. In the same way even the $n/2m_i$ additive correction quickly becomes very small as m_i increases. The danger with the additive factor is that it is possible for some of the m_i to be small even when M is large. If in the previous example only ten cases were taken from group 1 then $n/2m_1$ would be 10/20 or 0.5 and $n/2m_2$ would be 10/180 or 0.056. Even so the correction is usually not great!

If you would like to try the unbiased version of the plug in estimator then make the following modifications and additions to the linear discriminant program given earlier:

```
1210 PRINT "UNBIASED ESTIMATE Y/N ";
1220 INPUT U$
1230 RETURN


2840 F(H)=F(H)+C(N+1,H)
2845 IF U$="Y" THEN F(H)=F(H)*(T-G)/
     (T-G-N-1)+N/M(H)/2
2846 F(H)=F(H)+LOG(P(H))
```

Notice that the correction for bias doesn't alter the calculation of the discriminant function coefficients, only the calculation of the discriminant scores. For most practical applications the standard plug in estimator can be used. However when the estimation of the probabilities of group membership is important then the unbiased estimate is worth using (see later and [1]).

Linear and quadratic discriminant functions for other distributions

The most popular method of classification is most certainly the linear discriminant function. The reason for this is partly that it is simple to understand and easy to use but the fact that it tends to work well in a range of situations also has to be taken into account. In other words even when the underlying distributions are not normal or have unequal covariance matricies the linear discriminant function tends to work quite well. One reason for this good-natured behaviour is that the Bayes' rule has the form of the linear discriminant function for any collection of groups with distributions of the form:

$$P(\mathbf{x} \mid G_i) = K(\mathbf{A})f(\sqrt{(\mathbf{x} - \boldsymbol{\mu}_i)'\mathbf{A}(\mathbf{x} - \boldsymbol{\mu}_i)})$$

where $K(\mathbf{A})$ is a normalising constant and $f(\mathbf{x})$ is an arbitrary non-negative function (sufficiently well behaved to be integrable [2]). This equation may look a little complicated but the family of distributions that it describes is easily characterised in terms of the probability contours of the distributions. The distributions described by the above equation all have elliptical probability contours and only differ in the rate at which the probability decreases away from the mean. In other words, the distributions have the same shape as the multivariate normal, they just decrease more or less rapidly. A large number of distributions do have this elliptical shape and unless a distribution has a very odd shape a linear discriminant function will be appropriate. What does alter with the rate of decrease of probability is the relative importance of the discriminant functions belonging to each group. For example in the two group case the rule:

if

$$f_1(\mathbf{x}) - f_2(\mathbf{x}) > \ln(P(G_2)/P(G_1))$$

assign to group 1
else assign to group 2

may have to be modified to:

if

$$f_1(\mathbf{x}) - f_2(\mathbf{x}) > c \ln(P(G_2)/P(G_1))$$

assign to group 1
else assign to group 2

62 Classification Algorithms

to take account of non-normality in the data – c is a constant that depends on the distribution. If the distributions are known then it is possible to work out the value of the constant – for the multivariate normal c=1 for example – however it is normally necessary to find the value of c by trial and error. This accounts for the well known fact that a linear discriminant function can often give better results if the a priori probabilities are 'adjusted' away from their true values. Adjusting the a priori probabilities corresponds to adding a constant to each discriminant function and this is another way of making a correction for lack of normality in the underlying distributions. In practice adjusting the linear discriminant functions in this way has to be performed with some care due to the difficulties in estimating the performance of a classification rule, a subject which is dealt with in the next chapter.

In the same way it can be shown that the quadratic discriminant function is appropriate for a family of distributions like that described above but with the additional freedom that the covariance matrices are allowed to be different for each group. That is each distribution must have an elliptical shape but the orientation of the ellipses of constant probability can vary from group to group. Once again the relative importance of each discriminant function may be different from that suggested by the normal theory and this can be taken into account by adding a constant.

What the above argument does not explain is why the linear discriminant function also seems to work quite well when the covariance matrices are unequal. The reason for this is that treating the groups as if they had equal covariance matrices is equivalent to replacing each of the different covariance matrices by an 'average' covariance matrix. Thus, as long as the covariance matrices are not grossly dissimilar the linear discriminant functions will be quite close to the quadratic discriminant functions in the regions where the groups are most dense. In other words, although the quadratic and linear discriminant functions give very different results a long way from the group means, they give similar results near the means where, of course, most of the cases to be classified occur. Once again treating groups as if they had equal covariance matrices can require that the linear discriminant functions are adjusted by the addition of a constant determined by trial and error. Sometimes with small samples the situation arises where linear discriminant functions work better than quadratic discriminant functions even though it is known that the covariance matrices are different. The reason for this is to do with the number of parameters to be estimated. To make a reasonably accurate estimate of the quadratic discriminant function, with its large number of parameters, requires more data than the linear discriminant function.

To summarise:

Some Practical Considerations **63**

(1) The quadratic and linear discriminant functions are appropriate for a wide range of distributions.

(2) Linear discriminant functions perform as well as quadratic functions unless there is a great deal of difference in the covariance matrices.

(3) To account for non-normality in data that shows elliptical symmetry it is often necessary to multiply each discriminant function by a 'weight' that is determined by trial and error.

(4) To account for lack of equality in the covariance matricies it is often necessary to multiply each linear discriminant function by a 'weight' that is determined by trial and error.

In short it is always worth trying a linear discriminant function!

Other criteria of classification

As mentioned many times Bayes' rule is optimal if minimum TEC is required. However if other measures of optimality are used then other rules will be desired. It is difficult to think of a more natural measure of how well a rule does than the number of cases it misclassifies but often there are more important considerations than the gross error rate. For example three common measures are:

(1) *Minimum cost* – if there is a penalty or cost associated with misclassifying a case that belongs to group i as belonging to group j then we might want to find a rule that minimises total cost rather than total misclassification rates.

(2) *Minimax error* – if there are a number of unknowns about the situation or if the parameters are subject to variation with time then we could be interested in finding a rule that minimises the maximum possible error – the so called minimax rule.

(3) *Fixed error rate* – it may be that the error rate for misclassification into one group in particular is more important than the rest. In this case it is desirable to use a rule that gives a predetermined value of error for this group subject to minimising the error rates for the other groups.

Even though each of these criteria are different in intent, notice that they are, as you might expect, connected with the error rate. In Chapter 10 a number of criteria for constructing discriminant functions which are not directly connected to the error rate are discussed. All that now remains is to derive

Classification rule for minimum total cost **

If we assign costs of penalties for an incorrect classification, we can derive a rule which minimises the expected loss. If we incur a cost c_{ij} when we classify a case from the ith group into the jth group ($c_{ii}=0$), then the rule which minimises the expected loss is:

assign the case **x** to the kth group if

$$\sum_i P(G_i)P(\mathbf{x} \mid G_i)c_{ki} < \sum_j P(G_j)P(\mathbf{x} \mid G_j)c_{mj}$$

for all $m \neq k$. This may look complicated but as $P(G_i)P(\mathbf{x}|G_i)$ is proportional to $P(G_i|\mathbf{x})$ the sum:

$$\sum_i P(G_i)P(\mathbf{x} \mid G_i)c_{ki}$$

is proportional to:

$$\sum_i P(G_i \mid \mathbf{x})c_{ki}$$

which can be thought of as the expected cost of assigning **x** to group k and obviously we should assign the case to the group for which this is a minimum. This is clearly an extension of Bayes' rule and any of the classification rules derived from Bayes' rule can be modified to include costs. For example in the multi-group normal case we have:

assign to the kth group if

$$L_k < L_j \qquad \text{for all } j \neq k$$

where:

$$L_j = \sum_{i \neq j} P(\mathbf{x} \mid G_i)P(G_i)c_{ji}$$

$$= \sum \frac{1}{(2\pi)^{n/2}|\Sigma|^{1/2}} \exp[-\tfrac{1}{2}(\mathbf{x} - \boldsymbol{\mu}_i)'\Sigma^{-1}(\mathbf{x} - \boldsymbol{\mu}_i)]P(G_i)c_{ji}$$

As before, we can cancel the common factor $1/(2\pi)^{n/2}$ from all of the L_js to arrive at the least cost classifier.

Some Practical Considerations

If we assume common covariance matrices we can cancel the $|\Sigma|^{1/2}$, and the $\exp(x'\Sigma^{-1}x)$, from each term to obtain

$$L_j = \sum_{i \neq j} \exp(f_i) P(G_i) c_{ji}$$

where f_i is the usual linear discriminant function. This minimum cost rule is not easy to use because of the presence of the uncancelled exponential function in each term.

If we set $c_{ij} = c$, i.e. equal costs, then we recover the Bayes' rule. Thus the Bayes' rule minimises the expected loss if all the misclassification costs are equal.

Minimax classifier **

Suppose that in the two group case $P(G_1)$ and $P(G_2)$ are either not known or are known to vary. For any classification rule the error rate will vary with $P(G_1)$ (and hence $P(G_2) = 1 - P(G_2)$). The minimax rule gives the smallest value for the maximum error as $P(G_1)$ varies. It thus protects us from doing very badly indeed. The minimax rule is the Bayes' rule but with the 'cut off' point adjusted to give equal errors in both groups. Thus:

if

$$\frac{P(x \mid G_1)}{P(x \mid G_2)} > B$$

then assign to group 1
otherwise assign to group 2

where B is adjusted to give equal errors in both groups. In the normal equal covariance case this becomes

$$f_1 - f_2 > 0 \quad \text{then assign to group 1}$$
$$f_1 - f_2 < 0 \quad \text{then assign to group 2}$$

which is the usual rule but without any values of $P(G_1)$.

Fixed error rate classifier **

The Bayes' rule minimises the total error rate. In the two group case we can split this total error into two parts, E_1, the error rate due to misclassifying cases from group 1, and E_2, the error rate due to misclassifying cases from group 2. The Neyman Pearson or likelihood ratio rule minimises E_1 subject to E_2 being equal to some *fixed* value E_0, and is equal to:

66 Classification Algorithms

if

$$\frac{P(x \mid G_1)}{P(x \mid G_2)} > u \qquad \text{then assign to group 1}$$

$$< u \qquad \text{then assign to group 2}$$

where the constant u is adjusted to make $E_2 = E_0$.

For the linear discriminant function this becomes:

if

$$f_1 - f_2 > \ln u \qquad \text{assign to group 1}$$

$$< \ln u \qquad \text{assign to group 2}$$

where ln(u) is the solution to the equation

$$\Phi\left(\frac{\ln u - \delta^2/2}{\delta}\right) = E_0$$

Φ is the standard cumulative normal. The corresponding theoretical value for E_1 is:

$$E_1 = \Phi\left(\frac{\ln u + \delta^2/2}{\delta}\right)$$

or

$$E_1 = \Phi\left(\frac{\ln u - \delta^2/2}{\delta}\right) - 0.5$$

For other rules the value of u can be found from the solution to the equation:

$$E_0 = \int_{R_1} P(x \mid G_2) \, dx$$

where R_1 is the region in which x is classified as group 1. In general the value of u that produces a given error rate is difficult to find.

Alternatives to the plug in estimate of a classifier

As already mentioned a number of times, the most obvious way of obtaining an estimate of the linear or quadratic discriminant function is to substitute the sample values of the population parameters in the classification rule. This leads to the 'plug in' estimate of the classification rule which has been discussed earlier in this chapter. It is important to always remember that this method or any other method of estimation doesn't give *the* Bayes' rule, only something that approximates to it. The plug in version of a classifier has few theoretical results to recommend it, but it is the best known and most often used estimation procedure. For completeness and to show that there are alternatives to the plug in estimate two other methods of estimation are described in the sections below. However, they will not be pursued any further in this book and the interested reader should see Reference [3] for more information. Both of the alternative methods of estimation discussed use Bayesian arguments but to go into the details of the Bayesian approach to statistics is beyond the scope of this book (interested readers should see Reference [4]). However it is worth saying that most of the philosophical and practical difficulties in using the Bayesian approach are due to the use of probability to represent degrees of belief rather than the relative frequency of occurrence of an event (see also Chapter 10). It is also important to realise that although Bayes' rule is derived using Bayes' theorem it isn't dependent on the Bayesian approach to statistics in any way nor does its use imply that Bayesian methods in the broadest sense are being used. (The following sections marked ** are not easy and may be omitted on first reading.)

The semi-Bayesian estimate **

If we have a population classification rule C_p then a Bayesian estimate based on a sample X from the population is $E(C_p|X)$, i.e. the posterior mean of C_p. This clearly depends on the assumption of some prior distribution for C_p, and here we meet with the usual philosophical problems of Bayesian estimates.

For the two-group discriminant function w_p and the 'non-informative' prior $p(\mu_1, \mu_2, \Sigma)$, we have:

$$E(w_p | \bar{x}_1, \bar{x}_2, S) = w_s + \frac{1}{2n}\left(\frac{1}{m_1} - \frac{1}{m_2}\right)$$

given that

$$p(\mu_1, \mu_2, \Sigma) \propto |\Sigma|^{(n+1)/2}$$

68 Classification Algorithms

where $\bar{x}_1$ and $\bar{x}_2$ are the sample means for the two groups, S is the sample covariance matrix, w_s is the usual plug in estimate of the linear discriminant function, n is the number of variables and m_1 and m_2 are the number of cases measured in each group. Hence the Bayesian estimate of w_p is the same as the plug in estimate when $m_1 = m_2$ and closely related otherwise. $E(C_p|X)$ has the property of minimising $E(C_p-c)^2$ where c is an estimate of C_p, but there seems to be little gain in abandoning the simple linear discriminant function in its favour.

The full Bayesian approach **

In the full Bayesian approach we use the Bayes' estimate of $P(x|G_i)$ which is of course $P(x|G_i,X)$ where X is a sample from the population. In the case of multivariate normality we have:

$$P(x \mid G_i, X_1, X_2, S)$$

$$= \int P(x \mid G_1, \mu_1, \mu_2, \Sigma) P(\mu_1, \mu_2, \Sigma^{-1} \mid \bar{x}_1, \bar{x}_2, S)\, d\mu_1\, d\mu_2\, d\Sigma^{-1}$$

$$= St\left(m_i - 1, \bar{x}_i, \left(1 + \frac{1}{m_i}\right)S_i\right)$$

where St is a multivariate student distribution. If the covariance matrices are equal, we have:

$$P(x \mid G_i, X_i, S) = St\left(M - G, \bar{x}_i, \left(1 + \frac{1}{m_i}\right)S\right)$$

There is evidence [3] that both the full Bayesian and semi-Bayesian estimates are superior to the plug in estimates but they are much more complex and hence are used infrequently. This might change as programs become available. For reasonably large sample sizes both methods produce results that are similar to the plug in estimate and for small sample sizes there is evidence that correcting the bias in the plug in estimate improves it to the point where there is little to be gained in using the more complicated Bayes' estimates [1].

Probabilities of classification

Although all that is needed to classify a case into one group or another is the value of the discriminant function for each group it is often useful to know the estimates of $P(G_i|x)$ for each group or just for the group with the largest discriminant function. If the distributions are known to be normal then

Some Practical Considerations 69

deriving estimates of $P(G_i|x)$ is fairly easy. In the case of equal covariance matrices and linear discriminant functions we have:

$$P(G_i \mid x) = \frac{\exp[f_i + \ln(P(G_i))]}{\sum_{j=1}^{G} \exp[f_j + \ln(P(G_j))]}$$

$$= \frac{\exp(f_i)P(G_i)}{\sum_{j=1}^{G} \exp(f_j)P(G_j)}$$

This equation has one problem – exp (f_i) can be very large. This can cause a computer to overflow or at least lead to inaccuracy when the divison is performed. A more practical form of the equation can be obtained by dividing top and bottom by $\exp[\max(f_k)]$ i.e. the largest of the EXP terms to give:

$$P(G_i \mid x) = \frac{\exp[f_i - \max(f_k)]P(G_i)}{\sum_{j=1}^{g} \exp[f_i - \max(f_k)]P(G_j)}$$

In the same way the discriminant score obtained from the quadratic discriminant function can be converted into probabilities:

$$P(G_i \mid x) = \frac{\exp[\max(d_k) - d_i]/P(G_i)}{\sum_{j=1}^{G} \exp[\max(d_k) - d_j]/P(G_j)}$$

An estimate of the probability of group membership for the largest discriminant function is easy to add to the linear discriminant program. Make the following modifications and additions:

```
2595 GOSUB 2700:REM FIND PROBABILITY
2600 PRINT J;TAB(3);"LARGEST IS FUNCTION ";
     L;"=";F(L);TAB(20);"PROB.=";P

2700 P=0
2710 FOR H=1 TO G
2720 IF F(H)-F(L)>-80 THEN P=P+EXP(F(H)-F(L))
2730 NEXT H
2740 P=1/P
2750 RETURN
```

70 Classification Algorithms

Subroutine 2700 calculates the probability using the equation given above. Notice that even though the largest discriminant function is subtracted from all the other values it is still possible to cause an error if F(H) is very much smaller than F(L) and so it is necessary to test in line 2720 for values that would cause the EXP function to fail due to 'underflow'.

In many situations it is more important to estimate $P(G_i|x)$ accurately than to simply assign new cases. In the same way that the plug in estimator is a biased estimate of the linear discriminant function so too are the estimates of the probabilities computed using it. However, in this case the bias is important even when the number of cases taken from each group is the same. The bias is also more important because the use of the EXP function in computing the probabilities tends to increase the effect of small differences in the discriminant functions. The obvious solution is to use the unbiased version of the plug in estimator, as described earlier, to compute the probabilities. Indeed if you have made the modifications to the linear discriminant program to compute the unbiased estimate then selecting this option will automatically result in unbiased estimates of the probabilities. In many ways the problem of bias in the estimation of $P(G_i|x)$ is not as serious as the assumption of normality. It is important to realise that, while a linear or quadratic discriminant function may give low error rates, this does not imply that the probability estimates based on them are valid. There are many distributions for which linear and quadratic discriminants are appropriate but the method of estimating $P(G_i|x)$ given above depends on multivariate normality.

The reject option

By examining the size of $P(G_i|x)$ you can gain an idea of how 'certain' the classification is. Clearly if the assignment is made with a value of $P(G_i|x)$ of 0.9 the classification is more certain than if $P(G_i|x)$ is around 0.5. It is possible to decide not to assign a case to any of the groups if the estimate of the probability of group membership is too low and this leads to the idea of a classification rule with a 'reject option'. Running this latest version of the linear discriminant program on the iris data reveals that in this case all of the correct assignments are associated with high probabilities of group membership whereas the misclassified cases are associated with low probabilities of group membership. If the cases which are assigned to a group on the basis of a low probability of group membership were 'rejected' (i.e. not classified) the total error rate would be reduced. In general it is always possible to improve the error rate of a classification rule by refusing to classify difficult cases!

It is not difficult to show that the optimum classification rule using a reject option is:

if $P(G_i|x)$ is the largest probability of group membership
then reject x if $P(G_i|x) < 1-t$
and assign to group i otherwise

where $0 \leq t \leq 1$. This is clearly nothing more than Bayes' rule with the extra condition that a case is rejected if the largest $P(G_i|x)$ is less than the reject threshold $1-t$. The reason for writing the reject threshold as $1-t$ is simply that t is related in various ways to the error rate for the rule. In particular it can be shown [5] that:

(1) The error rate decreases and the reject rate increases as t increases.

(2) The error rate is always less than $t \times 100\%$.

(3) t is the slope of the error/reject rate trade off curve.

The first result implies that it is always possible to trade error for rejects. The second result is not as useful as it appears because in practice t is always fairly large, for example 0.9 and knowing that the error rate is less than 90% is not very informative. The third result implies that the error rate reduction is most noticeable for large values of t, i.e for low rejection rates. This means that reject rules follow a law of diminishing returns as far as trading off error rates for reject rates is concerned. Rejecting a small proportion of cases can be expected to bring about a worthwhile reduction in the error rate but rejecting even more cases will not bring about as big reductions in the error rate.

The actual relationship between error rate and reject rate can be calculated if a particular distribution is assumed, e.g. multivariate normal, but in practice it is usual to obtain such information empirically. That is, a classification rule is repeatedly tested using different values of t and a graph of estimated error rate against estimated reject rate is drawn and a suitable working value for t is selected. There are many more interesting relationships between t and the error rate and it is possible to estimate the error rate from knowledge of how the reject rate varies with the value of t. This can be used to obtain estimates of the error rate when the correct assignment of the test sample is not known (see reference [6]).

Another approach to the problem of low probability of group membership is to test for 'outliers'. An outlier is a case that is so untypical of the groups that it is unlikely to have come from any of them. The standard test for a case x to have come from the groups under consideration is a multivariate T test [1] and this is much more complicated than the simple reject procedure outlined above. There is also a difference in intent between the reject and outlier procedure. The outlier procedure aims to detect and remove cases that are unlikely to have come from any of the groups whereas the reject procedure simply trades off error rate for reject rate. In other words, the reject procedure doesn't claim that the case comes from some group not under consideration it simply reserves judgment.

Missing values

In any application of statistics the problem of missing values arises and so it is with classification analysis. As the main techniques of classification depend on the use of the group means and either the common covariance matrix or the individual group covariance matrices, the problem of missing values can be treated as one of estimating a mean or covariance matrix using incomplete data. The most obvious method of handling a case with missing values of one or a number of variables is simply to omit the case in its entirety – thus reducing the sample size for that group by one. However if the total sample size is small or if missing values are very common omitting cases with missing values may result in some groups having virtually no cases at all! There are two main alternative approaches to this simple option – each element in the mean vector and the covariance matrix can be estimated from however many measurements are available or each missing value can be replaced by the mean for that measurement calculated from the available data. The first alternative results in a mean vector and a covariance matrix with elements that have been estimated from samples of different sizes. For example if in a sample of 100 ten cases are missing a value of variable 1, all of the elements of the mean vector would be based on a sample size of 100 apart from the first variable which would be based on a sample of 90. In the same way all of the elements of the covariance matrix would be based on a sample of size 100 apart from the elements in the top row and first column which would be based on a sample of 90. If your purpose is to obtain a good estimate of a linear or a quadratic discriminant function then this seems like a reasonable procedure unless the pattern of missing values is very extreme. However any statistics based on the mean or covariance matrix are not likely to be of use because they generally assume that the same sample size has been used throughout. The second option of substituting the mean in the estimation of the covariance matrix does at least allow standard programs to be used to derive the covariance matrix and discriminant functions and for this reason alone it is the most commonly used method of dealing with missing values. The rationale behind this method can be seen as substituting the best estimate of the missing measurement and this can be extended to other interpretations of 'best estimate'. For example it is possible to estimate the missing value from a regression using all the other variables. That is, if there are a number of cases with missing values of variable 1 then a regression equation is calculated using all the other variables with variable 1 as the dependent variable. Missing values of variable 1 can then be estimated using the regression equation and the values of the other variables in the cases affected. This use of a regression estimate for a missing value is clearly better than using the mean but it is very expensive in terms of computation.

The same set of problems can occur when using a discriminant function to classify new cases. Missing values in the calculation of a discriminant score can be treated in roughly the same way as in the estimation of the discriminant function, that is you can choose not to classify the case on the grounds of incomplete data or you can estimate the missing value by its mean or by using a regression estimate based on the remaining values. There is still much theoretical work to be done in the area of missing values in classification but for now the above procedures are practical and sufficient for most purposes.

References

1. Moran, M.A. and Murphy, B.J. (1979) 'A closer look at two alternative methods of statistical dicrimination'. *Applied Statistics*, **28**, 223–32.
2. Haralick, R.M. (1977) 'Pattern discrimination using ellipsoidally symmetric mutivariate density functions' *Pattern Recognition*, **9**, 89–94.
3. Aitchison, J., Habbema, J.D.F and Kay, J.W. (1977) 'A critical comparison of two methods of statistical discrimination' *Applied Statistics*, **26**, 15–25.
4. Lindley, D.V. (1965) *Introduction to Probability and Statistics from a Bayesian Viewpoint* (2 volumes): Cambridge University Press.
5. Chow, C.K., (1970) 'On optimum recognition error and reject tradeoff' *IEEE Transactions on Information Theory*, **IT-16**, 41–6.
6. Fukunaga, K. (1972) *Introduction to Statistical Pattern Recognition*: Academic Press.

Chapter Six
Evaluating Rules - Estimating Error Rates

Given that we have obtained a classification rule by some means then an obvious question to ask is 'how good is it?' In other words, if we use this rule, what percentage of cases will we misclassify in the long run? It should be noted that this question makes sense for *any* rule not just the Bayes' rule or those constructed by a particular statistical method. The way a classification rule was obtained does not affect the question 'how good is it?'

We can try and answer the question in two distinct ways:

(1) We can obtain statistical estimates of the performance of a rule by classifying samples from the population that the rule will be *used* on.

(2) We can use our theoretical assumptions about the populations, i.e. their normality, to produce a theoretical *prediction* for how a rule will perform.

Method 2 depends on the type of classification rule used and hence is highly specific. We will therefore deal with method 1 first, which leads to techniques which can be used with *any* rule.

It is important to notice that in this chapter we are concerned with the problem of estimating how good any given classifier is when working with a given population. There is a related but distinct question concerning the performance of the optimum or Bayes' classifier when working on a given population. In other words, if we knew the form of the Bayes' classifier, how well would it do? Obviously knowledge of the error rate of the best classifier could be used as a standard against which the error rate of any practical classification rule could be judged. Surprisingly it is possible to estimate the error rate of the Bayes' classifier without any knowledge of its form but a discussion of this technique is left until Chapter 9.

Statistical estimation of error rates

There are many techniques for statistical error estimation. We will discuss the four most important:

(1) Independent sample – unknown a priori probabilities

(2) Independent sample – known a priori probabilities

(3) The apparent error rate

(4) The 'leaving-one-out' and the jackknife rate

Other methods are encountered but these four have proved to be the most useful and easy to use.

Independent sample - unknown a priori probabilities

The most obvious way to test a classification rule is to take a new sample, i.e. one which was not used in the design of the classifier, and use the rule to classify the cases. The error rate is then simply estimated by the proportion of the sample misclassified. If the a priori probabilities of the groups are unknown then a straightforward random sample ignoring group structure should be used. This will provide examples from each group in the correct proportions for the estimate (compare with the next section).

If a sample of size M is drawn and e of them are misclassified, then:

$$E_1 = \frac{e}{M}$$

is an estimate of ϵ the true error rate. Two useful pieces of information about E_1 are:

(1) $E(E_1) = \varepsilon$

(2) $VAR(E_1) = \varepsilon(1 - \varepsilon)/M$

These tell us that E_1 is an unbiased estimate of ϵ and it is consistent (its spread or variance around the population error rate ϵ tends to zero as the sample size M increases). The expression for $VAR(E_1)$ may be used to find the standard error for E_1, (by the usual method of substituting sample values for unknown parameters in the expression for the variance:

$$SE(E_1) = \sqrt{\frac{E_1(1 - E_1)}{M}}$$

and approximate confidence intervals for E_1 (i.e. $E_1 \pm SE(E_1)$), although these must be used with caution in small samples. (In fact it is possible to obtain exact confidence intervals for E_1 and these are presented in [3].)

Independent samples with known a priori probabilities

If we know the a priori probabilities of the different classes then we can improve our error estimate by taking a stratified sample. If the a priori probability of a group G_i is P_i then we can take m_i samples from G_i where:

$$m_i = P_i M$$

That is, we take samples from each group such that the sizes are proportional to the probability of the group occurring.

We obtain the error estimate E_2 in a similar way to the previous technique by classifying each sub-sample and counting the total number misclassified. In this case we have:

$$E(E_2) = \varepsilon$$

(as was the case for E_1)

$$\text{VAR}(E_2) = \sum_{i=1}^{G} P_i e_i (1 - e_i)/M$$

where e_i is an estimate of the probability of misclassifying a case from group i given by:

$$e_i = \frac{E_i^*}{m_i}$$

where E_i^* is the number misclassified from group i. It can be shown that, for any M:

$$\text{VAR}(E_1) \geqslant \text{VAR}(E_2)$$

and thus a better estimate of the error rate can be obtained if *known* a priori probabilities are used.

The apparent error rate

This is the most commonly encountered and potentially the most misleading error estimate. If a classification rule is arrived at by using a sample, then an obvious estimate of the error rate can be obtained by classifying this same sample. This is the method introduced in Chapter 4 as part of both the linear discriminant and the quadratic discriminant programs and indeed it is the procedure used by most classification programs. The problem is that while it does lead to an estimate of the error rate it is a *biased* one. In fact it can be shown that the apparent error, as this estimate is called, leads to an estimate that is biased low. This is only to be expected as the classifier should do better on the sample it was designed for than on a new sample. If E_A is the apparent error rate then:

$$E(E_A) \leq \varepsilon$$

In other words, the apparent error rate is, on average, lower than the true error rate.

The optimistic bias in E_A has been the cause of many problems in applied classification. A classifier designed on a sample and evaluated on the same sample might give the impression of performing well, but when used in earnest usually proves to be a disappointment. However, this said, it must be pointed out that the bias decreases with sample size and hence, for large samples, E_A is a useful estimate of ε. It is always difficult to say what 'large' means but a common interpretation used in multivariate statistics is to regard a sample with more cases than ten times the number of variables as large.

There are three slightly different ways of obtaining E_A.

(1) If the a priori probabilities are known and a proportional sample has been used to design the classifier then E_A is simply e/M.

(2) If the a priori probabilities are unknown and a full random sample has been used to design the classifier then E_A is again simply e/M.

(3) If the a priori probabilities are either known to be P_i or are estimated by P_i and a disproportionate sample has been used to design the classifier, then:

$$E_A = \sum_{i=1}^{G} \frac{P_i E_i^*}{m_i}$$

where E_i^* is the number misclassified from group i and m_i is the number in the sample from group i.

These variations in E_A are simple but can cause trouble if the estimate of E_A produced by a computer program is used without inquiring which estimate is assumed. Most programs use methods 1 and 2, i.e they simply count the number misclassified and report it as a proportion of the total sample, and so care should be exercised with disproportionate samples. A modification to the linear discriminant program to enable it to report the correct error in all situations is given later.

The leaving-one-out method
Using an independent sample to test a classifier is very wasteful of cases. If it is difficult or expensive to obtain samples, then neither the independent

sample nor the apparent error rate are likely to be useful. A method which has characteristics of both is the 'leaving-one-out' method. We can think of the independent sample method as simply taking a single sample of size 2M and using half to design the classifier and the other half to test it. Why half? Why not use three-quarters to design the classifier and one-quarter to test it? In fact the use of various proportions to design and test the classifier is called the 'sample partitioning' method or the 'hold out' method and has received quite a lot of attention. Obviously the proportion of the sample used to design the classifier should be as large as possible so that it can be estimated reliably but it is also important that the proportion of the sample used to estimate the error rate is as large as possible for the same reason! Taking the 'hold-out' method to its logical conclusion, where the classifier is designed using the sample with one case removed and then tested by classifying the one left out, we have the 'leaving-one-out' method. An estimate of the error is obtained by repeating the procedure, each time leaving out a different case, until every case has been used to test the classifier. The error is then given by:

$$E_L = \frac{e}{M}$$

for a proportional sample, or:

$$E_L = \sum_{i=1}^{G} \frac{P_i e_i}{M}$$

for a disproportionate sample.

The leaving-one-out method has many disadvantages. It requires the design of M classifiers which can be a time-consuming business except in a few special cases such as the two group normal case and in some of the categorical methods described in Chapter 9. A more important problem is to which of the M classification rules does the error estimate refer. The answer is usually thought to be the rule designed using all M cases. Unfortunately the answer is more complicated.

The leaving-one-out method estimates the expected (or average) error of a classifier designed on a sample of size M−1. Notice that this does not refer to any *particular* classifier, but to the average performance of an M−1 classifier. This fact is usually ignored and the error estimate is taken to apply to the full classifier designed on the complete sample.

A third disadvantage of the leaving-one-out method is that, for a given sample size, it has a larger variance than the apparent error estimator. A discussion of this fact is postponed to the next section where we compare the two methods.

After mentioning these disadvantages the reader might be wondering why the leaving-one-out method is worth using. The single overpowering advantage is that the estimate of the expected error is unbiased. When carrying out initial studies to determine the feasibility of using statistical classification it is important to obtain an error estimate that is not too optimistic. Such studies are usually based on small samples and only the leaving-one-out method can provide an unbiased estimate in these cases.

Apparent error versus leaving-one-out error
Both E_A and E_L use only a single sample of size M to estimate the error rate. E_A is optimistically biased but this bias decreases with the size of the sample. E_L is an unbiased estimator of the average error of a classifier designed on a sample of size M−1. For a given sample size the variance of E_A is smaller than that of E_L. In small samples we would prefer E_L because the bias of E_A would be large. As the sample size is increased, however, we would tend to prefer E_A because even though it was biased, the bias would be small and so would the variance. A modification to enable the linear discriminant program to compute the leaving-one-out error rate is given later.

The jackknife estimate
Sometimes the leaving-one-out method is incorrectly referred to as a 'jackknife estimate'. In fact 'jackknifing' is a general technique for removing bias from any estimate. For example if t is an estimate of some parameter based on a sample of size M and t_j is an estimate of the same form as t but based on a sample of size M−1 obtained by leaving out the jth observation then:

$$T = Mt - \frac{(M-1)}{M} \sum_{j=1}^{M} t_j$$

is an improved estimate in the sense that it removes the bias of order 1/M from t. If the jackknife is applied to the apparent error E_A then the resulting procedure requires the design of M classifiers as in the case of the leaving-one-out method but, instead of classifying only the case left out, the jackknifed estimate classifies all of the cases used to design the classifier. In other words the jackknifed error rate is calculated by first calculating the apparent error in the usual way and then calculating the apparent error for each sub-sample obtained from the original sample by leaving out a single case. This is obviously a very time-consuming process and for this and other reasons the jackknifed error estimate has received very little theoretical or practical attention.

80 Classification Algorithms

Theoretical estimates of error

If we construct a classification rule assuming some distribution, then, by estimating the parameters of that distribution, a theoretical error estimate can be obtained. We can distinguish at least two types of error that might be of interest:

(1) The optimum error rate, i.e. the error associated with the Bayes' classifier.

(2) The actual error rate, i.e. the error associated with any estimated classifier.

As mentioned in the introduction an estimate of the error rate for the Bayes' rule would be of particular interest but, as will be explained, it is a little difficult to achieve! Theoretical error rates are usually only used for the normal two group equal covariance case and we will give the standard results for this.

Optimum error rate
For a two group normal case the optimum error rate (that is the error rate achieved by Bayes' rule) is given by:

$$\text{Bayes' error} = P_1 \int_{R_2} f_1(x)\,dx + P_2 \int_{R_1} f_2(x)\,dx$$

where R_1 and R_2 are the regions in which we classify a case as group 1 or group 2 respectively and $f_1(x)$ and $f_2(x)$ are the probability density functions for the two groups. This expression is perfectly general and doesn't depend on the form of f_1 or f_2. However for the normal case things are simpler. If $w_p(x)$ is the usual population discriminant function then:

$$\int_{R_2} f_1(x)\,dx$$

is the same as the probability that:

$$w_p(x) < \ln(P_1/P_2)$$

when x comes from group 1. In other words it is the probability that the rule will assign a case from group 1 into group 2. Recalling (see Chapter 5) that $w_p(x)$ is normal with mean $\delta^2/2$ and variance δ^2 in group 1:

$$\int_{R_2} f(x)\,dx = \Phi\left(\frac{\ln(P_2/P_1) - \delta^2/2}{\delta}\right)$$

where δ^2 is the population Mahalanobis distance squared and Φ is the cumulative standard normal distribution.

A similar expression for group 2 can be obtained in the same way and hence:

$$\text{Bayes' error} = P_1\Phi\left(\frac{\ln(P_2/P_1) - \delta^2/2}{\delta}\right) + P_2\Phi\left(\frac{\ln(P_2/P_1) + \delta^2/2}{\delta}\right)$$

The actual error rate

By an argument similar to that used in the last section the error rate for a linear discriminant function $w_s(x)$ constructed from a sample with means $\bar{x}_1$ and $\bar{x}_2$ and covariance matrix S is given by:

$$\text{error rate} = P_1\Phi\left(\frac{\ln(P_2/P_1) - E(w_s \mid G_1)}{\text{VAR}(w_s)^{1/2}}\right) + P_2\Phi\left(\frac{\ln(P_2/P_1) + E(w_s \mid G_2)}{\text{VAR}(w_s)^{1/2}}\right)$$

where the mean and variance of $w_s(x)$ are as given in Chapter 5.

To sum up: the expression given above is a theoretical estimate of the error rate produced by a particular discriminant function $w_s(x)$ assuming that the two populations are normal with equal covariance matrices.

The use of theoretical measures

The estimation of both the optimum and the actual error rates require knowledge of the population parameters. To be of any practical use we must substitute estimated values for these parameters into the two equations. In the case of the optimum error this gives:

$$\text{Bayes' error} = P_1\Phi\left(\frac{\ln(P_2/P_1) - D^2/2}{D}\right) + P_2\Phi\left(\frac{\ln(P_2/P_1) + D^2/2}{D}\right)$$

where D is the sample Mahalanobis distance.

In the case of the actual error rate, as substituting sample estimates for population values gives $D^2/2$ and $-D^2/2$ for the mean of $w_s(\mathbf{x})$ in group 1 and group 2 respectively and D^2 for the variance of $w_s(\mathbf{x})$ (see Chapter 5), the estimate of the error rate becomes:

$$\text{error rate} = P_1\Phi\left(\frac{\ln(P_2/P_1) - D^2/2}{D}\right) + P_2\Phi\left(\frac{\ln(P_2/P_1) + D^2/2}{D}\right)$$

which is the same as the estimate of the optimum error rate. Hence from a single sample we can only obtain one theoretical error estimate, which is usually taken to be an estimate of the actual error rate.

The actual error rate is only useful when the assumption of normality is *known* to hold. In large samples it is relatively unbiased and efficient but in small samples it must be treated with as much care as the apparent error rate. Some of the small sample bias can be removed by using a less biased estimate of D^2. That is:

$$D_*^2 = \left(\frac{m_1 + m_2 - n - 3}{m_1 + m_2}\right)D^2$$

In fact, when the normality assumption is valid, there is evidence [1] that the actual error rate using D^2 is one of the best methods available. It is always worth examining the value of this theoretical estimate to gain some idea of how well a classification rule is working. Gross differences between the theoretical error rate and other estimates of the error rate are a good indication that something is wrong with the underlying assumptions of the method – i.e. normality or equal covariance matrices.

Confusion matrices

Up to this point we have assumed that only the total error is of any interest to us. However the details of how the classifier makes its errors are usually of value. A simple method for displaying a full breakdown of error rates is the confusion matrix. A confusion matrix is a G×G contingency table of 'actual group' against 'classified group'. For example in the two group case:

		Actual		
		1	2	
Classified	1	E_{11}	E_{21}	m_{1c}
	2	E_{12}	E_{22}	m_{2c}
		m_{1a}	m_{1a}	

where E_{ij} is the number from group i classified as group j, m_{ia} is the number actually in group i and, m_{ic} is the number classified to group i.

The sample confusion matrix has a population counterpart with entries that are probabilities, e.g.

		Actual		
		1	2	
Classified	1	$P_1 \epsilon_{11}$	$P_2 \epsilon_{21}$	P_1'
	2	$P_1 \epsilon_{12}$	$P_2 \epsilon_{22}$	P_2'
		P_1	P_2	

Where P_1, P_2 are the a priori probabilities, ϵ_{ij} are the population error rates and P_1', P_2' are the proportions of the population assigned to group 1 and group 2 by the classification rule. The extension to more than two groups merely increases the number of rows and columns in the table to G where G is number of groups. It is interesting to note that P_i' does not always equal P_i (the a priori probability). That is, a classifier does not always divide the population up in the same ratio as that in which the groups actually occur. (This is even true of the Bayes' classifier!)

It is instructive to consider the form of the confusion matrix for two simple classification rules.

(1) Random assignment
If we simply assign each case as it occurs randomly to any one of the two groups, the population confusion matrix is:

84 Classification Algorithms

Actual

		1	2	
Classified	1	$P_1/2$	$P_2/2$	$1/2$
	2	$P_1/2$	$P_2/2$	$1/2$
		P_1	P_2	

and the total error rate is 0.5.

(2) A priori assignment
If we assign the cases randomly as before but with probabilities P_1 to group 1 and P_2 to group 2, the population confusion matrix is:

Actual

		1	2	
Classified	1	P_1^2	$P_1 \times P_1$	P_1
	2	$P_1 \times P_2$	P_2^2	P_2
		P_1	P_2	

and the total error rate is $2P_1P_2$.

The extension to more than two groups is obvious. In case 1 the entries in the ith column are P_i/G and in case 2 the diagonal terms are P_i^2 and the off-diagonal terms are P_iP_j.

These two cases indicate what sort of error rates and patterns of error rates can be achieved 'without really trying'. Case 1 corresponds to using no information about the populations and case 2 uses only the prior probabilities. (It is pleasing that the error in case 2 is always less than or equal to the error in case 1!) It is these two confusion matrices and error rates against which the performance of any classifier should be judged. Loosely speaking, if a classifier gives a pattern of errors not very far removed from case 1 or 2, then it cannot be using very much more information.

It is tempting to try and use the usual chi squared (χ^2) statistic as a measure of how far the observed confusion matrix differs from the expected. Some computer programs do this without saying what null hypothesis is being tested. If the usual χ^2 formula is used on a confusion matrix then, by default, the null hypothesis tested is that case 2 holds, i.e. that the classifier is equivalent to random assignment using the a priori probabilities. Whether this is the most appropriate null hypothesis to be testing is a matter of opinion, but in this case the following are true:

(1) If the a priori probabilities are known, then case 2 is what we can manage without using a designed classifier and so this represents the lowest performance expected from a classifier.

(2) As the classification performance improves χ^2 gets larger.

(3) As χ^2 gets larger, the classification performance does *not* necessarily improve.

(4) It is possible for a designed classifier to do *worse* than case 2.

(5) If the error rates are based on an independent sample, then the χ^2 statistic does indeed follow a χ^2 distribution with $(G-1)^2$ degrees of freedom as the sample size increases.

In practice the value of χ^2 obtained from a confusion matrix is of little value. It is usually computed from a matrix formed of apparent error estimates. In this case χ^2 is biased so one should not be surprised at large values and small significances!

The confusion matrix can be used to examine the way a classifier makes errors. By examining which groups are being confused, one can identify candidates for pooling or further work. A classifier might be satisfactory on a sub-set of the groups although giving poor results on the complete set. An intelligent examination of the confusion matrix, combined with various scatter plots (see 'feature selection' in Chapter 7), can provide information invaluable in the improvement of a classifier.

Extending the linear discriminant program

At this point it is obvious that the method used by the linear discriminant program developed in Chapters 4 and 5 to estimate the error rate is inadequate. There are many features that could be added but in this section the program is extended to include:

(1) A leaving-one-out estimate of the error rate.

(2) A confusion matrix.

(3) The option of specifying the prior probabilities or of having them estimated from the sample proportions.

To incorporate these changes add the following lines to the linear discriminant program. (Note: while only a few lines in subroutine 2500 have been altered the final subroutine is sufficiently different to make it worth quoting in its entirety.)

```
  60 GOSUB 3500:REM ESTIMATE ERROR RATE
  70 GOSUB 4500:REM ANALYSE ERROR PATTERN
  80 STOP

1105 T=0
1135 T=T+M(I)
1155 DIM D(G),E(G+1,G+1)
1162 FOR I=1 TO G
1163 P(I)=M(I)/T
1164 NEXT I
1165 PRINT "DO YOU KNOW THE PRIOR
     PROBS. Y/N";
1166 INPUT P$
1167 IF P$="N" THEN GOTO 1210

2200 REM

2500 GOSUB 7400:REM CLOSE FILE
2510 GOSUB 7200:REM OPEN INPUT FILE
2515 GOSUB 7300:GOSUB 7300
2516 E=0
2517 W=0
2520 FOR K=1 TO G
2530 PRINT "GROUP ";K
2540 FOR J=1 TO M(K)
2550 FOR I=1 TO N
2560 GOSUB 7300:REM READ R
2570 X(I)=R
2580 NEXT I
2585 IF E$="Y" THEN GOSUB 3800:
     REM FIND SMALLEST LOO DISCRIMINANT
2590 GOSUB 2800:
     REM FIND LARGEST DISCRIMINANT
2595 GOSUB 2700:REM FIND PROBABILITY
2600 PRINT J;TAB(3);"LARGEST IS FUNCTION ";
     L;"=";F(L);TAB(20);"PROB.=";P
2604 IF Q<>L AND E$="Y" THEN PRINT
     "***LEAVING ONE OUT ASSIGNS IT TO GROUP ";Q
2605 E(L,K)=E(L,K)+1
2606 E(L,G+1)=E(L,G+1)+1
2607 E(G+1,K)=E(G+1,K)+1
2608 IF Q<>K AND E$="Y" THEN W=W+P(K)/M(K)
2610 NEXT J
2620 PRINT:PRINT
2630 NEXT K
2640 PRINT
2655 IF E$="Y" THEN PRINT "LEAVING ONE OUT
     ESTIMATE   OF ERROR RATE=";W*100;"%"
2660 RETURN

3500 PRINT
3510 PRINT "DO YOU WANT THE LEAVING ONE OUT
```

```
              ERROR RATE (Y/N)";
3520 INPUT E$
3540 IF E$="N" THEN GOTO 3610
3550 A=(T-G)/(T-G-1)
3560 FOR I=1 TO N
3570 FOR J=1 TO N
3580 S(I,J)=-S(I,J)
3590 NEXT J
3600 NEXT I
3610 GOSUB 2500
3620 RETURN

3800 Y=0
3810 FOR I=1 TO N
3820 FOR L=1 TO N
3830 Y=Y+S(I,L)*(X(I)-A(I,K))*(X(L)-A(L,K))
3840 NEXT L
3850 NEXT I
3860 Y=(M(K)-1)*(T-G)/M(K)-Y
3865 Q=1
3870 FOR H=1 TO G
3880 U=0
3890 V=0
3900 FOR I=1 TO N
3910 FOR L=1 TO N
3920 U=U+S(I,L)*(X(I)-A(I,H))*(X(L)-A(L,K))
3925 V=V+S(I,L)*(X(I)-A(I,H))*(X(L)-A(L,H))
3926 NEXT L
3927 NEXT I
3928 D(H)=(V+U*U/Y)/A
3930 IF H=K THEN D(H)=D(H)*M(K)*M(K)/
     (M(K)-1)/(M(K)-1
3940 IF P$="Y" THEN D(H)=D(H)-LOG(P(H))
3950 IF P$="N" AND H<>K THEN D(H)=D(H)-
     LOG(M(H)/(T-1))
3960 IF P$="N" AND H=K THEN D(H)=D(H)-
     LOG((M(H)-1)/(T-1))
3965 IF D(H)<D(Q) THEN Q=H
3970 NEXT H
3980 RETURN

4500 E=0
4504 PRINT
4505 S=8
4506 E(G+1,G+1)=T
4507 PRINT TAB(15);"ACTUAL GROUP=
     COL/ASSIGNED GROUP=ROW"
4508 PRINT
4510 FOR I=1 TO G
4520 PRINT TAB(S*I);"I";I;
4530 NEXT I
4535 PRINT TAB(S*(G+1));"I"
```

```
4540 GOSUB 4900
4550 FOR I=1 TO G+1
4560 IF I<>G+1 THEN PRINT I;
4570 FOR J=1 TO G+1
4580 PRINT TAB(S*J);"I";E(I,J);
4590 NEXT J
4600 PRINT
4610 IF I<>G+1 THEN GOSUB 4900
4620 NEXT I
4625 PRINT
4630 FOR K=1 TO G
4640 J=(E(G+1,K)-E(K,K))/E(G+1,K)
4650 PRINT "GROUP ";K;TAB(10);J*100;
     "% MISCLASSIFIED"
4660 E=E+J*P(K)
4670 NEXT K
4680 PRINT
4690 PRINT "ESTIMATED ERROR RATE =";E*100;"%"
4700 RETURN

4900 PRINT " ";
4905 FOR K=1 TO G+2
4910 FOR L=1 TO S-1
4920 PRINT "-";
4930 NEXT L
4940 IF K<>G+2 THEN PRINT "+";
4950 NEXT K
4960 PRINT
4970 RETURN
```

Following these modifications and additions, the program asks if the user knows the prior probabilities. If the answer is 'no' they are estimated by the number of cases in each group, otherwise the user is asked to supply them. Then the analysis proceeds as before until the file is about to be re-read so as to estimate the apparent error rate. At this point the user is asked if the leaving-one-out error rate should be calculated. If the answer is 'yes' then the leaving-one-out discriminant scores are calculated along with the standard discriminant scores. The leaving-one-out scores are not reported but if they lead to a different classification than the standard discriminant scores then this fact is indicated by a suitable message. Finally the leaving-one-out error rate is reported, taking account of the prior probabilities, along with a confusion matrix for the errors produced by the standard linear discriminant functions. A χ^2 statistic is not calculated on the confusion matrix because it adds very little information over a careful examination of the error pattern. It is important to notice that all of the error rates reported by this version of the program take into account the prior probabilities of the groups whether they are estimated or supplied. Also, while it is still possible to compute and use the unbiased form of the linear discriminant

Evaluating Rules – Estimating Error Rates   89

functions, the leaving-one-out estimate uses the standard plug in estimator.

Details of the error rate modifications **
The most complicated modification to the linear discriminant program is most certainly the addition of the leaving-one-out error estimate. For each case it is necessary to adjust both the means and the inverse covariance matrix to account for its omission from the sample. If case x* belonging to group k is deleted from the sample (using * to indicate a quantity calculated with x* omitted from the sample), it is not difficult to show that:

$$\bar{x}_i^* = \bar{x}_i \qquad \text{if } i \neq k$$

$$\bar{x}_i^* = \bar{x}_i - \frac{1}{(m_i - 1)}(\bar{x}^* - \bar{x}_i) \qquad \text{if } i = k$$

and

$$S^* = \frac{(M - G)}{(M - G - 1)} S - \frac{m_k}{(m_k - 1)(M - G - 1)}(x^* - \bar{x}_k)(x^* - \bar{x}_k)'$$

A standard matrix result states that if:

$$B = A - vv'$$

then it can be shown that:

$$B^{-1} = A^{-1} - \frac{A^{-1}vv'A^{-1}}{(1 - v'A^{-1}v)}$$

As S^* is related to S in the same way that B is to A, this equation gives us a way of expressing the inverse of S^* in terms of S^{-1}. That is:

$$S^{*-1} = \frac{1}{a}\left(S^{-1} + \frac{S^{-1}z_k z_k' S^{-1}}{h_k - z_k' S^{-1} z_k}\right)$$

where

$$h_k = \frac{(m_k - 1)(M - G)}{m_k}$$

$$a = \frac{(M - G)}{(M - G - 1)}$$

90 Classification Algorithms

and

$$z_k = (x^* - \bar{x}_k)$$

It is possible to use this expression for S^{*-1} to correct the linear discriminant functions for the omission of x^* but it is easier to correct the quadratic discriminants from which the linear discriminants are derived. That is, if we calculate for each group:

$$d_i^* = (x^* - \bar{x}_i^*)' S^{-1}(x^* - \bar{x}_i^*)$$

and assign the case to the group with the smallest value of d_i^* then this will give the same results as using the linear discriminant functions. This should be obvious because the d_i^* are simply the quadratic terms that lead to the linear discriminant functions when the common factors are cancelled (see Chapter 3). After a little algebra it is not difficult to show that:

if $i \neq k$ then

$$(x^* - \bar{x}_i^*)' S^{*-1}(x^* - \bar{x}_i^*) = (x^* - \bar{x}_i)' S^{*-1}(x^* - \bar{x}_i)$$

$$= z_i' S^{*-1} z_i$$

$$= \frac{1}{a}\left(d_i + \frac{d_{ik}^2}{(h_k - d_k)}\right)$$

where

$$z_i = (x^* - \bar{x}_i)$$

$$d_i = z_i' S^{-1} z_i$$

and

$$d_{ik} = z_i' S^{-1} z_k$$

Notice that the terms d_i and d_{ik} involve the original means and the original inverse covariance matrix. If $i=k$ then the equation is only a little more complicated:

$$(x^* - \bar{x}_k^*)' S^{*-1}(x^* - \bar{x}_k^*) = \left(\frac{m_k}{m_k - 1}\right)^2 \frac{1}{a}\left(d_k + \frac{d_{kk}^2}{(h_k - d_k)}\right)$$

Which, apart from the $m_k/(m_k-1)$ factor at the start, is the same as the equation for the case $i \neq k$.

Using these equations to calculate the quadratic discriminant scores after omitting **x*** from the sample is straightforward. Subroutine 3800 calculates the leaving-one-out quadratic discriminant scores using the inverse covariance matrix in S and the group means in A. As well as correcting for the changes to the means and the inverse covariance matrix resulting from the omission of **x***, it is also necessary to adjust the estimates of the prior probabilities (lines 3940, 3950 and 3960). As well as calculating the leaving-one-out discriminant, subroutine 3800 also finds the group that the case is assigned to and passes its number back in Q. This information is used in subroutine 2500 to keep a count of the total number of cases misclassified (line 2608). Notice the way that adding P(K)/M(K) rather than one to Q for each case misclassified always gives a correct estimate of the total error of classification, no matter how the prior probabilities were obtained.

Compared to the leaving-one-out error estimate, adding the confusion table is simple. Instead of keeping a single error count the matrix E(G+1,G+1) is updated (lines 2605, 2606, and 2607) so that E(L,K) holds a count of the number of cases from group K assigned to group L, E(L,G+1) holds the number of cases assigned to group L and E(G+1,K) holds the number of cases in group K. Thus as the sample is classified the confusion matrix is constructed complete with the row and column sums. Subroutine 4500 prints the confusion matrix in the standard format and also works out the percentage of each group misclassified (line 4640) and the total error rate (line 4660).

The transistor data

If the new version of the program is run on the transistor data given in Chapter 4 then the standard and leaving-one-out assignments agree for all but the last case. The output of the last part of the program is:

```
     LEAVING ONE OUT ESTIMATE OF ERROR RATE= 12%

            ACTUAL GROUP=COL/ASSIGNED GROUP=ROW

                  I 1    I 2     I
            -----+-----+-----+-----
              1   I 10   I 2    I 12
            -----+-----+-----+-----
              2   I 0    I 8    I 8
            -----+-----+-----+-----
                  I 10   I 10   I 20
      GROUP 1    0% MISCLASSIFIED
      GROUP 2   20% MISCLASSIFIED

      ESTIMATED ERROR RATE = 4%
```

An examination of the confusion matrix suggests that group 2 is being wrongly assigned as a result of the large prior probability given to group one

92   Classification Algorithms

($P(G_1)=0.8$ and $P(G_2)=0.2$). As the transistor data doesn't satisfy the assumption of equal covariance matrices (it was analysed using the quadratic discriminant program in Chapter 4) then it is likely that adjusting the prior probabilities (as described in Chapter 5) away from their true values will produce a better overall error rate. Notice also that although the error rate is only 4% the pattern of errors may be unacceptable for the application in that 20% of the bad transistors are misclassified as good! The leaving-one-out estimate of the error rate is more pessimistic at 12% but it is sobering to realise that this difference is the result of changing the allocation of only *one* case!

Error rates and practice

The estimation of error is a separate step in the production of a classifier and should be viewed as such. It is worth remembering that it is often irrelevant how a classifier is obtained; it is only how it performs that is important. If, in a particular case, an ad hoc rule succeeds in having a low error rate and this error rate is known with some accuracy *then use it*! The only advantage of classifiers, which are theoretically optimal subject to many conditions, is that they have been found to be good in many cases, e.g. the linear discriminant function. In practice, it is never incorrect to use a classifier that works. Equally, their is no point in trying to use a poor but theoretically correct classifier.

However, this said, the reader should be warned that many studies in the past have failed because a rule that gave good results during the design phase failed when used in the field. This has tended to give classification theory something of a bad name among applied statisticians. This is almost entirely due to the misuse and misinterpretation of error estimates provided by standard computer programs.

Not all methods of error estimation have been covered here by any means. In particular, two remarkable methods have been ignored. The first is the K-NN method dealt with in Chapter 9 which estimates the error rate of the Bayes' classifier without knowing what that classifier is! The second is the reject rate method which allows the estimation of error rates using an additional sample, but without knowing the *true* classification of any of the cases in the additional sample! Details of the reject method can be found in Reference [2]. For general use the methods described are usually adequate and have the advantage that they can all be obtained from or using standard computer programs.

References

1. Lachenbruch, P.A. (1975) *Discriminant Analysis*: Hafner Press.
2. Fukunaga, K. (1972) *Introduction to Statistical Pattern Recognition:* Academic Press.
3. Highleyman, W.H. (1962) 'The design and analysis of pattern recognition experiments' *Bell System Technical Journal*, 41, 723-44.

Chapter Seven
Feature Selection - Canonical Analysis

One of the preoccupations of multivariate statistics in general is the reduction of the number of variables that have to be considered to reach a conclusion about the data being studied. In general the fewer variables involved in a problem the more likely we are to understand it and the more likely is it that any 'solution' will be practical. This is certainly true of classification where methods of reducing the number of variables involved in a classification rule, without severely affecting the rule's performance, are known collectively as 'feature selection'. The use of the word 'feature' originated in pattern recognition where a feature is some identifiable part which serves to distinguish between groups. However its use does not seem inappropriate when taken to mean any variable or combination of variables important for classification.

There are many reasons why we would want to use feature selection techniques. Some of these are:

(1) To investigate the causes of the differences between groups. (In other words, to discover why these groups can be classified so well.)

(2) To improve classification by discarding 'irrelevant' information.

(3) To reduce the number of dimensions to two (sometimes three), thus enabling a graphical representation of the group separation.

(4) To reduce the number of variables used in a classifier (resulting in the same or nearly the same performance for fewer measurements).

General formulation of the feature selection problem

If we are using a set of n measurements, **x**, in a classification rule, then we may state the feature selection problem in a fairly general form, thus:

> Find a matrix **A** (m×n) such that a classifier using **y** = **Ax** has the best error rate achievable.

(This is not the most general form because we are allowing only linear transformations, but, as these are the only type that we can handle, it is sufficient.) As the number of features is reduced to m, it is usual to add the condition that m is as small as possible without losing too much performance.

We can stipulate extra conditions on the matrix **A**, according to the type of solution we consider acceptable. It the matrix is allowed to be completely general then the resulting **y** will be made up of linear combinations of the **x** measurements. For example, for m=2 and n=3:

$$\begin{bmatrix} y_1 \\ y_2 \end{bmatrix} = \begin{bmatrix} a_{11}x_1 + a_{12}x_2 + a_{13}x_3 \\ a_{21}x_1 + a_{22}x_2 + a_{23}x_3 \end{bmatrix}$$

$$= \begin{bmatrix} a_{11} & a_{12} & a_{13} \\ a_{21} & a_{22} & a_{23} \end{bmatrix} \begin{bmatrix} x_1 \\ x_2 \\ x_3 \end{bmatrix}$$

This implies that although only m dimensions (measurements) are being used in a classifier we still have to *measure* n things to obtain them! This 'unconstrained' form of feature selection is clearly only useful for reducing the number of dimensions so that the reasons for the group differences can be seen.

If we need to reduce the number of measurements then this can be specified by constraining the matrix **A** to have only a single 1 in each row. For example, for m=2 and n=3:

$$\begin{bmatrix} y_1 \\ y_2 \end{bmatrix} = \begin{bmatrix} 1 & 0 & 0 \\ 0 & 0 & 1 \end{bmatrix} \begin{bmatrix} x_1 \\ x_2 \\ x_3 \end{bmatrix}$$

defines $y_1 = x_1$ and $y_2 = x_3$. This is usually referred to as the variable selection problem and is more simply stated as 'select m variables which give the best classification results'.

The matrix formulation allows us to pose the feature selection problem in a general way. However, as the solutions to the general unconstrained problem and the constrained or variable selection problem are so different, we will consider them separately. Unconstrained feature selection forms the subject of this chapter and constrained feature selection, or the variable selection problem, is dealt with in the next. In many ways unconstrained feature selection is very like principal components analysis or factor analysis [1] in that it seeks to represent the data using a smaller number of dimensions (obtained as linear combinations of the original variables) and constrained feature selection is very like the variable selection problem encountered as part of multiple regression [2].

Before we move on, it is worth making clear that, although there are a large number of techniques to select the best set of variables, there exists no complete solution to either form of the problem if, by best, we mean best error rate. In addition, the techniques which do exist are almost exclusively for either the normal case or apply only to the linear discriminant function. Any other distribution or classification rule can be handled only by hoping that the methods described are robust – i.e. that they are insensitive to changes in the conditions under which they were derived.

The normal or linear discriminant case

If we assume that our G groups each have a multivariate normal distribution with equal covariance matrices and hence use linear discriminant functions, or if we simply *choose* to use linear discriminant functions whatever the underlying distributions are, then a well-known procedure exists for feature selection. One cannot use the word solution here because, even in the normal case, the m linear combinations which give the *minimum error* classifier are *not* known (apart from the two group case where the linear discriminant itself is the best linear combination). This said, the procedure we are about to discuss – the canonical analysis method – has a great deal in its favour and, in practice, is used routinely.

Canonical analysis

As already mentioned there is no simple and efficient method of obtaining m linear combinations of the original variables that give the smallest error rate. Given that this is true, then our only practical option is to seek an alternative measure, related to error rate, for which we can find the optimum m linear combinations. Obviously any measure of the differences between the groups is a likely candidate. For example, if we can find m linear combinations that make the separation between the group means as large as possible then using these new variables will probably give a small error rate. Unfortunately it is not enough to concentrate on the differences between group means because these can be made as large as you please simply by multiplying by a constant (i.e. by scaling the data). A good measure of group separation has to take into account the differences between the means and how much the groups spread about the means.

The general case will be easier to understand if we first consider the two group case in two dimensions. The two groups can be represented by ellipsoids indicating the regions in which samples are likely to fall as in Fig. 7.1. (Also see Chapter 2.)

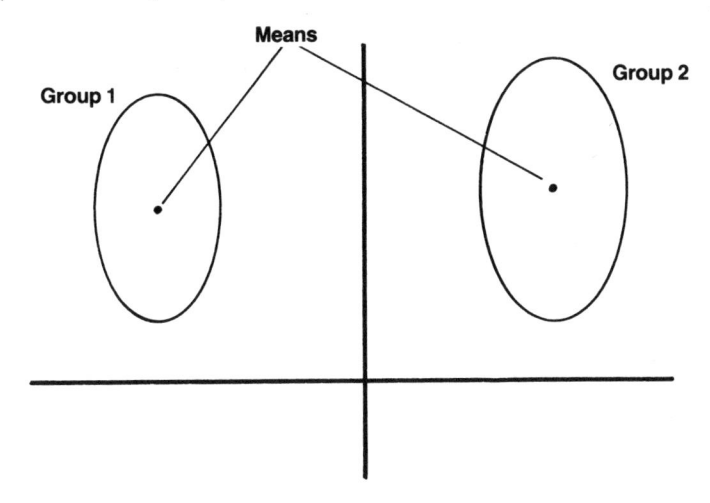

Fig. 7.1 Two groups with equal covariances

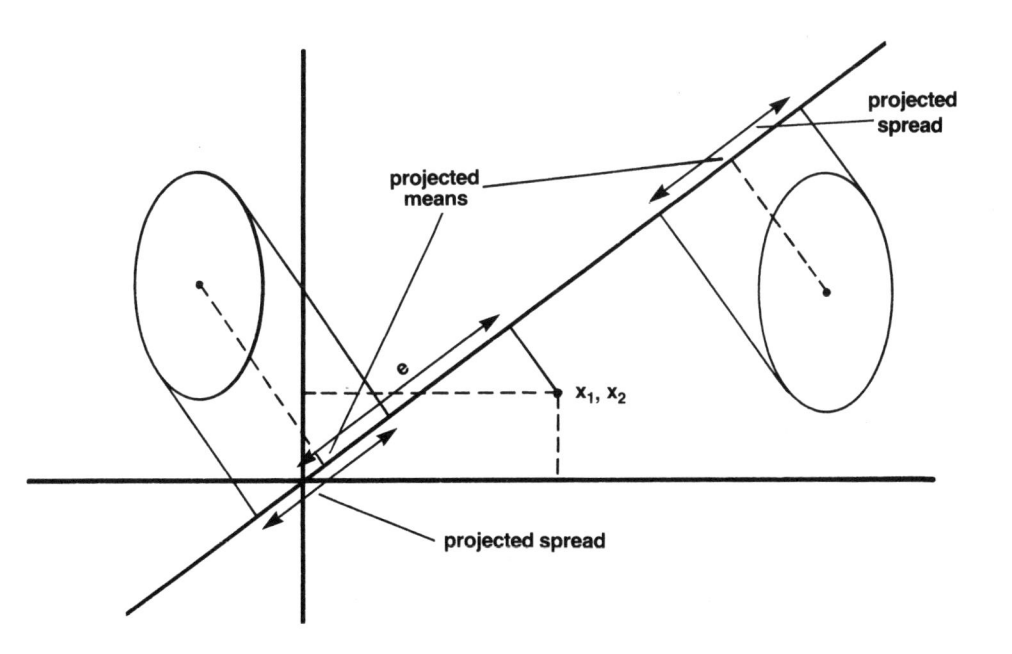

Fig. 7.2 Projected spreads

98 Classification Algorithms

Consider any arbitrary line drawn between the two groups. If we project the ellipsoids of spread and the means of the two groups onto this line (Fig. 7.2), we can see that the difference between the projected means depends on the angle of the line. Similarly, the size of the projected spread (variance) depends on the angle of the line.

Using distance measured along the line as a new variable, e, then e is given by the simple expression:

$$e = \sum_{i=1}^{2} v_i x_i = v_1 x_1 + v_2 x_2$$

where the vs are constants which define the orientation of the line. (e is the distance of the projection of any point x_1, x_2 from the origin.) Given this variable e we may form the 'within groups sums of squares' (SSW) and the 'between groups sums of squares' (SSB) for the two groups in exactly the same way as for a one-way ANOVA. If you are not familiar with one-way ANOVA then it is useful to think of SSW as measuring the spread of cases within any of the groups and SSB as measuring the spread of the groups, or more accurately the group means.

Now, for any orientation of the line, we can obtain values for SSB and SSW. If we are to use only this one dimension to classify the groups, the problem is what orientation the line should have. It would seem reasonable to use an orientation which maximises SSB or which minimises SSW. That is, making SSB large corresponds to finding an orientation which separates the group means as much as possible and making SSW small corresponds to finding an orientation which makes the groups as 'tight' as possible. In fact the best line is the one which maximises the ratio SSB/SSW. This is intuitively reasonable because, by asking for a large value of SSB/SSW, we obtain a line which makes SSW small and SSB large.

In the two group case the line which maximises SSB/SSW solves the feature selection problem exactly if we are using a linear discriminant. For, in this case, the linear discriminant *is* the line which maximises SSB/SSW. (To be more exact the coefficients are proportional to the corresponding coefficients of the linear discriminant function.)

Thus we may state the following in the general two group, n dimension case. If:

$$e = \sum_{i=1}^{n} v_i x_i$$

is the line which maximises SSB/SSW, then:

(1) e *is* the two group linear discriminant function w(**x**) (see the end of Chapter 3).

Feature Selection - Canonical Analysis   99

(2) In the *normal equal covariance* case, e is a complete solution to our feature selection problem, i.e. e gives the *same* error rate as the entire set of measurements **x**.

(3) In any other case e gives the *same* error rate as the linear discriminant function but, as always, this need not be the Bayes' rule.

(4) If we are not using the linear discriminant function, then e is not necessarily the best choice of a single dimension for classification.

The first three points are fairly straightforward, but the last deserves some discussion as, in practice, it is rare for e to be considered in any context other than linear discrimination. Suppose we are using a 1-nearest neighbour (1-NN) classifying rule (see Chapter 9). That is, for any case to be classified, find its nearest neighbour and assign it to the same group. Then, using the original sample, we would have to calculate an n-dimensional distance to determine the nearest neighbour to a given case. If we 'condense' the n measurements to one, e, then we simply have to subtract to find a case's nearest neighbour. There is no guarantee however that the rule using e would give good results in this case. (One would have to determine error rates, etc. to evaluate it.)

The point is that the fact that in the two group case e and the linear discriminant function are identical should not be allowed to confuse the purpose of finding e (i.e. to reduce the dimension of the classification space) and of using the linear discriminant for classification.

Multigroup canonical analysis

If we have G groups we can still compute SSB and SSW for any line in the n-dimensional space in exactly the same way as in the two group case. We can also form SSB/SSW and find the line which maximises this ratio. However unlike the two group case this line doesn't give the same result as classifying using all of the original variables. This suggests that it might be worth trying to find other lines which maximise the ratio of SSB to SSW. If we try to go on and find another line which maximises SSB/SSW, it is clear that we must add another condition, otherwise we would get our first solution again! The standard extra condition is to require the scores on the second line to be *uncorrelated* with the scores on the first. Then we can go on to try to find a third line, then a fourth, etc.

This is reminiscent of the procedure involved in principal components (PC) analysis [1] and in fact the mathematics is closely related. In PC analysis we find a line which maximises the projected total sums of squares and then a second and a third. etc., each subject to the extra condition of being uncorrelated with the previous lines. Each of these lines is known as an 'eigenvector' and the value of the sums of squares (in fact variance) associated with each is called an eigenvalue. In exactly the same way we call each line which maximises SSB/SSW an eigenvector (alternative names are canonical vector and canonical eigenvector) and the value of SSB/SSW associated with it an eigenvalue. The similarity between PC analysis and canonical analysis is striking but one important difference exists – in PC analysis there are, in general, n eigenvectors corresponding to non-zero eigenvalues, but in canonical analysis there are only min(G−1,n) eigenvectors with non-zero eigenvalues. As G (the number of groups) is normally smaller than n (the number of measurements), what this means is that we can usually only obtain G−1 eigenvectors. Thus, in the two group case, only one eigenvector with a non-zero SSB/SSW exists, i.e. after the first eigenvector (the discriminant function) any line uncorrelated with it gives a zero value for SSB/SSW. As we shall see, this fact is important, but first, let us summarise our position:

(1) We try to find lines which maximise SSB/SSW and are mutually uncorrelated.

(2) Such lines are called eigenvectors.

(3) Each line e_i is associated with a value of SSB/SSW which it maximises – this value is known as an eigenvalue (written λ_i).

(4) There are at most min(G−1,n) eigenvectors with non-zero eigenvalues.

If we recall our aim in carrying out canonical analysis, viz. feature selection, we should expect a classification rule based on a subset of the e_i to do as well as a classification rule based on *all* the data i.e. **x**. However, as in the two group case, this will not in general be true. For example if we are using a 1-NN rule (see the last section), then, although we would expect that using only the first k eigenvectors would give a reasonably good error rate, it is almost certain that there exists another set of k linear combinations that produces a lower error rate. In other words, the eigenvectors are a good choice but not necessarily the best. However, if we have the normal equal covariance case, or if we are using linear discriminant functions, then the following is true:

> Linear discriminant functions constructed using only the eigenvectors with non-zero eigenvalues give the *same* results as linear discriminant functions constructed using the original measurements.

In other words, if we are using linear discriminant functions we can get the same result by using just the min(G−1,n) eigenvectors corresponding to

Feature Selection – Canonical Analysis

non-zero eigenvalues as by using all of the data. This implies that all the information used by the linear discriminant functions is contained in just these few eigenvectors. This can be very useful when G is 2 or 3 because a one- or two-dimensional plot can be used to examine all the important information in a sample. When G is greater than 3, no two-dimensional plot can represent the groups with complete accuracy. However in exactly the same way that the first two principal components can be used to plot the data in two dimensions as faithfully as possible, so the first two eigenvectors can be used to plot the data in two dimensions so as to represent the group structure as accurately as possible. An examination of data plotted on the first two principal components can give information on outliers etc. Similarly, a plot using the first two eigenvectors can provide information on outliers, group structure and on why certain cases are misclassified. When interpreting such plots it is worth knowing that the linear discriminant function constructed using the eigenvectors is equivalent to assigning a case to the group to whose mean it is closest. This is because each eigenvector is constructed to be uncorrelated with the rest and hence the within-groups covariance matrix is diagonal (see Chapter 2) and, as it is only the ratio SSB/SSW that is fixed, we can scale the eigenvectors (multiplying by a constant) to make the diagonal elements of the covariance matrix equal to one. That is, the within-groups covariance matrix using the eigenvectors is $\mathbf{I}$, the identity matrix (see Appendix 1). This means that the linear discriminant functions constructed using the eigenvectors instead of the original measurements have a very simple form:

$$J_i = \boldsymbol{\mu}_i' \boldsymbol{\Sigma}^{-1} \mathbf{e} + \boldsymbol{\mu}_i' \boldsymbol{\Sigma}^{-1} \boldsymbol{\mu}_i$$
$$= \boldsymbol{\mu}_i' \mathbf{I}^{-1} \mathbf{e} + \boldsymbol{\mu}_i' \mathbf{I} \boldsymbol{\mu}_i$$
$$= \boldsymbol{\mu}_i' \mathbf{e} + \boldsymbol{\mu}_i' \boldsymbol{\mu}_i$$

which is an expression that only involves the group means. In fact it can be shown to be related simply to the distance of the case from the group means. Thus, as long as the prior probabilities are equal, classification using the eigenvectors is simply a matter of assigning a case to the group with the closest mean.

So far we have only considered discarding the eigenvectors with zero eigenvalues. We have found that for the linear discriminant case nothing is lost, but what happens if we discard even more eigenvectors? In the normal case it is certain that, if we use only $m < \min(G-1, n)$ eigenvectors, we will lose classifying power and also that there exists another set of m linear combinations which will give a smaller error rate. In other words, even for the normal case we have not solved the feature selection problem for

102   Classification Algorithms

m<min(G—1,n). For any other case we have no theoretical reasons for preferring the canonical eigenvectors, only the intuitive appeal of directions which maximise SSB/SSW. We will return to the question of discarding eigenvectors when we discuss significance testing.

The geometry of canonical analysis

If we consider two groups, then it is obvious that their means lie on a straight line irrespective of the number of dimensions we measure, i.e. two points define a straight line (Fig. 7.3). If we consider three groups, it is equally clear that their means define a plane (Fig. 7.4).

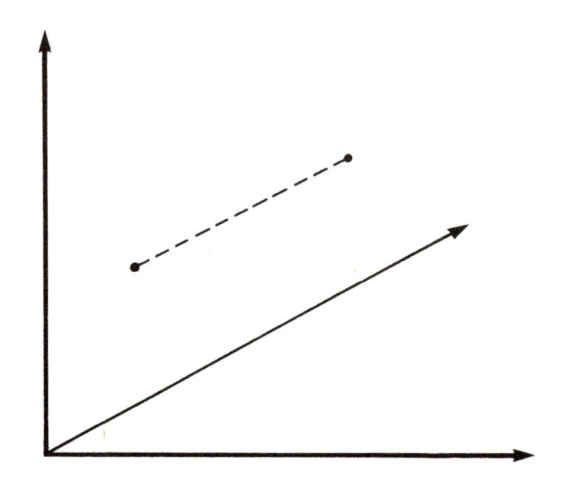

Fig. 7.3   Two means define a line

In general the means of G groups define a flat (G—1)-dimensional surface – called a hyperplane. (As a (G—1)-dimensional thing cannot be imagined, let alone drawn, for G greater than 4, we will use G = 3 as an illustration throughout.) The number G—1 is reminiscent of the number of non-zero eigenvalues in canonical analysis. In fact the usual G—1 necessary eigenvectors all lie in the G—1 hyperplane defined by the group means. For example, in the two group case, the single eigenvector lies along the line joining the two means. In the three group case the two vectors lie in the plane as shown in Fig. 7.5. It is possible for the G means to define a hyperplane of less than G—1 dimensions – for example, in the three group case, all the means might lie on a line (Fig. 7.6). This is known as degeneracy and is the

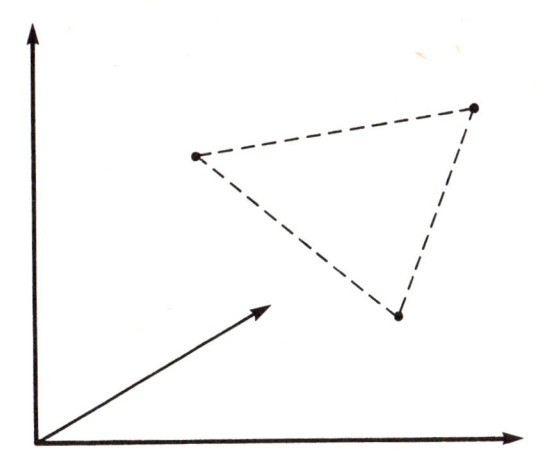

Fig. 7.4 Three means define a plane

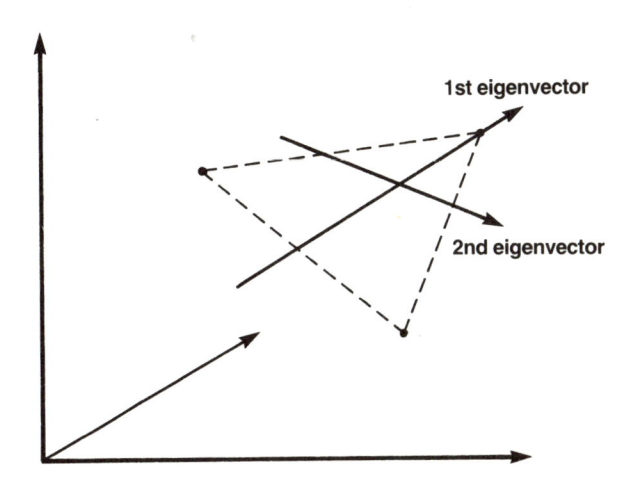

Fig. 7.5 The two eigenvectors lie in the plane defined by the means

reason why there might be *fewer* non-zero eigenvalues than G−1. Similarly, if n is smaller than G−1 then the means *must* be degenerate. For example, in the four group case with n = 2 (see Fig. 7.7), all the means lie in a plane! You should now be able to understand the statement:

There are at most min(G−1,n) non-zero eigenvalues.

In most practical cases n is much greater than G−1 and the number of

104 Classification Algorithms

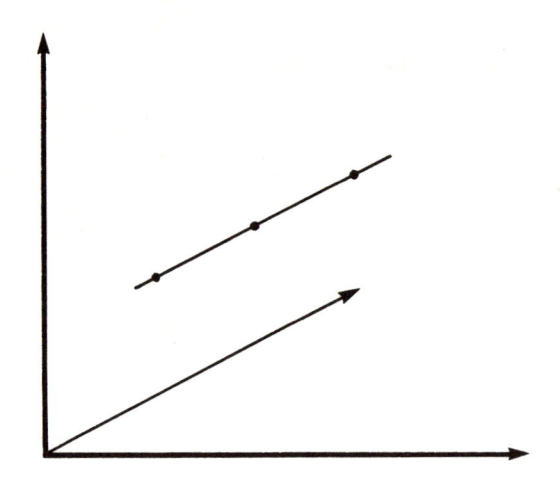

Fig. 7.6 Three means can lie on a line

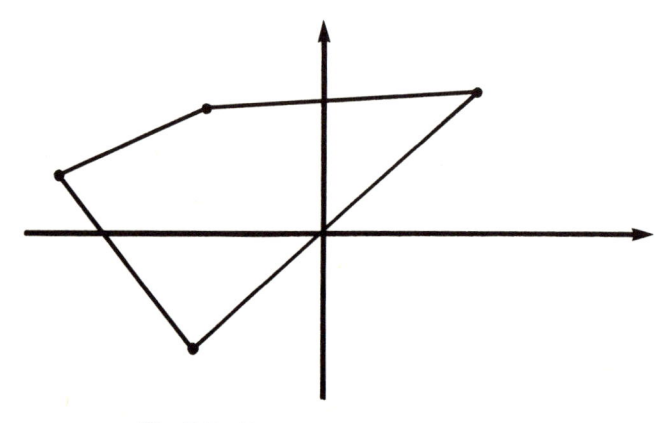

Fig. 7.7 Four means can lie on a plane

non-zero eigenvalues is exactly G−1. The fact that only these G−1 are necessary when using linear discriminants tells us that only information about the differences in the means is being used. For, in the G−1 dimensional hyperplane, the means of the groups are different, but, when viewed in the remaining dimensions they are *identical*. The three group case should make this clear (Fig. 7.8). This is another intuitive justification for using the canonical eigenvectors for other classification rules – if the population means are not different then most rules perform poorly.

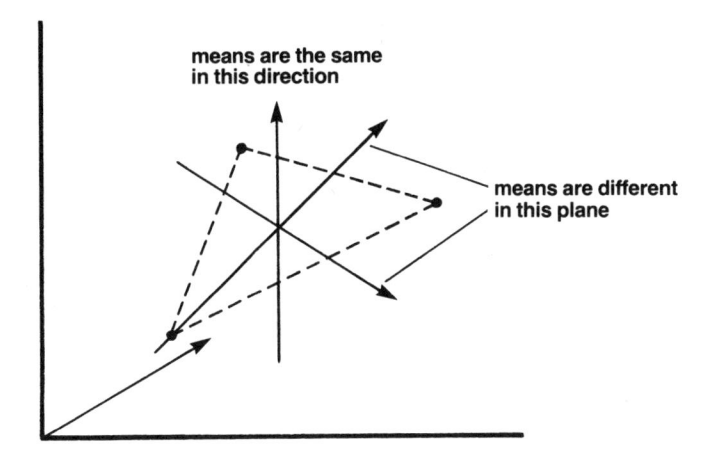

Fig. 7.8 Between groups variation for three groups

A canonical analysis program

The following program can be used to perform a canonical analysis of data stored in a disk file in the format described in connection with the linear and quadratic discriminant programs. The first part of the program is superficially similar to the linear discriminant program but there are enough differences to make it worth entering from scratch. You can check that you have entered the program correctly by comparing its output on the iris data with the results given in the next section. The program works out the means and the common covariance matrix both of which are printed as intermediate results. Then all G−1 eigenvectors and eigenvalues are calculated and printed. As the eigenvectors and eigenvalues are being calculated a slowly reducing quantity called DELTA is printed to show how the calulation is progressing – the calculation is complete when DELTA is zero. Finally the program constructs a scatter plot on the first two eigenvectors. In this version of the program the eigenvectors are scaled so that the within groups variance for each of the variables is one. This is useful because, as mentioned in a previous section, classification using linear discriminant functions is equivalent to assigning a case to the nearest group mean on the scatter diagram.

```
10 GOSUB 1000:REM GET PARAMETERS
20 GOSUB 2000:REM MAKE S AND MEANS
30 GOSUB 3000:REM PRINT STATS
40 GOSUB 4000:REM CALCULATE BETWEEN
```

```
            COVARIANCES B
     50 GOSUB 6000:REM FACTOR S
     60 GOSUB 6500:REM INVERT FACTORS
     70 GOSUB 5000:REM FORM FINAL MATRIX IN E
     80 GOSUB 8000:REM FIND EIGENVECTORS OF E
     90 GOSUB 4500:REM CONVERT TO CANONICAL
            VECTORS
    100 GOSUB 3500:REM PRINT RESULTS
    110 IF G>2 THEN GOSUB 9000:REM PLOT FIRST
            TWO VECTORS
    120 STOP

   1000 PRINT "CANONICAL ANALYSIS"
   1010 PRINT
   1020 PRINT "DATA FILE NAME ";
   1030 INPUT F$
   1040 GOSUB 7200:REM OPEN INPUT FILE
   1050 GOSUB 7300:N=R:REM READ R
   1060 GOSUB 7300:M=R
   1070 PRINT "CASES=";M;"VARIABLES=";N
   1080 PRINT "NUMBER OF GROUPS ";
   1090 INPUT G
   1100 DIM M(G)
   1110 FOR I=1 TO G
   1120 PRINT "NUMBER OF CASES IN GROUP ";I;
   1130 INPUT M(I)
   1140 NEXT I
   1150 PRINT
   1160 DIM S(N,N),B(N,N),H(N,N),X(N),T(N),
            A(N,G),C(N,N),E(N,N)
   1170 RETURN

   2000 FOR K=1 TO G
   2010 FOR J=1 TO M(K)
   2020 FOR I=1 TO N
   2030 GOSUB 7300
   2040 A(I,K)=A(I,K)+R
   2050 X(I)=R
   2055 IF K=1 AND J=1 THEN T(I)=R
   2060 NEXT I
   2070 FOR I=1 TO N
   2080 FOR L=1 TO I
   2090 S(L,I)=S(L,I)+(X(L)-T(L))*(X(I)-T(I))
   2100 NEXT L
   2110 NEXT I
   2120 NEXT J
   2130 NEXT K
   2140 FOR K=1 TO G
   2150 FOR J=1 TO N
   2160 FOR I=1 TO J
   2170 S(I,J)=S(I,J)-(A(I,K)-M(K)*T(I))*
            (A(J,K)-M(K)*T(J))/M(K)
   2180 NEXT I
```

```
2190 NEXT J
2200 T=T+M(K)
2210 NEXT K
2230 FOR J=1 TO N
2240 FOR I=1 TO J
2260 S(J,I)=S(I,J)
2270 NEXT I
2280 NEXT J
2290 RETURN

3000 FOR K=1 TO G
3010 PRINT:PRINT
3020 PRINT "GROUP ";K;" MEANS ON ";M(K);
     " CASES"
3030 FOR I=1 TO N
3040 PRINT "VARIABLE ";I;"=";A(I,K)/M(K)
3050 NEXT I
3060 NEXT K
3070 PRINT
3080 PRINT
3085 PRINT "COVARIANCE MATRIX"
3090 FOR I=1 TO N
3100 FOR J=1 TO I
3110 PRINT TAB((J-1)*6);INT(S(I,J)*100/
     (T-G))/100;
3120 NEXT J
3130 PRINT
3140 NEXT I
3150 PRINT
3160 RETURN

3500 PRINT
3510 PRINT "CANONICAL VECTOR    EIGENVALUE
         PERCENT"
3520 FOR I=1 TO G-1
3530 PRINT TAB(10);I;TAB(20);X(I);TAB(35);
     X(I)/E*100;"%"
3540 NEXT I
3550 PRINT
3560 PRINT
3570 PRINT "VARIABLE    CANONICAL VECTORS"
3580 FOR J=1 TO G-1
3590 PRINT TAB(10*J+3);J;
3600 NEXT J
3610 PRINT
3620 FOR I=1 TO N
3630 PRINT I;
3640 FOR J=1 TO G-1
3650 PRINT TAB(J*10);B(I,J);
3660 NEXT J
3670 PRINT
3680 NEXT I
3690 RETURN
```

```
4000 FOR I=1 TO N
4010 T(I)=0
4020 NEXT I
4030 FOR K=1 TO G
4040 FOR I=1 TO N
4050 FOR J=1 TO I
4060 B(I,J)=B(I,J)+A(I,K)*A(J,K)/M(K)
4070 NEXT J
4080 T(I)=T(I)+A(I,K)
4090 NEXT I
4095 NEXT K
4100 FOR I=1 TO N
4110 FOR J=1 TO I
4120 B(I,J)=B(I,J)-T(I)*T(J)/T
4130 B(J,I)=B(I,J)
4135 H(I,J)=S(I,J)/(T-G)
4136 H(J,I)=H(I,J)
4140 NEXT J
4150 NEXT I
4160 RETURN

4500 E=0
4505 FOR I=1 TO G-1
4510 X(I)=0
4515 L=1
4520 FOR J=1 TO N
4530 IF E(J,J)>X(I) THEN X(I)=E(J,J):L=J
4540 NEXT J
4550 E(L,L)=0
4555 E=E+X(I)
4560 FOR J=1 TO N
4570 B(J,I)=0
4580 FOR K=1 TO N
4590 B(J,I)=B(J,I)+C(J,K)*S(K,L)
4600 NEXT K
4610 NEXT J
4620 NEXT I
4630 FOR K=1 TO G-1
4640 A=0
4650 FOR I=1 TO N
4660 FOR J=1 TO N
4670 A=A+H(I,J)*B(I,K)*B(J,K)
4680 NEXT J
4690 NEXT I
4700 A=SQR(A)
4710 FOR I=1 TO N
4720 B(I,K)=B(I,K)/A
4730 NEXT I
4740 NEXT K
4750 RETURN

5000 FOR I=1 TO N
5010 FOR J=1 TO N
```

```
5020 S(I,J)=0
5030 FOR K=1 TO N
5040 S(I,J)=S(I,J)+B(I,K)*C(K,J)
5050 NEXT K
5060 NEXT J
5070 NEXT I
5080 FOR I=1 TO N
5090 FOR J=1 TO N
5100 E(I,J)=0
5110 FOR K=1 TO N
5120 E(I,J)=E(I,J)+C(K,I)*S(K,J)
5130 NEXT K
5140 NEXT J
5150 NEXT I
5160 RETURN


6000 S(1,1)=SQR(S(1,1))
6010 FOR J=2 TO N
6020 S(1,J)=S(1,J)/S(1,1)
6030 NEXT J
6040 FOR I=2 TO N
6050 FOR K=1 TO I-1
6060 S(I,I)=S(I,I)-S(K,I)*S(K,I)
6070 NEXT K
6080 S(I,I)=SQR(S(I,I))
6085 IF I+1>N THEN GOTO 6150
6090 FOR J=I+1 TO N
6100 FOR K=1 TO I-1
6110 S(I,J)=S(I,J)-S(K,I)*S(K,J)
6120 NEXT K
6130 S(I,J)=S(I,J)/S(I,I)
6140 NEXT J
6150 NEXT I
6160 RETURN


6500 FOR K=1 TO N
6510 FOR I=N TO 1 STEP -1
6520 C(I,K)=0
6530 IF I=K THEN C(I,K)=1
6535 IF I=N THEN GOTO 6570
6540 FOR J=I+1 TO N
6550 C(I,K)=C(I,K)-S(I,J)*C(J,K)
6560 NEXT J
6570 C(I,K)=C(I,K)/S(I,I)
6580 NEXT I
6590 NEXT K
6600 RETURN

7200 OPEN "I",#1,F$
7210 RETURN

7300 INPUT#1,R
7310 RETURN
```

110 *Classification Algorithms*

```
7400 CLOSE #1
7410 RETURN
8000 V=0
8010 FOR I=1 TO N
8020 FOR J=1 TO N
8030 S(I,J)=0
8040 IF I=J THEN S(I,I)=1
8050 V=V+E(I,J)*E(I,J)
8060 NEXT J
8070 NEXT I
8080 V=SQR(2*V)/N/100000
8090 K=1
8100 P=1
8110 Q=2
8120 Z=E(P,Q)
8130 FOR I=1 TO N-1
8140 FOR J=I+1 TO N
8150 IF Z<ABS(E(I,J)) THEN Z=ABS(E(I,J)):
     P=I:Q=J
8160 NEXT J
8170 NEXT I
8175 PRINT "ITERATION ";K;"DELTA =";Z-V
8180 IF Z<V THEN RETURN
8190 GOSUB 8500
8200 K=K+1
8210 GOTO 8100

8500 IF E(P,P)=E(Q,Q) THEN C=.707:S=C:
     GOTO 8550
8510 A=2*E(P,Q)/(E(P,P)-E(Q,Q))
8520 X=ATN(A)/2
8530 C=COS(X)
8540 S=SIN(X)
8550 FOR I=1 TO N
8560 Z=E(P,I)
8570 E(P,I)=C*Z+S*E(Q,I)
8580 E(Q,I)=C*E(Q,I)-S*Z
8590 NEXT I
8600 FOR I=1 TO N
8610 Z=E(I,P)
8620 X=S(I,P)
8630 E(I,P)=C*Z+S*E(I,Q)
8640 E(I,Q)=C*E(I,Q)-S*Z
8650 S(I,P)=C*X+S*S(I,Q)
8660 S(I,Q)=C*S(I,Q)-S*X
8670 NEXT I
8680 RETURN

9000 GOSUB 7400:REM CLOSE FILE
9010 GOSUB 7200:REM OPEN INPUT FILE
9020 GOSUB 7300:GOSUB 7300
9030 DIM Z(T),Y(T),D(T)
```

```
9031 V=0:A=0
9034 I=1
9035 L=1:S=1:P=1:Q=1
9040 FOR K=1 TO G
9045 FOR H=1 TO M(K)
9050 FOR J=1 TO N
9060 GOSUB 7300:REM READ R
9070 Z(I)=Z(I)+R*B(J,1)
9080 Y(I)=Y(I)+R*B(J,2)
9090 NEXT J
9100 IF Z(I)>Z(L) THEN L=I
9110 IF Z(I)<Z(S) THEN S=I
9120 IF Y(I)>Y(P) THEN P=I
9130 IF Y(I)<Y(Q) THEN Q=I
9135 D(I)=K
9140 I=I+1
9145 NEXT H
9146 NEXT K
9155 A=60:B=25
9160 L=Z(L):S=Z(S)
9170 P=Y(P):Q=Y(Q)
9180 FOR I=1 TO T
9190 Z(I)=INT((Z(I)-S)/(L-S)*(A-1)+1)
9200 Y(I)=INT((Y(I)-Q)/(P-Q)*(B-1)+1)
9210 NEXT I
9220 GOSUB 9600
9221 PRINT
9222 FOR I=1 TO A
9223 PRINT TAB(I);"-";
9224 NEXT I
9225 PRINT
9226 J=1
9230 FOR I=1 TO B
9240 PRINT "I";
9250 IF Y(J)>I THEN GOTO 9290
9255 IF J=T THEN GOTO 9290
9256 IF Z(J)=Z(J-1) THEN GOTO 9270
9260 PRINT TAB(Z(J));CHR$(D(J)+48);
9270 J=J+1
9280 GOTO 9250
9290 PRINT TAB(A+1);"I"
9300 NEXT I
9310 FOR I=1 TO A
9320 PRINT TAB(I);"-";
9330 NEXT I
9340 PRINT
9350 RETURN

9600 FOR I=1 TO T-1
9610 K=I
9620 FOR J=I+1 TO T-1
9630 IF Y(J)<Y(K) THEN K=J
9635 IF Y(J)=Y(K) AND Z(J)<Z(K) THEN K=J
```

```
9640 NEXT J
9650 Z=Y(I)
9660 Y(I)=Y(K)
9670 Y(K)=Z
9680 Z=Z(I)
9690 Z(I)=Z(K)
9700 Z(K)=Z
9710 Z=D(I)
9720 D(I)=D(K)
9730 D(K)=Z
9740 NEXT I
9750 RETURN
```

A canonical analysis of Fisher's iris data

The iris data has been analysed a number of times in earlier chapters but so far no attempt has been made to examine the distribution of the three groups graphically. As there are only three groups of iris all of the information used by the linear discriminant functions to classify them can be seen in a plot of the data on the only two (G−1=2) canonical vectors. If the iris data is analysed using the program given in the previous section the results are:

```
CANONICAL ANALYSIS
DATA FILE NAME ?IRIS
CASES= 150 VARIABLES= 4
NUMBER OF GROUPS ? 3
NUMBER OF CASES IN GROUP  1 ?  50
NUMBER OF CASES IN GROUP  2 ?  50
NUMBER OF CASES IN GROUP  3 ?  50


GROUP  1   MEANS ON   50  CASES
VARIABLE   1 = 5.006
VARIABLE   2 = 3.428
VARIABLE   3 = 1.462
VARIABLE   4 = 0.246


GROUP  2   MEANS ON   50  CASES
VARIABLE   1 = 5.936
VARIABLE   2 = 2.77
VARIABLE   3 = 4.26
VARIABLE   4 = 1.326


GROUP  3   MEANS ON   50  CASES
VARIABLE   1 = 6.588
VARIABLE   2 = 2.974
VARIABLE   3 = 5.552
VARIABLE   4 = 2.026
```

```
COVARIANCE MATRIX
 0 .26
 0 .09   0.11
 0 .16   0.05   0.18
 0 .03   0.03   0.04   0.04


CANONICAL VECTOR     EIGENVALUE          PERCENT
      1               32.3243           99.1249 %
      2                0.285371          0.87511 %


VARIABLE    CANONICAL VECTORS
               1          2
    1     -0.85279    0.0302752
    2     -1.52342    2.16107
    3      2.22376   -0.935407
    4      2.7976     2.84088
```

```
 -----------------------------------------------------------------
I                                         2                         I
I                                                                   I
I                                                 33                I
I                 1                     22 2   2                    I
I                                        2 2   22   2               I
I                                     2      2      2      3        I
I           1                             2 2                       I
I           1 11                          2   2 2   3 2      3   3  I
I           111                       2    2 2               3      3I
I            1                            222  2         3          I
I           11 1                          222           333         I
I         1111                           22  22        3 33 3    3  I
I          111                        2      22   2 3  3            I
I         1 1   11 1                        2                3      I
I          1111                                       33    3  3    I
I         1 1                               2            3  3  3    I
I           1   1                                     2  3          I
I       I 1      1   1                            2      3   3      I
I      I1     1                                          3     3    I
I      I1 1                                              3 33       I
I                                                        3 3        I
I                                                                3  I
I                                                        3 33       I
I                                                     3             I
I                                                                   I
 -----------------------------------------------------------------
```

If you examine the scatter plot you will be able to see the details of the group separation that has been indicated by the error rates reported by the classification programs. It is clear that group 1 is well separated from groups 2 and 3 but 2 and 3 are quite close together. Even though groups 2 and 3 are close together they are quite distinct and this accounts for the good performance of the classifiers used in earlier chapters. It is also interesting to notice that the first eigenvector accounts for a large proportion of the within groups to between groups variation and this suggests that it might be worth using this linear combination alone to classify the irises – however more of this idea later.

114   Classification Algorithms

Algebra of canonical analysis **

Thus far we have given no details of the calculation of the canonical vectors and this is obviously necessary before the inner workings of the canonical analysis program given in the previous section can be described. The mathematical details given in this section are not easy to follow and require some knowledge of matrix theory. It is quite possible to use and interpret canonical analysis without following the mathematical details of its derivation so this section (and the next) may be skipped if desired.

We require a vector $\mathbf{v}$ such that $y = \mathbf{v}'\mathbf{x}$ maximises

$$\lambda_i = \frac{\mathbf{v}'\mathbf{B}\mathbf{v}}{\mathbf{v}'\mathbf{W}\mathbf{v}}$$

where $\mathbf{B}/(G-1)$ = Between groups covariance matrix
$\mathbf{W}/(n-G)$ = Within groups covariance matrix

$$\mathbf{v}'\mathbf{B}\mathbf{v} = \text{SSB} \quad \text{of } y$$

$$\mathbf{v}'\mathbf{W}\mathbf{v} = \text{SSW} \quad \text{of } y$$

We can find $\mathbf{v}$ either by noting that λ is a ratio of quadratic forms and hence can be maximised in the usual way [3], or by the longer, but more elementary, method of differentiating λ with respect to $\mathbf{v}$ and equating the derivative to zero in the standard way:

$$\frac{d\lambda}{d\mathbf{v}} = \frac{2[\mathbf{B}\mathbf{v}(\mathbf{v}'\mathbf{W}\mathbf{v}) - (\mathbf{v}'\mathbf{B}\mathbf{v})\mathbf{W}\mathbf{v}]}{(\mathbf{v}'\mathbf{W}\mathbf{v})^2} = 0$$

(This expression can be obtained by finding $d\lambda/d\mathbf{v}_i$ for each i and collecting the terms.) On dividing top and bottom by $\mathbf{v}'\mathbf{W}\mathbf{v}$, we have:

$$\frac{2[\mathbf{B}\mathbf{v} - \lambda\mathbf{W}\mathbf{v}]}{\mathbf{v}'\mathbf{W}\mathbf{v}} = 0$$

which is equivalent to:

$$\mathbf{B}\mathbf{v} = \lambda\mathbf{W}\mathbf{v}$$

a generalised eigenvalue problem.

If $\mathbf{W}$ is non-singular (i.e. $\mathbf{W}^{-1}$ exists), this may be reduced to an ordinary eigenvalue problem:

$$\mathbf{W}^{-1}\mathbf{B}\mathbf{v} = \lambda\mathbf{v}$$

The only problem with this expression is that $\mathbf{W}^{-1}\mathbf{B}$ is not necessarily a symmetric matrix and in general a complete set of eigenvectors is only guaranteed to exist for a symmetric matrix (and a number of other well defined classes of matrices). Without presenting a proof we will state that a complete set of eigenvectors exists and we will write $\mathbf{V}$ for the matrix of such eigenvectors. (In fact $\mathbf{V} = \mathbf{A}\mathbf{L}^{-1/2}\mathbf{B}$ where $\mathbf{A}$ is the eigenvector matrix of $\mathbf{W}$, $\mathbf{L}$ is its corresponding diagonal matrix of eigenvalues and $\mathbf{B}$ is the eigenvector matrix of the symmetric $\mathbf{L}^{-1/2}\mathbf{A}\mathbf{B}\mathbf{A}\mathbf{L}^{-1/2}$.)

Thus

$$\mathbf{W}^{-1}\mathbf{B}\mathbf{V} = \mathbf{V}\Lambda$$

where Λ is a diagonal matrix of eigenvalues λ_i.

The following results are also true. (Again no formal proof will be presented.)

(1) $\mathbf{V}'\mathbf{B}\mathbf{V}$, $\mathbf{V}'\mathbf{W}\mathbf{V}$ and $\mathbf{V}'\mathbf{T}\mathbf{V}$ are diagonal ($\mathbf{T} = \mathbf{B}+\mathbf{W}$).
This shows that the new variables are uncorrelated between groups, within groups and within the total sample.

(2) By choice of normalisation any of $\mathbf{V}'\mathbf{B}\mathbf{V}$, $\mathbf{V}'\mathbf{W}\mathbf{V}$ or $\mathbf{V}'\mathbf{T}\mathbf{V}$ can be made equal to $\mathbf{I}$ the matrix identity.

(3) $\mathbf{V}'\mathbf{V}\neq\mathbf{I}$ – the new variables may be uncorrelated, but they are not *orthogonal*.

(4) There are $\min(\text{rank}(\mathbf{B}), \text{rank}(\mathbf{W}))$ non-zero eigenvalues.

(5) The maximum rank of $\mathbf{B}$ is $G-1$ and of $\mathbf{W}$ is n.

It is interesting to note that the usual method of finding the canonical vectors is to factor $\mathbf{W}$ into the product $\mathbf{D}'\mathbf{D}$ where $\mathbf{D}$ is a non-singular lower triangular matrix, i.e. $\mathbf{W} = \mathbf{D}'\mathbf{D}$, and then solve the related problem:

$$\mathbf{D}^{-1}\mathbf{B}\mathbf{D}'^{-1}\mathbf{V}^* = \mathbf{V}^*\Lambda$$

using the standard methods for symmetric matrices (as

$$\mathbf{D}^{-1}\mathbf{B}\mathbf{D}'^{-1}$$

is symmetric) for $\mathbf{V}^*$ and then find $\mathbf{V}$ using:

$$\mathbf{V} = \mathbf{D}'^{-1}\mathbf{V}^*$$

More details of how the eigenvectors and eigenvalues are calculated are given in the next section.

Technical details of the canonical analysis program **

The canonical analysis program essentially follows the order of computation suggested in the previous section, no attempt has been made to optimise the program for storage or speed to make it easier to follow the calculation. Subroutines 1000, 2000 and 3000 are similar to those used in the linear discriminant program – 1000 gets the relevant parameters, 2000 computes the within groups sums of squares and cross products matrix (stored in S(N,N)) and the group means (stored in A(N,G)) and subroutine 3000 prints the results. Subroutine 4000 then forms the between groups sums of squares and cross products matrix from the means (stored in B(N,N)) and the within groups covariance matrix (stored in H(N,N)). Then subroutine 6000 finds a lower triangular matrix, **D** such that **D'D=S**, using the Cholesky decomposition – the result overwrites the contents of S. Subroutine 6500 uses back-substitution to find the inverse of the lower triangular matrix stored in S and the result is stored in C(N,N). Subroutine 5000 forms the matrix product:

$$\mathbf{D}^{-1}\mathbf{B}\mathbf{D}'^{-1}$$

storing the result in E(N,N) – at the end of this subroutine C(N,N) still contains the inverse of **D** for later use. Subroutine 8000 uses the classical Jacobi method to find all of the eigenvalues and eigenvectors of E(N,N). When the subroutine is finished the eigenvalues are stored in the diagonal elements of E and the eigenvectors are stored in S. The Jacobi method consists of a number of iterations, each one reducing the magnitude of an off-diagonal element. Obviously when all the off-diagonal elements are zero the result is a diagonal matrix with the eigenvalues as the diagonal elements. The only trouble is that an off-diagonal element that was zeroed in one iteration can be made non-zero by a subsequent iteration. Fortunately the process does converge with the off-diagonal elements growing ever smaller. Although there are faster methods of finding the eigenvectors and eigenvalues of a symmetric matrix the Jacobi method has the advantage that it is simple and can be programmed in very few lines. The variable V (line 8080) controls the accuracy of the results – the smaller the value of V the more accurate the answer but the longer the time taken! Subroutine 8000 prints out the difference between V and the largest off-diagonal element in the matrix so that the user can follow the progress of the calculation. Once the eigenvectors and eigenvalues have been found the program's task is nearly done. Subroutine 4500 converts the eigenvectors of E to those of:

$$\mathbf{W}^{-1}\mathbf{B}$$

Feature Selection – Canonical Analysis

that is, the canonical vectors that we require, by multiplying S by $\mathbf{D}^{-1}$. The final eigenvectors are also scaled by subroutine 4500 so that $\mathbf{V'WV = I}$ (i.e. the within groups variance of each of the new variables $\mathbf{v'x}$ is one). Finally subroutine 9000 computes the values of the first two canonical vectors for each case in the sample and plots a scatter diagram. The method used to plot the scatter diagram is very slow because it only uses the simple PRINT and PRINT TAB(X) statements to position the output. This routine is capable of being greatly speeded up by the use of a PRINT TAB(X,Y) statement but this has been avoided as it is machine specific.

A summary of the subroutine structure and array use of the canonical analysis program is presented in Table 7.1.

Table 7.1

Canonical analysis subroutine use

Subroutine	Action
1000	Get parameters and set up arrays
2000	Calculate covariance matrix and means
3000	Print means and covariance matrices
3500	Print canonical vectors and eigenvalues
4000	Calculate between group covariance
4500	Convert to canonical vectors
5000	Calculate E
6000	Factor covariance matrix
6500	Invert factors
7200	Open input file
7300	Read a value into R
7400	Close file
8000	Find eigen values of E
8500	Jacobi iteration
9000	Re-read file and plot 1st and 2nd canonical vectors
9600	Sort values in Y and Z

Array use

Array	Purpose
M(G)	Number of cases in each group
S(N,N)	Within groups covariance matrix and general work matrix
B(N,N)	Between groups covariance matrix and canonical vectors
H(N,N)	Within groups covariance matrix

118 *Classification Algorithms*

X(N)   Used to read in data and later to hold eigenvalues
T(N)   Stores working means
A(N,G)   Group means
C(N,N)   Inverse of factors of within groups covariance matrix
E(N,N)   Jacobi iteration matrix

Significance testing and the selection of eigenvectors **
From the previous discussion of the geometry of canonical eigenvectors the reader may already be convinced that it is not safe to discard any of the non-zero eigenvectors. However, many programs give significance levels for each of the canonical vectors and suggest selection procedures based on these. For this reason we will cover the usual methods of significance testing and try to outline when this might be useful. In this section it is assumed that the reader is familiar at least with ANOVA and preferably its multivariate extension MANOVA. It is worth mentioning at this point that the techniques of canonical analysis are used for the same purpose within MANOVA [4].

If the groups are multivariate normal with equal covariance matrices we may use the usual test of the hypothesis H_{o1} i.e. are the group means identical? This is a one-way MANOVA using Wilks' lambda and is normally quoted at the start of a canonical analysis. If this is significant we reject H_{o1} and conclude that there is evidence for differences in the means that is unlikely to have arisen by chance alone. After finding the first eigenvector we can go on to test the hypothesis H_{o2}, i.e., in the remaining space, are the group means identical? If this is significant we can extract the next eigenvector and test the hypothesis H_{o3}, i.e. is there no difference between the means in the remaining space? Either we will find all G−1 eigenvectors and stop or we will find an H_{oi} which is not significant. If the latter happens, we must ask ourselves if there is any point in extracting any more eigenvectors because we have no evidence that any difference between the means in the remaining space is due to anything other than random sampling. In other words, in the remaining space the differences between the means as small enough to have arisen by chance alone.

The technical details of the sequence of significance tests are as follows:

If $\lambda_1, \lambda_2, \ldots, \lambda_p$ are the non-zero eigenvalues and L is the Wilks' lambda test for differences in the original sample, we have:

$$\frac{1}{L} = (1 + \lambda_1)(1 + \lambda_2) \cdots (1 + \lambda_p)$$

and

$$V = -(m - 1 - (n + G)/2) \ln L$$
$$= (m - 1 - (n + G)/2)[\ln(1 + \lambda_1) + \ln(1 + \lambda_2) +$$
$$\cdots + \ln(1 + \lambda_p)]$$

which is approximately χ^2 with $G(n-1)$ degrees of freedom. The expression for Wilks' lambda given above suggests a decomposition of the statistic suitable for testing each hypothesis in turn. That is:

$$V_i = [m - 1 - (n + G)/2] \ln(1 + \lambda_i)$$

are approximately independent χ^2 with $G+n-2i$ degrees of freedom. ($m =$ number of cases, $n =$ number of variables and $G =$ number of groups.)

Using the V_i statistics the successive tests are:

H_o	χ^2	df
means are different	V	$G(n-1)$
means are different after removing first eigenvector	$V-V_1$	$G(n-1)-(G+N-2)$
means are different after removing second eigenvector	$V-V_1-V_2$	$G(n-1)-(G+N-2\times 2)$
$\vdots$	$\vdots$	$\vdots$
means are different after removing ith eigenvector	$V-V_1-V_2 \ldots -V_i$	$G(n-1)-(G+N-2i)$

The logic behind rejecting all those eigenvectors following non-significance is a little vague. In the population there is no reason for leaving out any of the non-zero eigenvectors – each one improves the classification performance. However, if we are using sample estimates for the population parameters, this need not be so. If the difference between the means could have arisen by random sampling fluctuation alone then the use of this difference in classification could make the performance worse. In other words we can reduce the variance of the discriminant functions by leaving out non-significant canonical vectors. It should be noted however that for an eigenvector to be non-significant its eigenvalue λ must be small. This implies that SSB is small and that the actual effect of the eigenvector on classification is small. Therefore, whether we leave it in or out may be immaterial.

All this said, it must be admitted that there are very few theoretical or empirical studies giving useful information on the effect of ignoring non-significant eigenvectors.

The structure of discrimination

Apart from plotting the cases, the canonical vectors have another important use. This is the examination of the structure of the discrimination. If we are interested in what makes our groups different we can use the canonical vectors to discover features of importance. An eigenvector's effect on classification is clearly related to the size of its eigenvalue. If we take the most important and try to interpret its coefficients, we have a situation exactly mirroring PC or factor analysis where we try to name the important factors. In this process of interpretation we have all the usual problems of arbitrary scales. If all the variables are measured in the same units then the relative contribution of each variable in each eigenvector is simply proportional to the appropriate coefficient, i.e. if the ith eigenvector is:

$$e_i = \sum_j v_{ij} x_j$$

then the importance of x_3 is proportional to v_{i3}. If, however, the variables are measured in different scales, we have to standardise the coefficients to take this into account. This is done by multiplying each by the standard deviation of the corresponding variable, i.e.

$$v_{ij}^* = s_j v_{ij}$$

where s_j is the within groups standard deviation of variable j.

Whether we use the standardised or unstandardised eigenvectors, our problem is the same – by examining the relative magnitudes of the vs we have to 'name' the eigenvectors in the same way as we name 'factors' in principal component analysis. If we succeed then we can say that the groups differ mostly because of this characteristic and give its name the eigenvector with the largest eigenvalue.

This interpretation process is usually very difficult and can be made easier in two ways:

(1) By examining the arrangement of the groups on each eigenvector in turn.

(2) By 'rotating' the eigenvectors using the usual VARIMAX or PROMAX methods of factor analysis (see [1]).

The first suggestion is easily carried out and is usually the most helpful in building other theoretical knowledge into the solution. For example, if we had three groups labelled schizophrenic, manic depressive and normal, and, on the first canonical vector, the schizophrenic and manic depressive groups are close and the normal is well separated, then we might be tempted to name it 'psychotic v. normal'.

The second suggestion is almost as easy to carry out, given the availability of a computer program for factor analysis. However, as the theory and varieties of methods to be employed are the same as for factor analysis, the reader is referred to standard texts on factor analysis [1] and [2]. In practice the rotated solutions are usually as difficult to interpret as the original and lack the 'ordering' of the original according to importance.

Extending the canonical analysis program

From the preceding discussion it is clear that the two facilities that the canonical analysis program lacks is the ability to quote significance levels relevant to each of the canonical eigenvectors and to provide standardised versions of the canonical eigenvectors. Standardising the canonical eigenvectors is simply a matter of multiplying each of the coefficients by the appropriate standard deviation and this is a small change to the previous program. Working out values of Wilks' lambda and its associated χ^2 value is also easy but it is also worth adding a subroutine to give the significance level of χ^2. The following changes and additions should be made to the canonical analysis program given earlier:

```
3500 PRINT
3510 PRINT "CANONICAL VECTOR     EIGENVALUE
     PERCENT";
3512 PRINT TAB(45);"CHI        DF
     SIGNIFICANCE"
3514 U=G*(N-1) :GOSUB 3900
3515 PRINT TAB(11);"0";TAB(45);V;TAB(50);
     G*(N-1);TAB(60);W
3520 FOR I=1 TO G-1
3525 V=V-T(I)
3530 PRINT TAB(10);I;TAB(20);X(I);TAB(35);
     X(I)/E*100;"%";
3532 U=G*(N-1)-(G+N-2*I)
3534 GOSUB 3900
3535 IF I<>G-1 THEN PRINT TAB(45);V;TAB(50);
     G*(N-1)-(G+N-2*I);TAB(60);W
3540 NEXT I
3550 PRINT
3560 PRINT
```

```
3570 PRINT "VARIABLE     STANDARDISED CANONICAL
       VECTORS"
3580 FOR J=1 TO G-1
3590 PRINT TAB(10*J+3);J;
3600 NEXT J
3610 PRINT
3620 FOR I=1 TO N
3630 PRINT I;
3640 FOR J=1 TO G-1
3650 PRINT TAB(J*10);B(I,J)*SQR(H(I,I));
3660 NEXT J
3670 PRINT
3680 NEXT I
3690 RETURN

3900 R=1
3910 FOR J=U TO 2 STEP -2
3920 R=R*J
3930 NEXT J
3935 IF V>20*U OR V>160 THEN W=0:RETURN
3940 W=V^(INT((U+1)/2))*EXP(-V/2)/R
3945 IF INT(U/2)=U/2 THEN GOTO 3960
3950 J=SQR(2/V/3.14159)
3955 GOTO 3965
3960 J=1
3965 L=1:M=1
3970 U=U+2:M=M*V/U
3975 IF M<.0001 THEN W=1-J*W*L:RETURN
3980 L=L+M
3990 GOTO 3970

4750 FOR I=1 TO G-1
4760 T(I)=(T-1-(N+G)/2)*LOG(1+X(I))
4770 V=V+T(I)
4780 NEXT I
4790 RETURN
```

The changes to subroutine 3500 are extensive enough to warrant listing the entire routine but subroutine 4500 only requires the addition of five lines. Subroutine 3900 is entirely new and will return the significance level of χ^2 (stored in V) with U degrees of freedom in W.

An example of the structure of discrimination

If the modified canonical analysis program is used to examine the iris data once again then the following additional results are obtained:

CANONICAL VECTOR	EIGENVALUE	PERCENT	CHI SQU.	DF	SIG.
0			546.692	9	0.0
1	32.3243	99.1249	36.527	4	3.576E-07
2	0.2854	0.8751			

VARIABLE	STANDARDISED CANONICAL VECTORS	
	1	2
1	-0.123158	0.0222624
2	-0.115805	0.836453
3	0.684635	-1.46636
4	0.371904	1.92293

(The means, covariance matrices and the scatter diagram are of course unaffected by the modifications.) The first value of χ^2 is a straightforward test of the difference between the group means. In this case it has a significance level so small that it is reported as zero and hence there is almost certainly a real difference between the group means! (Recall that the significance level gives the probability of obtaining the result by chance alone and hence a small significance implies that the differences between the group means are unlikely to have resulted by chance.) The second value of χ^2 tests for any remaining group differences after removing the variation along the first canonical eigenvector. This too is significant at a level that would normally be considered to provide excellent evidence for a group difference. Thus the three group means are sufficiently different in two distinct directions to require both canonical eigenvectors to describe them – that is they lie in a two dimensional plane. If the second value of χ^2 had not proved significant then we could have concluded that there was no difference between the groups after the first eigenvector had been extracted and hence the group means were close to being in a straight line on the scatter diagram. As it is we have to conclude that the group means are close to lying on a straight line but there is sufficient difference between them along the second canonical eigenvector to make it unlikely that this difference arose by chance alone.

Even though the second χ^2 value is large enough to make the differences in the group means along the second canonical eigenvector more than just the result of random sampling the amount of group separation along this new variable is remarkably small. This is a paradox familiar to applied statisticians – the result is statistically significant but practically insignificant. Even a significant canonical eigenvector can be ignored if its contribution to the group differences is very small. In this case calculating discriminant functions using only the first canonical eigenvector results in almost the same error rate as using the original variables. To classify cases using only the first canonical vector all that it is necessary to do is to calculate its value for each of the three group means e.g. for group 1:

$$-0.852797 \times 5.006 - 1.52342 \times 3.428 + 2.22376 \times 1.462 + 2.7976 \times 0.246$$
$$= -5.55204$$

and assign each case according to the group canonical eigenvalue mean to which its own canonical eigenvector value is closest. (Notice that the unstandardised coefficients have to be used.) An equivalent procedure is to calculate the canonical vector 'score':

$$v_1 x_1 + v_2 x_2 + v_3 x_3 + v_4 x_4$$

for each case in the sample, where v_1 to v_4 are the coefficients of the first canonical eigenvector and x_1 to x_4 are the four measured variables, and submit the resulting data on the single new variable to the linear discriminant program. The generalisation of these ideas to cases involving more than two canonical eigenvectors is straighforward – if all but P canonical eigenvectors are rejected as being unimportant then classification can be achieved either by computing P canonical vector scores and assigning to the group with the closest mean or by submitting the canonical vector scores to the linear discriminant program.

Looking at the size of the coefficients on the first standardised canonical eigenvector reveals a very different pattern to that in the unstandardised form. Although it is difficult to find a suitable name to describe this 'feature' it is possible to see that it has roughly the form:

(petal length − sepal length) + (petal width − sepal width)

and this may be useful in understanding the differences in the species. In this case a rotation of the two canonical eigenvectors would almost certainly result in features that were easier to interpret but a description of this technique is beyond the scope of this book – see Reference [1] or [2] for more information.

Relation to canonical correlation **

It is worth noting that canonical analysis is nothing more than canonical correlation using the measured variables as one set and dummy variables indicating which group a case belongs to as the other – hence the name canonical analysis. The dummy variable coding is simple. If there are G groups, we create G−1 new variables. Then each of the first G−1 groups is associated with a variable and the fact that a case belongs to a particular group is indicated by a 1 in its associated variable and 0s in the rest.

Membership of the Gth group is indicated by 0s in all G−1 variables. For example, if G=4, we would use three dummy variables a, b and c as follows:

	a	b	c
case in group 1	1	0	0
case in group 2	0	1	0
case in group 3	0	0	1
case in group 4	0	0	0

The canonical eigenvectors and eigenvalues are then obtained by running a canonical correlation on the measured variables and the dummy variables as the independent and dependent sets of variables respectively. The canonical analysis eigenvectors are simply the canonical variables constructed on the measured variables and the eigenvalue, $\lambda_i \propto SSB/SSW$, is obtained from the canonical correlation r_i using

$$\lambda_i = \frac{r_i^2}{1 - r_i^2}$$

The significance tests etc. provided by a canonical correlation program, are all analogous to the canonical analysis case.

This procedure can be useful in two cases:

(1) If a good canonical analysis program is not available.

(2) If the numerical accuracy of a canonical analysis program is in doubt.

Programs and practice

This chapter on canonical analysis is very long for a technique that is concerned not with classification but with feature selection. Indeed the use of canonical analysis is rarely essential unless we wish to explore the reasons for good classification or test whether there really are differences between the groups. Although the significance tests associated with canonical analysis assume multivariate normality the rest of the procedure is based on considerations of maximising a very reasonable measure of group separation and as such it can be applied when the variables are not normal. On the other hand canonical analysis is closely linked with linear discrimination and many of its optimal properties apply only to this type of classification rule. In particular, even using all G−1 eigenvectors will still result in a loss of performance if you are using quadratic discriminant functions. It is also true that there is no equivalent to canonical analysis for quadratic discriminant functions and this implies that when the covariance matrices are different information from outside the hyperplane defined by the means is used [5].

However canonical analysis has caused so much confusion in the past that it is important to understand its purpose. A number of classification programs (SPSS for example) confuse feature selection and classification – indeed the name discriminant function or discriminant vector is sometimes used for the canonical eigenvectors. It is probably the availability of programs which carry out stepwise variable selection (see next chapter) and canonical analysis, automatically rejecting non-significant eigenvectors, that have led to the misunderstanding. The programs behave correctly but they integrate the feature selection and classification steps so closely that it is difficult for a novice user to tell what is happening.

References

1. Child, D. (1970) *The Essentials of Factor Analysis*: Holt, Rinehart and Winston.
2. Maxwell, A.E. (1977) *Multivariate Analysis in Behavioural Research*: Chapman and Hall.
3. Shilov, G.E. (1977) *Linear Algebra*: Dover.
4. Chatfield, C. and Collins, A.J. (1980) *Introduction to Multivariate Analysis*: Chapman and Hall.
5. Decell, H. P., Odell, P. L. and Coberly, W. A. (1981) 'Linear dimension reduction and Bayes' classification' *Pattern Recognition*, **13**, 241–3.

Chapter Eight
Feature Selection - Variable Selection

Even if, using canonical analysis, we succeed in reducing the number of dimensions used in classification to m, we still have to measure all of the n original variables because each of the new variables is a linear combination of all of the old measurements. If our objective is to reduce the number of measurements we make, then we must use another method – variable selection. What we would like to do is to select the best m variables where 'best' means lowest error rate. This is similar to the variable selection problem in regression analysis [1], where we attempt to find the best m variables to predict the dependent variable.

In fact all the arguments used in the regression case can be applied to the classification case with one important difference. In the regression case the measure of best is usually taken to be R^2 (the multiple correlation coefficient), which gets bigger as the predictive power improves, and this can be calculated quickly and efficiently. In the classification case the measure of best is the error rate and for most classifiers, calculating this quantity is very time-consuming and needs a large sample. Because of this difference, the variable selection problem for classification is usually carried out by trying to find a set of variables which maximise some measure which we hope is closely related to the error rate of the resulting classifier. (This is of course exactly the approach used in unconstrained feature selection covered in the previous chapter.) This said, we will move on to consider the possible methods of finding a set of m variables which maximises some (unspecified) measure and then we will consider some possible choices for these measures of 'best' which are in common use. It should be noted that the first part of this discussion relates to any classifier, but the second is exclusively concerned with multivariate normality.

Variable selection techniques

We can identify four different methods of selecting a 'best' set of m variables.

(1) Complete subsets

This is the most direct method and consists simply of finding every possible subset of size m of the variables and calculating the measure of best (or goodness) on each. Our solution is simply the set with the largest value of our measure.

Although this procedure is guaranteed to find the best m variables, it suffers from one enormous disadvantage. If m and the number of variables is at all large the number of subsets to be considered is very large, usually much too large to make the complete subset method viable. (However there has been some recent work which has made the complete subset method more practical [2], [3].)

(2) Stepwise forward

This is the most usual and well-known method of variable selection The method is conceptually simple. First we find the single variable which maximises our measure of goodness. Then we find the variable which, when paired with our previously selected variable, maximises the measure of goodness. (Note that, at the second stage, we have not examined every pair of variables but only those containing the variable selected at stage one.) We then proceed in the same way to find a third variable which maximises the measure of goodness when added to our previous two and so on until we have selected m variables.

It is clear that we have not necessarily found the best set of m variables – because we have not considered every possible subset of size m – but we hope that we have, at least, a reasonable set. This risk of obtaining a suboptimal solution is also true of the next two methods.

(3) Stepwise backward

The stepwise backward method works like the stepwise forward method, except that we start with all the variables and, at each stage, discard the variable which results in the smallest lowering of our measure of goodness. We stop, of course, when we are left with m variables. It is important to realise that, although the stepwise forward and stepwise backward methods are very similar in their appearance, they can produce different results even when using the same measure of goodness.

(4) Full stepwise

We can combine the forward stepwise method with the backward stepwise method to produce a method which has properties of both. The full stepwise method works by, at each stage, examining the decrease in the measure of goodness produced by removing a variable. If the decrease is below a specified threshold the variable is removed. If no variable meets this criterion a variable is added by the usual forward stepwise method. The logic behind this method is that if a variable which was entered at an earlier step can be replaced by a combination of variables at a later stage then it should be eliminated.

It should be noted that each of these procedures has no claim to statistical validity. They are heuristic procedures for selecting the best variables in a given sample. Any results in future samples must either be taken on trust or verified by testing the classifier on an independent sample. In other words, any significance levels associated with the final classifier are almost certainly erroneous. Also of importance is the fact that none of the procedures is inherently related to any particular measure of 'best', although most stepwise procedures are based on an assumption of multivariate normal distributions.

Finally, in all our methods, we have assumed that m – the number of variables to be selected – is fixed. This is rarely the case, however, and the very nature of a stepwise procedure invites us to examine successive values for m. Hence, in practice, we need some sort of 'stopping rule' to tell us when there is no point in adding another variable. A number of possible stopping rules are described later. In practice it is important to make a clear distinction between the measure used for selection and the measures used for stopping in any stepwise procedure.

Measures used in stepwise methods

A brief list of some of the measures which are used in stepwise procedures is given below – it should be remembered that the criterion we would like to use, if it were possible, is the error rate. Also, although each of the measures could be used with any classifier, they were specifically designed with the multivariate normal equal covariance case in mind.

(1) Wilks' lambda
Wilks' lambda is a multivariate measure of group differences that has already been introduced in connection with canonical analysis in the previous chapter. It is given by:

$$L = \frac{|W|}{|W + B|}$$

where $|W|$ and $|B|$ are the determinants of the within and between sums of squares and cross products matrices respectively. This may be converted to an approximate F ratio to test the group differences. F increases as the groups move apart or as the within group spread decreases. Wilks' lambda decreases as F increases. Thus we can either try to maximise the multivariate

F ratio or minimise lambda. Roughly speaking a determinant of a covariance matrix or a sums of squares and cross products matrix is related to the volume that the data occupies in the sample space (see Appendix 1). As $|\mathbf{W}+\mathbf{B}|=|\mathbf{T}|$, where T is the total sums of squares and cross products matrix (that is ignoring any group structure), Wilks' lambda can be thought of as the ratio of the volume of the within groups spread to the volume of the total spread of the data. Thus a stepwise procedure based on Wilks' lambda tries to separate the group means and reduce the group dispersions at the same time.

(2) Mahalanobis D^2
Maximising the Mahalanobis D^2 between the two *closest* groups, i.e. maximising the minimum D^2 between each pair, tends to separate the two closest groups. As in the case of Wilks' lambda we could use the F test associated with D^2 instead and this has the advantage of taking the group sizes into account.

(3) The residual
Minimising

$$R = \sum (1/(1 + D_{ij}/4))$$

(where D_{ij} is the Mahalanobis distance between the ith and jth groups), also tends to separate groups which are close together. You can think of the residual as a weighted average of all the Ds between the groups. However its original derivation is such that each term in the sum is an estimate of the proportion of unexplained variance of a dummy dependent variable defining each pair of groups when regressed on the classification variables.

(4) The conditional F ratio
The conditional F ratio is the univariate F ratio, associated with a particular variable, testing the difference between the group means conditional on the variables already entered in the equation. (In other words it is the F ratio used in an analysis of covariance to test for group differences on x_j using all the variables already selected as covariates.) It is a measure of how much a given variable contributes to the group differences given the variables already included. The F ratio is proportional to the ratio of the between groups sums of squares and the within groups sums of squares and so it is easy to see that large values of F correspond to well separated groups. The conditional F ratio is slightly different from the other measures in that it is calculated on *each* variable and the variable with the largest value is included. Hence, in this case, there is no overall measure which is being maximised.

It should be emphasised once again that any statistical properties, e.g.

Feature Selection – Variable Selection

significance levels, etc., of these measure are only valid if each of the groups is multivariate normal with equal covariance matrices.

Stopping rules

As was mentioned earlier, if we do not have a particular value of m in mind, we require some rule for stopping a stepwise procedure. This could take the form of not adding any more variables when the change in our measure of goodness was not 'significant', where significance can mean simply 'important' or take its more usual statistical meaning. A particularly common stopping rule is to refuse to add any more variables when none of the conditional F ratios of the remaining variables is significant at some level or other. This is reasonable no matter what measure of goodness we are trying to optimise.

A typical stepwise procedure

To illustrate some of these ideas we will discuss an actual stepwise procedure as implemented in BMD07M [4]. (This is similar to the SPSS procedure DISCRIMINANT [5].)

BMD07M uses a stepwise procedure with several choices of the criterion to be optimised in the forward direction and a single selection procedure for the backward direction. At each step the conditional F ratios are computed for each variable. If a variable which has already been selected has a non-significant F ratio, then it is removed. If more than one variable satisfies this condition, then the one with the smallest F ratio is removed. (The significance level for removing a variable can be changed by the user.) This constitutes the backward part of the stepwise procedure. If none of the variables are removed then the variable not already selected, which creates the largest change in one of the measures of goodness, is selected. The measures of goodness which can be selected by the user include the Mahalanobis D^2, the residual and the conditional F ratio. It should be obvious that any variable which enters at one step because it produces a maximum change in the criterion of interest, could be removed at a later stage because it is non-significant.

The only stopping rule included in BMD07M uses the conditional F ratios. If none of the remaining variables have a significant F value then the stepwise procedure is terminated.

Many other facilities are included in BMD07M and the reader is referred to the BMD Manual [4] for further details. The SPSS procedure DISCRIMINANT is similar but includes extra measures of goodness.

Each stepwise program is likely to have variations particular to itself. The best way to understand any unfamiliar program is to:

132 Classification Algorithms

(1) Discover whether a forward part is implemented and what it is optimising or selecting on.

(2) Discover whether a backward part is included and what it is optimising or selecting on.

(3) Identify the stopping rule.

The dangers of stepwise procedures

Most of the warnings associated with stepwise regression apply to stepwise discrimination. In particular, the final significance level of the group separation is not valid. After all, we have selected the best variables from a larger set. A significant difference between the groups at the 0.01 level is impressive but is much less so if it has been obtained by selecting the best m variables from say 100 initial variables. (Remember, a 0.01 significance level implies that we are likely to get a result at least as good once in one hundred purely by chance!) Remember, stepwise discrimination is not *yet* a statistical procedure! This said, it must be admitted that cautious use of stepwise programs *can* improve the performance of classifiers.

A stepwise discriminant program

The final addition to the linear discriminant program developed in Chapters 4, 5 and 6 turns it into a very useful forward stepwise analysis program. The selection criterion used is the conditional F ratio for each variable – this is easy to compute, good in practice and plays the dual role of a stopping rule. (It is relatively easy to extend the program to use other selection criteria and to include a backward step.) The stepwise program (listed below) can be created from the version of the linear discriminant program given in Chapter 6 by making changes (addition, modification or deletion as indicated by the final listing) to the following lines: 35, 1000, 1155, 2250, 2290, 2300, 2310, 2320, 2330, 2340, 2550, 2570, 3040, 3110, 3580 and 3600 to 3609. Also the following subroutines are either new or changed sufficiently to make it worth re-entering them: 1500, 4000, 6000, 9000, 9500, 8200, 9800, 8500 and 8800.

You should check that the program that results from these changes is identical to the complete listing and that it gives the same results on the test data in this and previous chapters. The stepwise linear discriminant program is:

```
10 GOSUB 1000:REM GET PARAMETERS
20 GOSUB 2000:REM MAKE S AND MEANS
```

Feature Selection - Variable Selection

```
  30 GOSUB 3000:REM PRINT STATS
  35 GOSUB 1500:REM COMPUTE TOTAL SSCP
  40 GOSUB 4000:REM CALCULATE DISC.
  50 GOSUB 5000:REM PRINT RESULTS
  60 GOSUB 3500:REM ESTIMATE ERROR RATE
  70 GOSUB 4500:REM ANALYSE ERROR PATTERN
  80 STOP
1000 PRINT "STEPWISE LINEAR DISCRIMINANT"
1010 PRINT
1020 PRINT "DATA FILE NAME ";
1030 INPUT F$
1040 GOSUB 7200:REM OPEN INPUT FILE
1050 GOSUB 7300:N=R:REM READ R
1060 GOSUB 7300:M=R
1070 PRINT "CASES=";M;"VARIABLES=";N
1080 PRINT "NUMBER OF GROUPS ";
1090 INPUT G
1100 DIM M(G)
1105 T=0
1110 FOR I=1 TO G
1120 PRINT "NUMBER OF CASES IN GROUP ";I;
1130 INPUT M(I)
1135 T=T+M(I)
1140 NEXT I
1150 PRINT
1155 DIM D(G),E(G+1,G+1),H(N,N),V(N),W(N),
     Z(N,G)
1160 DIM S(N,N),X(N),T(N),C(N+1,G),A(N,G),
     F(G),P(G)
1162 FOR I=1 TO G
1163 P(I)=M(I)/T
1164 NEXT I
1165 PRINT "DO YOU KNOW THE PRIOR PROBS. Y/N";
1166 INPUT P$
1167 IF P$="N" THEN GOTO 1210
1170 FOR I=1 TO G
1180 PRINT "PRIOR PROB. FOR GROUP ";I;"=";
1190 INPUT P(I)
1200 NEXT I
1210 PRINT "UNBIASED ESTIMATE Y/N";
1220 INPUT U$
1230 RETURN

1500 FOR I=1 TO N
1510 T(I)=0
1520 NEXT I
1530 FOR K=1 TO G
1540 FOR I=1 TO N
1550 FOR J=1 TO I
1560 H(I,J)=H(I,J)+A(I,K)*A(J,K)/M(K)
1570 NEXT J
```

```
1580 T(I)=T(I)+A(I,K)
1590 NEXT I
1600 NEXT K
1610 FOR I=1 TO N
1620 FOR J=1 TO I
1630 H(I,J)=H(I,J)-T(I)*T(J)/T
1640 H(I,J)=H(I,J)+S(I,J)
1650 H(J,I)=H(I,J)
1660 NEXT J
1670 NEXT I
1680 RETURN

2000 FOR K=1 TO G
2010 FOR J=1 TO M(K)
2020 FOR I=1 TO N
2030 GOSUB 7300
2040 A(I,K)=A(I,K)+R
2050 X(I)=R
2055 IF K=1 AND J=1 THEN T(I)=R
2060 NEXT I
2070 FOR I=1 TO N
2080 FOR L=1 TO I
2090 S(L,I)=S(L,I)+(X(L)-T(L))*(X(I)-T(I))
2100 NEXT L
2110 NEXT I
2120 NEXT J
2130 NEXT K
2140 FOR K=1 TO G
2150 FOR J=1 TO N
2160 FOR I=1 TO J
2170 S(I,J)=S(I,J)-(A(I,K)-M(K)*T(I))*
     (A(J,K)-M(K)*T(J))/M(K)
2180 NEXT I
2190 NEXT J
2200 REM
2210 NEXT K
2230 FOR J=1 TO N
2240 FOR I=1 TO J
2260 S(J,I)=S(I,J)
2270 NEXT I
2280 NEXT J
2290 RETURN

2500 GOSUB 7400:REM CLOSE FILE
2510 GOSUB 7200:REM OPEN INPUT FILE
2515 GOSUB 7300:GOSUB 7300
2516 E=0
2517 W=0
2520 FOR K=1 TO G
2530 PRINT "GROUP ";K
2540 FOR J=1 TO M(K)
2550 FOR I=1 TO Z
```

```
2560 GOSUB 7300:REM READ R
2570 X(W(I))=R
2580 NEXT I
2585 IF E$="Y" THEN GOSUB 3800:
     REM FIND SMALLEST LOO DISCRIMINANT
2590 GOSUB 2800:REM FIND LARGEST DISCRIMINANT
2595 GOSUB 2700:REM FIND PROBABILITY
2600 PRINT J;TAB(3);"LARGEST IS FUNCTION ";
     L;"=";F(L);TAB(20);"PROB. =";P
2604 IF Q<>L AND E$="Y" THEN PRINT
     "***LEAVING ONE OUT ASSIGNS IT TO GROUP ";Q
2605 E(L,K)=E(L,K)+1
2606 E(L,G+1)=E(L,G+1)+1
2607 E(G+1,K)=E(G+1,K)+1
2608 IF Q<>K AND E$="Y" THEN W=W+P(K)/M(K)
2610 NEXT J
2620 PRINT:PRINT
2630 NEXT K
2640 PRINT
2655 IF E$="Y" THEN PRINT "LEAVING ONE OUT
     ESTIMATE  OF ERROR RATE=";W*100;"%"
2660 RETURN

2700 P=0
2710 FOR H=1 TO G
2720 IF F(H)-F(L)>-80 THEN P=P+EXP(F(H)-F(L))
2730 NEXT H
2740 P=1/P
2750 RETURN
2800 FOR H=1 TO G
2810 F(H)=0
2815 FOR I=1 TO N
2820 F(H)=F(H)+X(I)*C(I,H)
2830 NEXT I
2840 F(H)=F(H)+C(N+1,H)
2845 IF U$="Y" THEN F(H)=F(H)*(T-G-N-1)/
     (T-G)+N/M(H)/2
2846 F(H)=F(H)+LOG(P(H))
2850 NEXT H
2860 L=1
2870 P=F(1)
2880 FOR H=2 TO G
2890 IF F(H)>P THEN P=F(H):L=H
2900 NEXT H
2910 RETURN

3000 FOR K=1 TO G
3010 PRINT:PRINT
3020 PRINT "GROUP ";K;" MEANS ON ";M(K);
     " CASES"
3030 FOR I=1 TO N
3040 PRINT "VARIABLE ";I;"=";A(I,K)/M(K)
```

```
3050 NEXT I
3060 NEXT K
3070 PRINT
3080 PRINT
3085 PRINT "COVARIANCE MATRIX"
3090 FOR I=1 TO N
3100 FOR J=1 TO I
3110 PRINT TAB((J-1)*6);INT(S(I,J)/(T-G)*
     100)/100;
3120 NEXT J
3130 PRINT
3140 NEXT I
3150 PRINT
3160 RETURN

3500 PRINT
3510 PRINT "DO YOU WANT THE LEAVING ONE OUT
     ERROR RATE (Y/N)";
3520 INPUT E$
3540 IF E$="N" THEN GOTO 3610
3550 A=(T-G)/(T-G-1)
3560 FOR I=1 TO N
3570 FOR J=1 TO N
3580 S(I,J)=-S(I,J)*(T-G)
3590 NEXT J
3600 FOR J=1 TO G
3602 Z(I,J)=A(V(I),J)/M(J)
3603 NEXT J
3604 NEXT I
3605 FOR I=1 TO N
3606 FOR J=1 TO G
3607 A(I,J)=Z(I,J)
3608 NEXT J
3609 NEXT I
3610 GOSUB 2500
3620 RETURN

3800 Y=0
3810 FOR I=1 TO N
3820 FOR L=1 TO N
3830 Y=Y+S(I,L)*(X(I)-A(I,K))*(X(L)-A(L,K))
3840 NEXT L
3850 NEXT I
3860 Y=(M(K)-1)*(T-G)/M(K)-Y
3865 Q=1
3870 FOR H=1 TO G
3880 U=0
3890 V=0
3900 FOR I=1 TO N
3910 FOR L=1 TO N
3920 U=U+S(I,L)*(X(I)-A(I,H))*(X(L)-A(L,K))
3925 V=V+S(I,L)*(X(I)-A(I,H))*(X(L)-A(L,H))
```

Feature Selection – Variable Selection   137

```
3926 NEXT L
3927 NEXT I
3928 D(H)=(V+U*U/Y)/A
3930 IF H=K THEN D(H)=D(H)*M(K)*M(K)/
     (M(K)-1)/(M(K)-1)
3940 IF P$="Y" THEN D(H)=D(H)-LOG(P(H))
3950 IF P$="N" AND H<>K THEN D(H)=D(H)-
     LOG(M(H)/(T-1))
3960 IF P$="N" AND H=K THEN D(H)=D(H)-
     LOG((M(H)-1)/(T-1))
3965 IF D(H)<D(Q) THEN Q=H
3970 NEXT H
3980 RETURN

4000 FOR I=1 TO N
4010 V(I)=I
4020 NEXT I
4030 GOSUB 6000
4040 PRINT
4050 PRINT "FINAL SOLUTION REACHED"
4060 Z=N
4070 N=K-1
4080 FOR I=1 TO Z
4090 FOR J=1 TO Z
4100 IF V(J)=I THEN W(I)=J
4110 NEXT J
4120 NEXT I
4130 RETURN

4500 E=0
4504 PRINT
4505 S=8
4506 E(G+1,G+1)=T
4507 PRINT TAB(15);"ACTUAL GROUP=COL/ASSIGNED
     GROUP=ROW"
4508 PRINT
4510 FOR I=1 TO G
4520 PRINT TAB(S*I);"I";I;
4530 NEXT I
4535 PRINT TAB(S*(G+1));"I"
4540 GOSUB 4900
4550 FOR I=1 TO G+1
4560 IF I<>G+1 THEN PRINT I;
4570 FOR J=1 TO G+1
4580 PRINT TAB(S*J);"I";E(I,J);
4590 NEXT J
4600 PRINT
4610 IF I<>G+1 THEN GOSUB 4900
4620 NEXT I
4625 PRINT
4630 FOR K=1 TO G
4640 J=(E(G+1,K)-E(K,K))/E(G+1,K)
```

```
4650 PRINT "GROUP ";K;TAB(10);J*100;
     "% MISCLASSIFIED"
4660 E=E+J*P(K)
4670 NEXT K
4680 PRINT
4690 PRINT "ESTIMATED ERROR RATE =";E*100;"%"
4700 RETURN

4900 PRINT " ";
4905 FOR K=1 TO G+2
4910 FOR L=1 TO S-1
4920 PRINT "-";
4930 NEXT L
4940 IF K<>G+2 THEN PRINT "+";
4950 NEXT K
4960 PRINT
4970 RETURN

5000 PRINT
5010 PRINT "DISCRIMINANT FUNCTIONS"
5020 PRINT
5030 FOR K=1 TO G
5040 PRINT "GROUP ";K
5050 FOR I=1 TO N
5060 PRINT "C(V";V(I);") =";C(I,K)
5070 NEXT I
5080 PRINT "CONSTANT =";C(N+1,K)
5090 PRINT
5100 NEXT K
5110 RETURN

6000 K=1
6010 GOSUB 9000:REM COMPUTE AND PRINT F
     RATIOS
6020 GOSUB 9500:REM SELECT VARIABLE
6030 IF I$="N" THEN RETURN
6040 GOSUB 8200:REM SWEEP S AND H
6050 GOSUB 9800:REM CALCULATE DISCRIMINAN
     FUNCTIONS
6060 GOSUB 8500:REM PRINT DISCRIMINANT
     FUNCTIONS
6070 K=K+1
6080 IF K>N THEN RETURN
6090 GOTO 6010

7200 OPEN "I",#1,F$
7210 RETURN

7300 INPUT#1,R
7310 RETURN

7400 CLOSE  #1
```

Feature Selection – Variable Selection

```
7410 RETURN

8200 FOR I=1 TO N
8210 IF I=K THEN GOTO 8260
8220 FOR J=1 TO N
8230 IF J=K THEN GOTO 8250
8240 S(I,J)=S(I,J)-S(I,K)*S(K,J)/S(K,K)
8245 H(I,J)=H(I,J)-H(I,K)*H(K,J)/H(K,K)
8250 NEXT J
8260 NEXT I
8270 FOR I=1 TO N
8280 IF I=K THEN GOTO 8310
8290 S(K,I)=S(K,I)/S(K,K)
8295 H(K,I)=H(K,I)/H(K,K)
8300 S(I,K)=S(I,K)/S(K,K)
8305 H(I,K)=H(I,K)/H(K,K)
8310 NEXT I
8320 S(K,K)=-1/S(K,K)
8325 H(K,K)=-1/H(K,K)
8330 RETURN


8500 PRINT TAB(25);"DISCRIMINANT FUNCTIONS"
8510 PRINT TAB(30);"GROUP"
8520 FOR L=1 TO G
8530 PRINT TAB(L*10);L;
8540 NEXT L
8550 PRINT
8560 FOR I=1 TO K
8570 PRINT "VAR ";V(I);
8580 FOR L=1 TO G
8590 PRINT TAB(L*10);C(I,L);
8600 NEXT L
8610 PRINT
8620 NEXT I
8630 PRINT "CONST=";
8640 FOR L=1 TO G
8650 PRINT TAB(L*10);C(K+1,L);
8660 NEXT L
8670 PRINT
8680 PRINT
8690 RETURN

8800 PRINT
8810 PRINT "WHICH VARIABLE DO YOU WANT TO
     INCLUDE (ENTER 0 FOR NONE)";
8820 INPUT I
8830 IF I=0 THEN RETURN
8840 L=0
8850 FOR J=K TO N
8860 IF I=V(J) THEN L=J
8870 NEXT J
```

```
8880 IF L=0 THEN PRINT "VARIABLE NON-
     EXISTANT OR ALREADY INCLUDED":GOTO 8800
8890 F=L
8895 I$="Y"
8896 RETURN

9000 PRINT:PRINT
9010 PRINT "STEP ";K
9020 PRINT "VARIABLES IN THE EQUATION =";K-1
9030 IF K=1 THEN GOTO 9090
9040 FOR I=1 TO K-1
9050 PRINT " VARIABLE ";V(I);"F RATIO ";
9060 T(I)=(S(I,I)-H(I,I))/H(I,I)*(T-G-K)/(G-1)
9070 PRINT T(I);"WITH ";G-1;" AND ";T-G-K;
     " DEGREES OF FREEDOM"
9080 NEXT I
9090 PRINT:PRINT
9100 PRINT "VARIABLES NOT IN THE EQUATION =";
     N-K+1
9110 FOR I=K TO N
9120 PRINT " VARIABLE ";V(I);"F RATIO ";
9130 T(I)=(H(I,I)-S(I,I))/S(I,I)*(T-G-K+1)/
     (G-1)
9140 PRINT T(I);"WITH ";G-1;" AND ";T-G-K+1;
     " DEGREES OF FREEDOM"
9150 NEXT I
9160 RETURN


9500 F=K
9510 FOR I=K TO N
9520 IF T(I)>T(F) THEN F=I
9530 NEXT I
9535 PRINT
9540 PRINT "VARIABLE ";V(F);"HAS THE LARGEST
     F VALUE (";T(F);")"
9541 PRINT "INCLUDE Y/N";
9544 INPUT I$
9545 IF I$="N" THEN GOSUB 8800:
     REM HAND SELECTION
9546 IF I$="N" THEN RETURN
9547 IF I$<>"Y" THEN GOTO 9541
9548 IF K=F THEN RETURN
9550 FOR I=1 TO N
9560 P=S(F,I):S(F,I)=S(K,I):S(K,I)=P
9570 P=H(F,I):H(F,I)=H(K,I):H(K,I)=P
9580 NEXT I
9590 FOR I=1 TO N
9600 P=S(I,F):S(I,F)=S(I,K):S(I,K)=P
9610 P=H(I,F):H(I,F)=H(I,K):H(I,K)=P
9620 NEXT I
9630 P=V(K):V(K)=V(F):V(F)=P
```

```
9640 RETURN

9800 FOR L=1 TO G
9810 FOR I=1 TO K
9815 C(I,L)=0
9820 FOR J=1 TO K
9830 C(I,L)=C(I,L)-A(V(J),L)*S(I,J)
9840 NEXT J
9845 C(I,L)=C(I,L)*(T-G)/M(L)
9850 NEXT I
9855 C(K+1,L)=0
9860 FOR I=1 TO K
9870 C(K+1,L)=C(K+1,L)+C(I,L)*A(V(I),L)
9880 NEXT I
9890 C(K+1,L)=-C(K+1,L)/(2*M(L))
9900 NEXT L
9910 RETURN
```

The program first goes through all of the now familiar steps of asking for the file name, the number in each group etc. and then prints the means and common covariance matrix. From this point the program behaves somewhat differently in that instead of deriving discriminant functions based on all of the avaliable variables it selects and uses variables one at a time. At each step the F ratio adjusted for all the variables already selected for each variable is quoted and the user is offered the choice of including the variable with the largest F ratio in the discriminant functions. As already described, this is quite a reasonable choice as each F ratio can be regarded as a measure of how much the groups are separated by the variable concerned after accounting for the variables already selected. (The F ratio is proportional to a ratio of the between groups sums of squares and the within groups sums of squares.) If the user decides not to include this variable, because there are theoretical reasons for preferring a different variable or just to see what will happen, then the program will accept the user's choice of variables not already selected to include in the discriminant functions. If none of the variables are considered worth adding, because the maximum F ratio is small or because of a desire to test the performance of the discriminant functions constructed so far, then selecting variable 0 causes the stepwise portion of the program to terminate. If a variable is included at each step then the stepwise portion of the program terminates when all of the variables have been included. At each step after the first, F ratios for variables already selected are also quoted and these can be used to detect variables that have become redundant at a later step due to a combination of variables that have been selected. A variable that has been selected but is discovered to have a small F ratio after other variables have been selected should be removed from the equation. As no backward step is included in this program an alternative is to re-run the program on the same data but, at each step reject the variable that 'develops' the small F ratio and see the effect that this has. The linear discriminant functions for each group are also printed at each step.

When the stepwise section of the program is completed the final discriminant functions are printed and then the file is re-read and error estimates are calculated as in the previous version of the program. The only difference is that if only a subset of the available variables is selected then, as you would expect, only those variables are used in the classification.

Details of the stepwise procedure **
The essential method of stepwise discrimination is already contained in the very first linear discriminant analysis program listed in Chapter 4. The calculation of the inverse covariance matrix using the sweep operator (see Chapter 4) by its very nature proceeds a variable at a time. After N sweeps, one on each of the variables, the result is minus the inverse covariance matrix. However after each sweep the intermediate result contains minus the inverse covariance matrix of the variables that have been 'swept'. To be more precise if variables 1 to k have been swept then the result can be thought of as composed of four square submatrices:

$$\begin{bmatrix} -S^{-1} & A \\ A & W \end{bmatrix}$$

S^{-1} is the inverse covariance matrix (k×k) for the k variables that have been swept and A and W are (n−k) × (n−k) matrices whose meanings will be discussed later. It should be clear that all that has to be done to implement a stepwise inversion of the covariance matrix is to select each variable in turn, move its row and column in the covariance matrix into the position following the variable that has just been swept and then sweep the entire matrix using the selected variable as the pivot. After the sweep the inverse matrix can be used along with the means to calculate discriminant functions for the variables that have been selected.

The only remaining difficulty is how to select the variable at each step. This involves computing suitable statistics for each variable taking into account the variables that have already been selected. Fortunately the submatrix W introduced earlier is a within groups covariance matrix adjusted for the variables already selected. The conditional F ratios described in an earlier section are proportional to the ratio of the between groups sums of squares and the within groups sums of squares adjusted for the variables already selected. Thus, if instead of sweeping the covariance matrix we sweep the sums of squares and cross products matrix, the diagonal elements of W will supply the adjusted within groups sums of squares for each variable. Finding adjusted between groups sums of square is a little more difficult. At first thought it would seem that the most obvious way is to form the between groups sums of squares and cross products matrix and subject that to the sweep operator but the between groups sums of squares and cross products matrix is singular and hence it doesn't have an inverse (see Appendix 1). The solution is to form and sweep the total sums of squares and cross products matrix and find the adjusted between groups sums of squares using:

$$\begin{pmatrix} \text{adjusted between groups} \\ \text{sums of squares} \end{pmatrix} = \begin{pmatrix} \text{adjusted total} \\ \text{sums of squares} \end{pmatrix} - \begin{pmatrix} \text{adusted within groups} \\ \text{sums of squares} \end{pmatrix}$$

If variable k has not yet been selected then its conditional F ratio is:

$$F = \left(\frac{t_{kk} - w_{kk}}{w_k}\right)\left(\frac{M - G - q}{G - 1}\right)$$

(with G−1 and M−G−q degrees of freedom) where t_{kk} and w_{kk} are the corresponding diagonal elements of the total and within groups sums of squares and cross products matrices after already being swept on q variables, G is the number of groups and M the number of cases. The corresponding equation if variable k has already been selected is:

$$F = \left(\frac{w_{kk} - t_{kk}}{t_{kk}}\right)\left(\frac{M - G - q + 1}{G - 1}\right)$$

(with G−1 and M−G−q+1 degrees of freedom).

The rest of the details of the program are straightforward. Subroutine 1500 is added to form the total sums of squares and cross products in H(N,N) and subroutine 2000 is modified to give the within groups sums of squares and cross products matrix rather than the covariance matrix. Also subroutine 2000 is modified to return the group totals rather than means − this simplifies some of the later calculations. Subroutine 6000 controls the order of operation during stepping. It calls other subroutines to derive F ratios and to sweep the matrices. Subroutine 9000 computes and prints the F ratios using the arrays H and S and the equations given earlier. Subroutine 9500 finds the largest F ratio in the set of variables not yet selected and offers the user the option of including the corresponding variable. Subroutine 8200 sweeps both S and H to find both the inverse matrix corresponding to the variables already selected and to find the adjusted sums of squares for

144 *Classification Algorithms*

the F ratios in subsequent steps. (Sweeping both matrices is not the most efficient way to find the adjusted total sums of squares but it is easy to implement and understand.) Finally subroutine 9800 computes the discriminant function based on the variables selected and subroutine 8500 prints the results. Once the stepwise portion of the program is complete then the rest of the program proceeds much as before. The only complication is that the need to exchange rows and columns of the matrices as the variables are selected alters the order of the variables. The array V is used to keep track of where the results for each variable are stored. The contents of V(1) give the number of the variable that the first discriminant function coefficient is associated with, V(2) the second, and so on. Various existing parts of the program have to be altered so that this new order of the variables is taken into account.

The subroutine structure of the stepwise discriminant program is given in Table 8.1.

Table 8.1

Stepwise discriminant subroutine use

Subroutine	Action
1000	Get parameters
1500	Calculate total SSCP matrix in H
2000	Calculate within SSCP matrix in S and means
2500	Classify cases
2700	Calculate discriminant functions
3000	Print means and within groups covariance matrix
3500	Get ready to calculate leaving-one-out discriminant functions
3800	Calculate leaving-one-out discriminant functions
4000	Begin stepwise selection
4500	Print confusion matrix and error rates
4900	Print confusion matrix dividing line
5000	Print discriminant functions
6000	Stepwise selection loop
7200	Open F$ for input
7300	Read a value into R
7400	Close F$
8200	Sweep S and H
8500	Print intermediate discriminant functions
8800	Manual selection of variables

Feature Selection - Variable Selection

9000   Compute and print F ratios
9500   Find largest F ratio and select variable
9800   Calculate discriminant function coefficients

Stepwise analysis of Fisher's iris data

The results of the stepwise portion of the analyis of the iris data can be seen below:

```
STEP   1
VARIABLES IN THE EQUATION = 0

VARIABLES NOT IN THE EQUATION = 4
   VARIABLE  1 F RATIO  119.264 WITH  2  AND  147  DEGREES OF FREEDOM
   VARIABLE  2 F RATIO   49.1597 WITH 2  AND  147  DEGREES OF FREEDOM
   VARIABLE  3 F RATIO  1180.17 WITH  2  AND  147  DEGREES OF FREEDOM
   VARIABLE  4 F RATIO  960.017 WITH  2  AND  147  DEGREES OF FREEDOM

VARIABLE  3 HAS THE LARGEST F VALUE ( 1180.17 )
INCLUDE ? Y
                        DISCRIMINANT FUNCTIONS
                                GROUP
              1           2           3
VAR  3     7.89478     23.0039     29.9807
CONST=    -5.77108    -48.9984    -83.2265


STEP   2
VARIABLES IN THE EQUATION = 1
   VARIABLE  3 F RATIO  1164.12 WITH  2  AND  145  DEGREES OF FREEDOM

VARIABLES NOT IN THE EQUATION = 3
   VARIABLE  2 F RATIO   43.0937 WITH 2  AND  146  DEGREES OF FREEDOM
   VARIABLE  1 F RATIO   35.223 WITH  2  AND  146  DEGREES OF FREEDOM
   VARIABLE  4 F RATIO   24.7986 WITH 2  AND  146  DEGREES OF FREEDOM

VARIABLE  2 HAS THE LARGEST F VALUE ( 43.0937 )
INCLUDE ?Y
                        DISCRIMINANT FUNCTIONS
                                GROUP
              1           2           3
VAR  3    -1.14217     18.4796     26.0059
VAR  2    30.256       15.1477     13.3079
CONST=   -51.0239     -60.3411    -91.9812


STEP   3
VARIABLES IN THE EQUATION = 2
   VARIABLE  3 F RATIO  1098.31 WITH  2  AND  144  DEGREES OF FREEDOM
   VARIABLE  2 F RATIO   42.5033 WITH 2  AND  144  DEGREES OF FREEDOM
```

```
VARIABLES NOT IN THE EQUATION = 2
   VARIABLE  1 F RATIO  12.7609 WITH  2  AND  145  DEGREES OF FREEDOM
   VARIABLE  4 F RATIO  34.6272 WITH  2  AND  145  DEGREES OF FREEDOM

VARIABLE  4 HAS THE LARGEST F VALUE ( 34.6272 )
INCLUDE ?Y
                        DISCRIMINANT FUNCTIONS
                                GROUP
                    1          2          3
   VAR  3        3.0624    18.2174    23.0845
   VAR  2       35.2666    14.8353     9.82643
   VAR  4      -24.785      1.54546   17.2212
   CONST=      -59.637    -60.3746   -96.1394


STEP  4
VARIABLES IN THE EQUATION = 3
   VARIABLE  3 F RATIO  38.3057 WITH  2  AND  143  DEGREES OF FREEDOM
   VARIABLE  2 F RATIO  53.9133 WITH  2  AND  143  DEGREES OF FREEDOM
   VARIABLE  4 F RATIO  34.1495 WITH  2  AND  143  DEGREES OF FREEDOM

VARIABLES NOT IN THE EQUATION = 1
   VARIABLE  1 F RATIO   4.94162 WITH  2  AND  144  DEGREES OF FREEDOM

VARIABLE  1 HAS THE LARGEST F VALUE ( 4.94162 )
INCLUDE ?Y
                        DISCRIMINANT FUNCTIONS
                                GROUP
                    1          2          3
   VAR  3      -16.8361     5.06666   12.7225
   VAR  2       23.4916     7.05326    3.69469
   VAR  4      -17.2237     6.54266   21.1587
   VAR  1       23.8563    15.7664    12.423
   CONST=      -85.5512   -71.6934  -103.167
```

From step one it can be seen that variable 3 – petal length – has a very large F ratio and on this basis alone it is worth examining the degree of discrimination attainable using only this variable. (This is left as an instructive exercise for the reader!) However even after variable 1 has been added there is sufficient discriminatory power in the other three variables to make it worth adding them – if any variable is to be rejected then it should be variable 1 which has least to add to the other three. Notice the way that the F ratio corresponding to variable 3 goes down when variable 4 is added – this is because much of its discriminatory power can be obtained as a linear combination of variable 2 and variable 4. Even so, variable 3 is still worth including! After the stepwise selection of variables the program goes on to estimate the error rate of the final equation. As an exercise you might like to find out how good discriminant functions based on each single variable, each pair and each triplet are!

Testing if a subset of the variables is necessary

A very simple version of the variable selection problem is the testing of the hypothesis that a set of the variables in a two group discriminant function has zero coefficients. Although this is less than the full feature selection problem, if the groups are known to be multivariate normal with equal covariance matrices, an exact solution exists.

The statistic

$$F = \frac{(m_1 + m_2 - n - 1)}{n - n'} \frac{C(D_n^2 - D_{n'}^2)}{1 + CD_n^2}$$

has an F distribution with $n-n'$ and m_1+m_2-n-1 degrees of freedom, where:

- n = number of variables in the full function
- n' = number of variables in the function when the variables in question have been left out
- D_n^2 = the Mahalanobis D on the full n variables
- $D_{n'}^2$ = the Mahalanobis D on the reduced n' variables
- m_1, m_2 = are the number of cases in groups 1 and 2 respectively

$$C = \frac{m_1 m_2}{(m_1 + m_2)(m_1 + m_2 - 2)}$$

If F is significant then we reject the hypothesis that the n' variables are zero. It is important to remember that *repeated* use of this statistic to test various subsets is prone to the same problems of false significance levels as stepwise regression.

Overview of feature selection

Feature selection has been confused with classification on many occasions. Indeed some aspects of feature selection have dominated the classification literature. Rather, feature selection should be seen as a separate and distinct step from the construction of a classification rule. It will be noticed that all the methods given in this and the previous chapter refer either to the multivariate normal, equal covariance case or to linear discriminant functions. This bias reflects the current state of knowledge and the frequency with which linear discriminant functions are used. Even so, a lot can be achieved with the intelligent use of existing techniques.

In Chapter 7 the feature selection problem was defined in general and we have since considered two versions of it – the unconstrained and the constrained problem. The unconstrained problem leads to canonical analysis, a method for exploring the differences between the groups. The constrained problem leads to stepwise variable selection, a method for finding the variables that are useful discriminators between groups. In practice there is nothing stopping us from using both feature selection techniques together. First stepwise variable selection could be used to reduce the number of variables to just those that were important and then canonical analysis could be applied to this set to investigate the reasons for the group's structure or just to eliminate the influence of dimensions in which the group means were identical. Normally following this, the linear discriminant functions would be derived and used as a classification rule but it is important to realise that this is not essential. Following variable selection and canonical analysis the information that has been gained about the variables and the group structure can be used to construct classification rules not based on the linear discriminant functions. For example the SPSS discriminant program allows the user to perform stepwise selection and canonical analysis, procedures which assume equal covariance matrices, and then offer the option of computing a set of quadratic discriminant functions which of course assumes that the covariance matrices are different! There is nothing wrong with this procedure as long as it results in a classification rule that performs well.

References

1. Maxwell, A.E. (1977) *Multivariate Analysis in Behavioural Research*: Chapman and Hall.
2. Narendra, P.M. and Fukanaga, K. (1977) 'A branch and bound algorithm for feature subset selection', *IEEE Transactions on Computers*, **C-26**, 917–22.
3. Roberts, S.J. (1984) 'A branch and bound algorithm for determining the optimal feature subset of given size', *Applied Statistics*, **33**, 236–41.
4. Dixon, W.J. (1983) *BMDP Statistical Software*, (revised printing): University of California Press.
5. Nie, N.H., Hull, C.H., Jenkins, J.G., Steinbrenner, K. and Brent, D.H. (1975) *SPSS - Statistical Package for the Social Sciences*, (second edition): McGraw-Hill.

Chapter Nine
Categorical Variables and Non-parametric Methods

All of the classification problems that have been examined in the earlier chapters of this book have assumed that the measurements made were continuous and either followed a normal distribution or could be assumed to follow a normal distribution. In practice many of the measurements made in the hope of classifying a case will be categorical and often it is impossible to regard these as continuous. In the same way the distribution of a set of variables may be clearly non-normal (for example it could be multi-modal or restricted to lie in a small range). In principle, constructing classification rules for categorical data is very easy, it is simply the direct application of Bayes' rule. However, in practice there are considerable difficulties to overcome due to the lack of sufficient data to estimate the complete rule. Categorical classification is now a fairly well developed subject but it draws extensively on advanced techniques used to analyse categorical data and so it is not possible to give anything more than an outline of the methods involved.

The problem of handling data without making any assumptions about its distribution, leads on to the subject of non-parametric classification. This too is a fertile field of study but unlike categorical classification it has not yielded any really practical classification rules. There is no doubt that non-parametric classification will develop further but for the moment there are still many unsolved problems and great difficulty in finding enough computer power to implement apparently simple rules. The second half of this chapter outlines some of the important ideas of non-parametric classification with an emphasis on practical classification rules.

Both categorical and non-parametric classification generally proceed by trying to estimate $P(\mathbf{x}|G_i)$ and then applying Bayes' rule using these estimates and this should be kept in mind while reading this chapter.

Categorical variables

As already mentioned, classification using categorical variables nearly always proceeds by attempting to estimate $P(\mathbf{x}|G_i)$ and then using Bayes' rule – there is therefore an obvious connection with non-parametric classification. However it is possible to approach the estimation of $P(\mathbf{x}|G)$ by postulating a parametric form and estimating the parameters by the usual methods, but this is rarely useful because of the lack of standard distributions for categorical variables. In a situation where the distribution of a categorical variable can be obtained by theoretical arguments then this is a viable and efficient method. In many cases a categorical variable will arise by direct measurement but the possibility of reducing a continuous variable to a number of categories should not be ignored as a way of avoiding making assumptions about its distribution. Indeed some writers [1], have suggested that this is always to be recommended! A particularly difficult classification problem arises when a mixture of categorical and continuous variables are measured. This is clearly another case where the possibility of converting continuous variables to categorical variables offers a solution but there are a number of methods of dealing with the problem directly and these are described later.

The contingency table

The contingency table [2] is the basic tool in categorical classification. Most people are familiar with the idea of a two-dimensional contingency table but for classification purposes it is necessary to consider multi-dimensional tables. Rather than go over the construction of a general contingency table from scratch, we will simply assume that on each object we measure n variables $v_1, v_2, \ldots v_n$ having $c_1, c_2, \ldots c_n$ respectively, and construct an n-dimensional table with $c_1 \times c_2 \ldots \times c_n$ cells. (Notice that any object will fall into one, and only one, such cell.) Corresponding to the sample table, there exists a population table with entries indicating the probability of a case falling into that cell. Fortunately we can illustrate all the problems that arise with a simple 2×2 table and generalise to multi-dimensional tables later. A 2×2 table and its population counterpart has the form:

Sample

	1	2	
1	f_{11}	f_{12}	f_{1+}
2	f_{21}	f_{22}	f_{2+}
	f_{+1}	f_{+2}	f_{++}

Population

	1	2	
1	P_{11}	P_{12}	P_{1+}
2	P_{21}	P_{22}	P_{2+}
	P_{+1}	P_{+2}	1

Categorical Variables and Non-parametric Methods

The notation f_{ij} is used to indicate the number of cases in the ijth cell and P_{ij} is used to indicate the probability of a case falling into the ijth cell. The '+' notation is used to indicate when a subscript has been summed over, i.e.

$$P_{+j} = \sum_i P_{ij} \qquad f_{++} = \sum_{ij} f_{ij}$$

This is a fairly standard notation for contingency table analysis.

When there are G groups under consideration we can either construct G individual contingency tables or use G as a categorical variable within a single table. Which is better depends on how the samples used to construct the table(s) have been obtained and on what additional procedures are being used. However in most cases it is easier to construct a single table.

Estimates of $P(X|G_k)$

It should be obvious that the number of cases in each cell of the sample table can be used to estimate the probabilities in the population table but exactly how depends on the way that the sample was obtained. If the sample was taken without reference to the group structure and a single table is constructed so that f_{ik} is the number of cases from group k that fall in category i, then the prior probabilities can be estimated by:

$$P(G_k) = \frac{f_{+k}}{f_{++}}$$

i.e., the number of cases in group k divided by the total number of cases. Similarly an estimate of $P(x|G_k)$ is given by:

$$P(x|G_k) = \frac{f_{ik}}{f_{+k}}$$

i.e., the number of cases from group k in category i divided by the total number of cases from group k. This gives for the Bayes' rule:

assign to group k if

$$\frac{f_{+k}}{f_{++}} \frac{f_{ik}}{f_{+k}} > \frac{f_{+j}}{f_{++}} \frac{f_{ij}}{f_{+j}}$$

or cancelling f_{+k}, f_{+j} and f_{++}

$$f_{ik} > f_{ij}$$

for all $j \neq i$

This is a very reasonable and easy-to-apply rule in that, given a contingency table constructed from a sample, it amounts to classifying future cases into the group that had the largest frequency count for that category.

If on the other hand individual samples of a given size had been taken from each group then the classification rule would be a little more complicated. The prior probabilities could no longer be estimated by f_{+k}/f_{++} because f_{+k}, the number of samples taken from group k, would have been fixed beforehand. Thus the prior probabilities either have to be known or have to be estimated by some other method. Also, although the estimate of $P(x|G_k)$ looks the same:

$$P(x \mid G_k) = \frac{f_{ik}}{f_{+i}}$$

it is different because f_{+i} is not a random quantity but fixed beforehand. Thus the classification rule becomes:

assign to group k if

$$P(G_k)\frac{f_{ik}}{f_{+k}} > P(G_j)\frac{f_{ij}}{f_{+j}}$$

for all $j \neq k$

and of course in this case no cancellation of f_{+k} and f_{+j} is possible.

Both of these classification rules are entirely general in the sense that they can be applied without any conditions having to be satisfied apart from the usual ones of random sampling. (In this case the estimates of the probabilities are maximum likelihood estimates.) The big drawback of this method is simply the number of parameters that have to be estimated. Even a small number of categories on a small number of variables implies a lot of cells. For example three variables with five categories, each on two groups, results in a table with 5×5×5×2 or 250 cells! Even with largish samples in practice many of the cells in a table will be empty or have very few cases and hence the estimates of the P_{ij} will often be poor. This is known as the 'sparse data' problem and it is the reason for most of the alternative methods suggested for handling categorical variables. However if there is enough data to estimate the probabilities then the classification rules described above are perfectly acceptable.

The classification table

The application of the two classification rules described in the previous section is made much simpler if a table summarising the way cases should be

Categorical Variables and Non-parametric Methods

assigned to groups is constructed. Such a table is often referred to as a 'classification table'. When a sample is taken to construct the classifier then not only are values of the categorical variables measured but the group that each case belongs to is also determined. In this way if n variables are measured the resulting contingency table is n+1-dimensional because of the addition of a variable indicating the group. However, when a case is measured in order to be classified, the group that it belongs to is not known and so we can think of the n measurements as determining which cell it falls into in an n-dimensional table. Now, for each cell in this table the classification rule associates one, and only one, group that a case falling into it should be assigned to. The classification table is simply an n-dimensional table whose entries are the number of the group that each cell is assigned to. If you think about it for a moment this corresponds to the division of the sample space in the theory of continuous variables.

For example suppose we have a sample of two variables each with two categories on two groups, then the sample contingency table would be 2×2×2:

Group 1
$g=1$

	x_1	1	2
x_2	1	5	3
	2	2	8

Group 2
$g=2$

	x_1	1	2
x_2	1	2	6
	2	7	4

Assuming that the sample was taken ignoring the group structure, we can apply the first classification rule. This implies, for example, that a case with $x_1=2$ and $x_2=1$ should be assigned to group 2($g=2$) because $f_{211}=3$ and $f_{212}=6$. Repeating this argument for each pair of cells, one in each table, gives:

	x_1	1	2
x_2	1	1	2
	2	2	1

for the classification table. Using this classification becomes simply a matter of reading the group number from the appropriate cell in the table.

Improved estimates of P_{ij}

It is rare that it is possible to collect sufficient data to estimate the probabilities in a contingency table with any reliability. The existence of zeros in the cells of a contingency table can either mean that P_{ij} is zero or that the sample was too small. The solution to the shortage of data is to 'smooth' the estimates of the cell probabilities. In most cases there are reasons for assuming that, even though in principle each cell probability can take on any value without reference to any other cell probability there will be regular patterns within the probabilities that can be used to improve the estimates. This idea will become clearer after a few examples of how a table can be 'smoothed'. There are three general approaches to improving cell estimates:

(1) Structural models

(2) Sampling models

(3) Pseudo-Bayes' estimates

(1) Structural models

By assuming various dependencies and independencies within the table, we can construct a model and then derive model estimates for the cell frequencies. For example, in the 2×2 case, we could assume the variables were independent (i.e. χ^2 non-significant). Independence implies that in the population the cell probabilities P_{ij} are given by:

$$P_{ij} = P_{i+}P_{+j}$$

This corresponds to a sample table in which each cell total was equal to the product of the row and column sums or marginals. In other words, if the variables are independent:

$$f_{ij} = f_{i+}f_{j+}$$

Using this relationship it is not difficult to see that:

$$\frac{f_{i+}f_{+j}}{f_{++}}$$

is an estimate of P_{ij}. Of course in practice f_{ij} will be different from $f_{i+}f_{+j}$ even if the variables are independent due to sampling variation. However if the variables are independent the estimate of P_{ij} based on row and column totals will have a smaller variance than the estimate based on f_{ij}. On the other hand if the variables are dependent the row and column sum estimate will be biased.

This simple example has all of the characteristics of applying more complicated models. First a model of the relationships between the variables is postulated and the pattern of observations that this model suggests has to be compared with those observed. As long as the discrepancy is not too great the model's predictions for the cell counts can be used in estimates of the probabilities and hence as part of a classification rule. If the model holds then these estimates will be better than the simple cell counts. If the model doesn't hold then these estimates will be biased and hence misleading (but possibly no more misleading than the original sample counts!).

The one problem with this procedure is of course the specification of suitable structural models. Fortunately this is not such a difficult problem now that the methods involved in log linear models have become commonplace. The description of a log linear model is beyond the scope of this book but suitable programs and explanations [3] are available elsewhere and once you know how to fit a log linear model to a contingency table the classification side of the problem is straightforward. The use of log linear models in categorical classification has not appeared in the literature to any great extent but this is one of the most promising methods and is sure to grow in popularity.

(2) Sampling models
The use of sampling models corresponds to the use of particular forms of distribution (e.g. normal) for $P(x|G_i)$ in the continuous case. The problem with this approach is that suitable and appropriate distributions are not really available for categorical variables. As a result complicated general expressions based on Walsh or Hadamar functions are often used. These are very specialised and beyond the scope of this book (see Reference [4] for more information). However the following example will demonstrate the fundamental principle that lies behind the sampling model approach.

If we have a variable with C categories we could proceed in the usual way and estimate P_i by f_i/f_+ but if we have reason to believe that the categories are generated by a binomial distribution (i.e. they are counts of the number of times an event with probability P occurs), then we could estimate P by:

$$\hat{P} = \frac{\sum_{i=1}^{C} if_i}{\sum_{i=1}^{C} f_i}$$

i.e. the mean of the distribution. The estimates of the cell probabilities would be given by the usual expression for the binomial distribution:

$$P_i = \frac{C!}{(C-i)!} \hat{P}^i (1-\hat{P})^{C-i}$$

156 Classification Algorithms

where x! stands for factorial x, i.e. $x(x-1)(x-2)(x-3) \ldots 1$. This use of the binomial corresponds exactly to the use of a normal distribution and estimates of the mean and standard deviation to estimate $P(x|G_i)$.

(3) Pseudo-Bayes' estimates **

The usual estimate of the cell probabilities is the maximum likelihood unbiased and minimum variance estimate. If we try to find a better estimate then we must leave the class of unbiased estimators. Finding better but biased estimators depends very much on the meaning assigned to the word 'better'. Traditionally the best sort of estimators have always been assumed to be unbiased but modern statistics suggests that it is often worth abandoning the requirement of unbiasedness in return for the estimate being on average closer to the value being estimated. An unbiased estimator will on average show no tendency to over-or underestimate a value but for most of the time it may be well away from the true value. On the other hand a biased estimator may show a tendency to always over- or underestimate a value but even so it may be closer to the true value for more of the time than an unbiased estimator (see Fig. 9.1). Of course there is no guarantee that a good but biased estimator exists or will be uniformly better than an unbiased estimator but this doesn't stop us from looking for one!

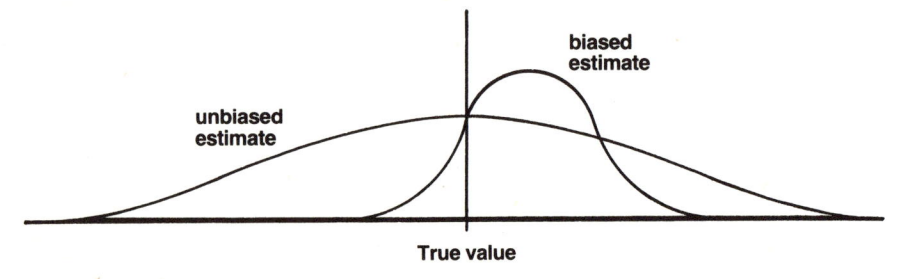

Fig. 9.1 A biased estimate is sometimes closer to the true value

The most common measure of how close an estimate is to the true value is the expected squared error loss function. If P* is an estimator of P then the expected squared error loss function is:

$$L(P, P^*) = E(|P - P^*|^2)$$

where $|x|$ means the absolute value of x and $E(x)$ is the expected or average value of x. We are looking for an estimator P* that minimises $L(P,P^*)$.

However, as L is a function of P* *and* P, an estimator could produce good results for some values of P and not others. It is possible to show that the usual estimate of the cell probabilities cannot be bettered for all values of P – in the jargon of decision theory f_{ij}/f_{++} is an 'admissible estimate'. Thus it seems that there is little point in trying to find a better estimator than f_{ij}/f_{++}. However, although it is not possible to find a P* that does better for all values of P, we can find an estimator that does *very* much better for some values of P. Such an estimator is the pseudo-Bayes' estimator, which is computed as follows:

(1) Select a priori table of probabilities λ_i.

(2) Compute the weight factor:

$$K = \frac{M^2 - \sum_i f_i}{\sum (f_i - M\lambda_i)^2}$$

(3) Compute the probability estimates:

$$P_i^* = \frac{f_i + K\lambda_i}{M + K}$$

where M is the total number of cases making up the table. We have used the subscript i to mean any particular cell in the table, usually labelled ijklmn ... depending on the dimension.

The prior table λ_i may be obtained in either of two ways:

(1) Using a priori theoretical considerations.

(2) Using the data f_i to suggest patterns of independence etc.

If all the λ_i are taken to be equal to M/C (where C is the total number of cells in the table), the pseudo-Bayes' estimate can be shown to be much better than f_{ij}/f_{++} for all values of P except those close to 0 or 1. The pseudo-Bayes' estimate and biased estimators in general are still not really an accepted part of general statistical practice because of the lack of a guarantee that they are always better than traditional unbiased estimators but they form a powerful alternative and deserve to be better understood.

Logistic models

The logistic model takes us away from an estimator of $P(x|G_i)$ in favour of an estimate of the likelihood ratio $P(x|G_i)/P(x|G_k)$. The logistic model is appropriate for any situation when the log of the likelihood ratio can be assumed to be linear. That is:

$$\frac{P(G_i \mid x)}{P(G_k \mid x)} = \exp(A_i + B_i'x)$$

where A_i and B_i are vectors of parameters to be estimated. The logistic method estimates A_i and B_i by maximum likelihood. However this is complicated and in general requires an iterative procedure. Of course the success of the logistic model depends on the extent to which the log of the likelihood ratio is linear in any given case. There are however a number of important cases where this can be shown to be exactly true:

(1) Multivariate normal with equal covariance matrices.

(2) Multivariate independent binary variables.

(3) Multivariate binary variables following a log linear model with equal second and higher order effects.

Because of cases 2 and 3 the logistic model can be seen as a sort of limited version of the approach using the log linear model.

In the normal equal covariance case:

$$B_i = \Sigma^{-1}\mu_i$$

and

$$A_i = -\tfrac{1}{2}\mu_i'\Sigma^{-1}\mu_i + \ln(P(G_i))$$

You should be able to see that in this case the parameters of the logistic model are nothing but the usual linear discriminant functions.

If the populations are non-normal, the discriminant functions are usually used as the starting values for the iteration. This leads us to believe that the linear discriminant function will do well whenever the logistic form is appropriate. In particular linear discriminant functions often work well for binary variables or a mixture of binary and normal variables.

Binary variables and linear discrimination

The previous section suggests that the computation of the linear discriminant functions on a mixed set of 0,1 variables and continuous variables should give reasonable results. This, in fact, is so, and the linear

Categorical Variables and Non-parametric Methods

discriminant functions are the most commonly used method for handling categorical variables. A good performance is not guaranteed but the results are often reasonable.

The fact that linear discriminant functions often do perform well on binary variables is however not a reason for not knowing or trying other methods of dealing with categorical variables. To a certain extent there is an overuse of linear discriminant functions and the assumption that if they do not work then nothing will. There are in fact a number of very simple situations in which it is possible to construct an efficient classifier using binary variables but the linear discriminant approach will fail. Once again it is worth recalling that any classification rule that works is a good rule but if a particular method doesn't work it could be that the method is at fault rather than there being no way of discriminating between the groups.

Any categorical variable can be coded as a set of binary variables so that the linear discriminant or logistic approach can be tried. For example, a variable with four categories can be recoded as two binary variables b_1, b_2 as:

x	b_1	b_2
0	0	0
1	0	1
2	1	0
3	1	1

The paradox of the constant Bayes' classifier

Consider the contingency table given below representing the estimates of the probabilities of a case falling in any given cell:

		Group 1	Group 2
x	1	0.2	0.5
	2	0.2	0.6
	3	0.7	0.2

and the prior probabilities $P(G_1)=0.1$ and $P(G_2)=0.9$. In this case what is the Bayes' rule? The surprising answer is that the optimal classification rule is to assign all of the cases to G_2 – i.e. the Bayes' rule is a constant! The error rate for G_1 is 100% and for G_2 is 0%. The total error rate is $100 \times P(G_1) +$

160 Classification Algorithms

$0 \times P(G_2) = 10\%$, and this is the smallest total error rate achievable! The constant rule problem can occur in any form of the Bayes' rule but categorical methods are particularly prone to it.

The difficulty stems from the fact that the TEC is not the criterion we are really interested in. It has to be realised that this sort of behaviour is not really the fault of the classification rule, it is a misunderstanding concerning the meaning of 'best' in the phrase 'the best rule'. For example if the above table corresponded to measurements made on patients and G_1 represented a benign disease group and G_2 a fatal but easily treatable disease. In this case it might be very reasonable to assign all of the cases to G_2 and treat the fatal disease even if this implies treating some patients unnecessarily. On the other hand if the treatment for the fatal disease was difficult, expensive and carried risks of its own then to treat patients without the disease would be most undesirable. Obviously the discussion of such cases is complicated and beyond the scope of this book but the general solution to the problem has already been described. Either:

(1) Assign costs to the different types of error and use a minimum cost classifier.

or

(2) Use the fixed error rate classifier – i.e. fix one error rate and minimise the other.

Details of these methods can be found in Chapter 5. The problem in any real situation is to find a way of fixing either the costs or the acceptable error rates.

Practical categorical classification

The whole subject of categorical classification is much too large to summarise in this chapter. The interested reader is directed to Reference [1] which is devoted entirely to the subject. In practice there are very few programs available for categorical classification and to an extent this is understandable. The most common methods in use involve either standard linear discriminant functions or log linear models. In the first case an existing linear discriminant program can be used and in the second a program for fitting general log linear models is all that is required. A general recommendation concerning categorical classification would be to first try linear discrimination and then move on to more sophisticated methods – particular the log linear model – if this failed.

Categorical Variables and Non-parametric Methods **161**

Non-parametric methods

Nearly all non-parametric classification methods are based on attempts to estimate $P(x|G_i)$, or at least to say in what regions $P(x|G_k)$ is larger than $P(x|G_j)$ (for all $j \neq k$).

The possible range of non-parametric procedures is limited only by the imagination and so the remainder of this chapter will describe four of the best known:

(1) Histogram estimates

(2) Parzen or kernel estimates

(3) Basis expansion methods

(4) Nearest neighbour estimates

The first three methods are concerned with finding direct estimates of $P(x|G_i)$ and using Bayes' theorem to construct a classifier. The fourth follows the same pattern but it results in a particularly simple and intuitive classification rule.

The problem of estimating $P(x|G_i)$

If we have a sample $x_1, x_2, x_3, \ldots x_{mi}$ from G_i, the problem of estimating $P(x|G_i)$ is easy to see. The fact that we have obtained the value x in the sample tells us nothing except that that value *can* occur, not how likely it is to occur. In a sense, the maximum likelihood estimate of $P(x|G_i)$ based on the sample is a series of points each with equal probability (i.e. a series of delta functions with weight $1/m_i$) (see Fig. 9.2). Although this is the maximum likelihood estimate, it is obviously not what we require. The condition which we are not including is of course that we expect $P(x|G_i)$ to be smooth. An exact solution to our problem would be a maximum likelihood estimate which satisfied some condition of smoothness – but this turns out to be mathematically intractable and so we use other methods.

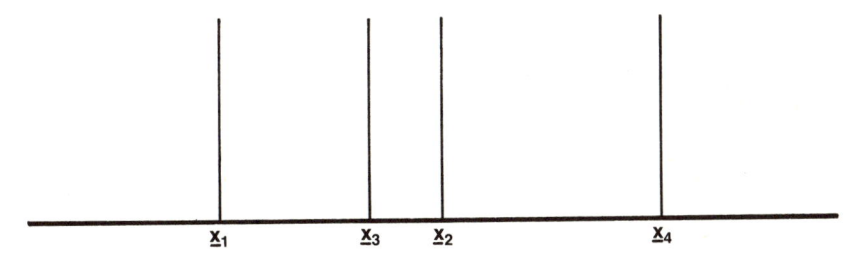

Fig. 9.2 Estimate of $P(x|G)$

162 Classification Algorithms

These methods are all attempts to produce smooth estimates of $P(x|G_i)$ however.

(1) Histogram method

The histogram is the most obvious and simple non-parametric method. Partition the sample space into mutually disjoint regions or cells $V_1, V_2, \ldots V_p$, each enclosing the same volume. It is not difficult to see that $P(x|G_i)$ can be approximated in each cell by f_i/m_i where f_j is the number of observations which fall into V_j. In one dimension this corresponds to the familiar notion of a histogram and indeed this approach can be thought of as a multi-dimensional histogram. The main trouble with this method is the amount of storage required for the f_j. For example, if we have n variables and use rectangular cells created by dividing each variable into p equal intervals, we have p^n cells in all. Obviously the problem is going to be getting enough data to ensure that most of the cells are not empty. This is exactly the same problem as encountered in estimating contingency table probabilities in categorical classification. The other problem is the selection of the basic cell size: too small and the estimate of $P(x|G_i)$ is not smooth enough (i.e. one observation in each cell); too large and the fine details of the distribution are lost (i.e. all the observations fall in one cell). In this case the size of the cell governs the amount of smoothing applied to the estimate of $P(x|G_i)$. Some attempts to solve these problems have involved the use of variable cell sizes [4] but in general the histogram method, for all its simplicity, is not practical.

(2) The Parzen or kernel estimate

The Parzen or kernel estimate achieves the smoothing of the estimate of $P(x|G)$ by supposing that each value that occurred in the sample raises the probability not only of that particular value occurring but also of values that are close to it occurring. The final value of the estimate of the probability of any value occurring is obtained by summing together all of the contributions from each value in the sample. This method is the most difficult from a mathematical point of view but it is fairly easy to imagine what is happening. The general Parzen estimate of $P(x|G)$ based on a sample of m_i values is:

$$P(x|G_i) = \frac{1}{m_i} \sum_{j=1}^{m_i} \frac{1}{h^n} K\left[\frac{x - x_j}{h}\right]$$

where
    n = number of dimensions
    K = a function known as the kernel of the estimate and
    h = a function of m_i

Although this formula looks complicated all it amounts to is surrounding

Categorical Variables and Non-parametric Methods 163

each value in the sample by a version of the kernel function centred on that value and estimating the probability at **x** by averaging all of the functions. This is easier to understand by way of an example.

The most common choice for a kernel function is the multivariate normal:

$$K\left(\frac{\mathbf{x} - \mathbf{x}_j}{h}\right) = \frac{1}{(2\pi)^{n/2}|\Sigma|^{-1/2}} \exp\left[\frac{(\mathbf{x} - \mathbf{x}_j)'\Sigma(\mathbf{x} - \mathbf{x}_j)}{h^2}\right]$$

and

$$h(m_i) = m_i^{-a/n}$$

where $0 < a < 1$

It is important to notice that Σ is nothing to do with the covariance matrix of the sample but is a smoothing parameter. However, we are left with the problem of selecting a value for Σ and it is usual to take S (the sample covariance matrix) for its value for then the covariance matrix of the Parzen estimate is:

$$\Sigma_p = (1 + h^2)\Sigma = (1 + h^2)S$$

All of this is easier to understand in the one dimensional case where the Parzen estimate is simply:

$$P(x \mid G_i) = \frac{1}{m_i} \sum_{j=1}^{m_i} \frac{1}{h} K\left[\frac{x - x_i}{h}\right]$$

Using a normal kernel in this expression, i.e.

$$K(y) = \frac{1}{(2\pi)^{1/2}} \exp\left[\frac{-Y^2}{2s^2}\right]$$

is equivalent to surrounding each point in the sample by a normal curve and summing the result as can be seen in Fig. 9.3.

The value of s in the kernel can now clearly be seen as a smoothing parameter. The larger the value of s used the smoother the estimate of $P(\mathbf{x}\, G_i)$. (Engineers will recognise the Parzen estimate as a filtering process on the sample with the kernel as the point spread function.)

The problems with the Parzen estimate are:

(1) The need to select a smoothing parameter or worse a kernel and a function $h(m_i)$.

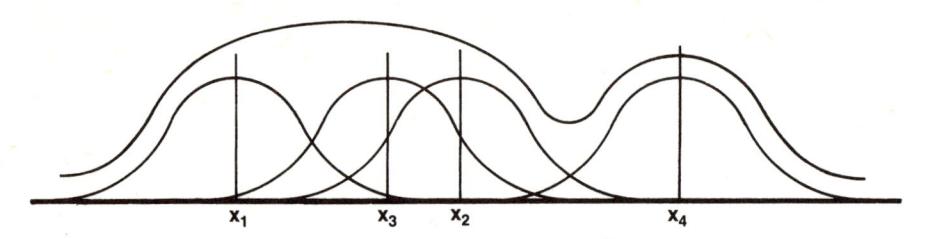

Fig. 9.3 Smoothed estimate of P(x|G)

(2) The complex form of the estimate resulting from most kernels.

(3) The amount of computation needed to work out the estimate increases rapidly with the sample size.

The first problem has been partially solved in that it has been shown that the particular kernel used has little effect on the results (although see the next section). As this is the case it makes sense to choose a kernel function that makes the computation of the estimate as easy as possible. Surprisingly one of the easiest kernel functions to work with is the normal. (For a listing of a FORTRAN program that calculates the Parzen estimate using normal kernels see Reference [5].) The second problem can be solved by using the normal kernel and then taking a polynomial expansion of the exponential function (see Reference [6]).

Conditions on the kernel function **
For the Parzen estimate to work the kernel must satisfy the following conditions:

(1)
$$\int_{-\infty}^{+\infty} K(z)\,dz = 1$$

i.e. must be normalised to 1.

(2)
$$\int_{-\infty}^{+\infty} K(z)\,dz < \infty$$

i.e. its magnitude must be integrable.

(3) $$\sup |K(z)| < \infty$$

i.e. it must be bounded.

(4) $$\lim_{z \to \infty} |zK(z)| = 0$$

i.e. it must go to 0 faster than $1/z$.

$h(m_i)$ must satisfy the following conditions for the estimator to have the named properties:

(1) $$\lim_{m_i \to \infty} h(m_i) = 0$$

for asymptotic unbiasedness.

(2) $$\lim_{m_i \to \infty} m_i h(m_i) = \infty$$

for asymptotic consistency.

(3) $$\lim_{m_i \to \infty} m_i h_n^2(m_i) = \infty$$

for uniform consistency.

If all these conditions are satisfied the estimate is asymptotically unbiased and consistent at all continuous points of $P(x|G_i)$. Needless to say all of these conditions are satisfied if the kernel is taken to be the normal distribution and $h(m_i)$ is

$$m_i^{-a/n}$$

with $0 < a < \frac{1}{2}$

(3) Basis expansion methods **

It is well known that there exist sets of functions which can be used to expand other functions as an infinite series, e.g. polynomials (giving the Taylor series) and sin and cos (giving the Fourier series). Expansions in

166 Classification Algorithms

more than one dimension are also possible but the notation and computation becomes a little complicated and so we will deal with the one-dimensional case.

If we expand an arbitrary function in terms of a set of basis functions $e_i(x)$:

$$f(x) = \sum_{i=1}^{\infty} c_i e_i(x)$$

we can determine the coefficients in the usual way:

$$c_i = \int w(x) e_i(x) f(x)\, dx$$

where $w(x)$ is an appropriate weight function such that:

$$\int w(x) e_i(x) e_j(x)\, dx = 0 \qquad \text{if } i \neq j$$

$$= 1 \qquad \text{if } i = j$$

If we treat $f(x)$ as a probability distribution and can express the c_i in terms of moments of the distribution, then we can fit a truncated series by the method of moments to a sample.

Practical difficulties are the selection of the e_i and ensuring that the truncated series (or the original series for that matter) represents a probability density function.

Standard forms of series expansions are the Edgeworth and the Charlier series (see Reference [1] for more details concerning categorical variables and Reference [7] for the continuous case).

(4) Nearest neighbour methods

Nearest neighbour methods are in a sense based on a 'reverse histogram' estimator. In the histogram method, the number of points falling into a fixed volume is used; in the nearest neighbour (NN) method, the volume which contains a fixed number of points is used as an estimator. We may define the K-NN estimate of $P(x|G_i)$, based on a sample of size m_i, as:

$$P_k(x \mid G_i) = \frac{K}{m_i} \frac{1}{A(K, x)}$$

where $A(K, x)$ is the volume which contains the K nearest sample points to x. To complete the definition we have to say what we mean by 'near' – in other

Categorical Variables and Non-parametric Methods

words we must define our metric. We can show that $P_k(x|G_i)$ is asymptotically unbiased and consistent if:

$$\lim_{K \to \infty} \frac{K}{m_i} = 0$$

As this condition is usually satisfied, the K-NN estimate is thus usually a good one.

In most cases it is appropriate to use the Euclidean metric which gives $A(K,x)$ the form of a sphere with radius r_k, i.e. the distance to the kth NN. In this case:

$$A(K, x) = \frac{2 r_k^n \pi^{n/2}}{n \Gamma(n/2)}$$

which is simply the volume of a sphere in n dimensions. Note: the Euclidean metric defines distance as:

$$d(x, y) = [(x_1 - y_1)^2 + (x_2 - y_2)^2 + \cdots (x_n - y_n)^2]^{1/2}$$

where $d(x,y)$ is the distance between x and y.

The problem with this method is the selection of K. In general K should be chosen to make r_k small enough for the probability to vary little through $A(K,x)$. As you might expect K plays the role of a smoothing parameter.

K-NN classification rule

By a slight modificiation the K-NN estimate can be turned into a classification rule that makes no reference to $A(K,x)$ and hence is easy to use.

If we have a sample of size M consisting of m_i samples from each group (i.e. $M = \Sigma m_i$) and find the Kth NN to x ignoring group membership, and if the K points contained in $A(K,x)$ consist of $K_1, K_2, \ldots K_g$ points from each group, we can estimate $P_k(x|G_i)$ by:

$$P_k(x | G_i) = \frac{K_i}{m_i} \frac{1}{A(K, x)}$$

Using this estimate in Bayes' rule gives:

assign to group i if

168 Classification Algorithms

$$P(G_i) \frac{K_i}{m_i} \frac{1}{A(K, x)} > P(G_j) \frac{K_j}{m_j} \frac{1}{A(K, x)}$$

for all $j \neq i$

Cancelling the factors $1/A(K,x)$ we have:

$$\frac{P(G_i)}{m_i} K_i > \frac{P(G_j)}{m_j} K_j$$

which is a very simple rule. If the sample sizes m_i are proportional to $P(G_i)$ ($m_i = MP(G_i)$), or if $P(G_i)$ is estimated by m_i/M, then the rule becomes:

$$K_i > K_j$$

which is the most usual form of the K-NN classification rule and amounts to assigning the new case to the group that the majority of its K nearest neighbours belong to.

The problem with this rule is the selection of K and the large amount of storage required. To a certain extent the first problem is artifical in that there are good theoretical reasons for supposing that the error rate of the 1-NN classifier will be better than any other value of K (see Reference [7]). Thus in most cases there is no need to consider anything more complicated than a nearest neighbour classifier. The second problem can be solved by removing all those points in the sample which are not 'important', i.e. do not influence the classification. These are located along the classification boundaries. An algorithm for this removal can be found in Reference [6]. Of all the non-parametric classifiers the nearest neighbour classifier is perhaps the most practical.

An estimate of the Bayes' error by the K-NN rule

Even though the K-NN rule is more difficult to use than say the linear discriminant function approach, it has one important advantage – it enables us to estimate the TEC of the true Bayes rule without knowing what form it takes. We can thus estimate the TEC of the best possible classifier and compare how well any rule that we are using is doing. It can be shown that:

$$\tfrac{1}{2} e_k \leqslant e^* \leqslant e_k$$

where
    e^* = the error rate of the Bayes' rule
    e_k = the error rate of the K-NN rule

Categorical Variables and Non-parametric Methods 169

Thus the K-NN error rate can be used to set rough limits on the error rate of the Bayes' classifier. The above relationship is an asymptotic result, becoming true only as the sample size tends to infinity, so estimates from finite sample sizes have to be treated with care. Even so it is remarkable to be able to gauge the size of the Bayes' error without knowing what the Bayes' rule is. Once again there are good theoretical grounds for assuming that the 1-NN rule will give a better estimate of the Bayes' error rate than any other value of K.

A 1-NN classifier program

The following program reads a data file in the format used for all the other classification programs presented in earlier chapters and then classifies each case using the 1-nearest neighbour rule. The final output is an estimate of the error rate for the 1-nearest neighbour rule and estimated bounds for the Bayes' error rate.

```
10 GOSUB 1000:REM GET PARAMETERS
20 GOSUB 2000:REM READ IN DATA
30 GOSUB 3000:REM CLASSIFY CASES
40 GOSUB 4000:REM PRINT ERROR RATE
50 GOSUB 5000:REM CLASSIFY NEW CASES
60 STOP

1000 PRINT "NEAREST NEIGHBOUR CLASSIFIER"
1010 PRINT
1020 PRINT "DATA FILE NAME ";
1030 INPUT F$
1040 GOSUB 7200:REM OPEN INPUT FILE
1050 GOSUB 7300:N=R:REM READ R
1060 GOSUB 7300:M=R
1070 PRINT "CASES=";M;"VARIABLES=";N
1080 PRINT "NUMBER OF GROUPS ";
1090 INPUT G
1100 DIM M(G)
1105 T=0
1110 FOR I=1 TO G
1120 PRINT "NUMBER OF CASES IN GROUP ";I;
1130 INPUT M(I)
1135 T=T+M(I)
1140 NEXT I
1150 PRINT
1160 DIM X(N,T+1),C(T)
1170 RETURN

2000 I=0
2010 FOR H=1 TO G
2020 FOR K=1 TO M(H)
2030 I=I+1
```

```
2040 C(I)=H
2050 FOR J=1 TO N
2060 GOSUB 7300:REM READ R
2070 X(J,I)=R
2080 NEXT J
2090 NEXT K
2100 NEXT H
2110 RETURN

3000 E=0
3010 FOR I=1 TO T
3020 S=I+1
3030 IF S>T THEN S=1
3040 J=S
3050 GOSUB 8000
3060 M=D
3070 FOR J=1 TO T
3080 IF I=J THEN 3110
3090 GOSUB 8000
3100 IF D<M THEN M=D:S=J
3110 NEXT J
3120 PRINT "NEAREST NEIGHBOUR TO ";I;"FROM G";
     C(I);" IS CASE ";S;"FROM G";C(S)
3130 IF  C(S)<>C(I) THEN E=E+1:PRINT "***";
3140 PRINT
3150 NEXTI
3160 RETURN

4000 PRINT
4010 PRINT "ERROR RATE=";E/T*100;"%"
4020 PRINT
4030 PRINT E/T/2*100;"%<=BAYES ERROR<=";
     E/T*100;"%"
4040 RETURN

5000 PRINT
5010 FOR I=1 TO N
5020 PRINT "VARIABLE ";I;"=";
5030 INPUT X(I,T+1)
5040 NEXT I
5050 S=1
5060 J=S:I=T+1
5070 GOSUB 8000
5080 M=D
5090 FOR J=2 TO T
5100 GOSUB 8000
5110 IF D<M THEN M=D:S=J
5120 NEXT J
5130 PRINT "CASE CLASSIFIED AS GROUP ";C(S);
     " CLOSEST CASE =";S
5140 GOTO 5000

7200 OPEN "I",#1,F$
```

```
7210 RETURN

7300 INPUT#1,R
7310 RETURN

7400 CLOSE #1
7410 RETURN

8000 D=0
8010 FOR K=1 TO N
8020 Q=X(K,I)-X(K,J)
8030 D=D+Q*Q
8040 NEXT K
8050 RETURN
```

Subroutine 2000 reads all of the data into an array X(N,T) and then subroutine 3000 proceeds to classify each case according to the group membership of its nearest neighbour. The measure of distance used is the conventional Euclidean metric, that is, the distance between case I and case J is given by

$$D^2 = (x_{i1} - x_{j1})^2 + (x_{i2} - x_{j2}) + \cdots (x_{in} - x_{jn})^2$$

Subroutine 4000 estimates both the error rate of the nearest neighbour classifier and the bounds on the Bayes' error rate. Finally subroutine 5000 will find the nearest neighbour of any new cases. The calculation of the distance between case I and case J is performed by subroutine 8000.

The subroutine structure of the program and its array use is given in Table 9.1.

A nearest neighbour classification of the iris data

If the iris data is analysed using the nearest neighbour program given above then the reported error rate is 4% which yields bounds on the Bayes' error of 2% to 4% which is very reasonable since the estimated error rate of the linear discriminant function is 2%. The estimated range of the Bayes' error is not always so tight. For example, the baby weight and height data results in a range of 25%–50% for the Bayes' error.

Practical non-parametric classification

Currently the only really practical non-parametric classification rule is the nearest neighbour classifier. However there are a number of other procedures that have been practically successful and could be called non-

Table 9.1

	1-NN Classifier subroutine use
Subroutine	Action
1000	Get parameters
2000	Read all data into X(N,T+1)
3000	Classify all cases
4000	Print error rate
5000	Classify new cases
7200	Open file F for input
7300	Read a value into R
7400	Close file
8000	Calculate distance between case I and case J

	Array use
Array	Purpose
X(N,T+1)	Holds all data in file F$
C(T)	Stores number of the group to which each case belongs

parametric. These are described in the next chapter. They have arisen in response to the needs of pattern recognition and artifical intelligence where the large numbers of variables and groups involved have tended to force the creation of ad hoc rules some of which have turned out to be based on good theory.

References

1. Goldstein, M. and Dillon, W.R. (1978) *Discrete Discriminant Analysis*: Wiley.
2. Reynolds, H.T. (1977) *Analysis of Nominal Data*: Sage University Papers.
3. Bishop, Y.M.M., Fienberg, S.E. and Holland, P.W. (1975) *Discrete Multivariate Analysis: Theory and Practice*: MIT Press.
4. Fukanaga, K. (1972) *Introduction to Statistical Pattern Recognition*: Academic Press.
5. Silverman, B.W. (1982) 'Kernel density estimation using the fast Fourier transform', *Applied Statistics*, **31**, 93–7.

6. Hart, P.E. (1968) 'The condensed nearest neighbor rule', *IEEE Transactions on Information Theory*, **IT-14**, 515-6.
7. Chen, C.H. (1973) *Statistical Pattern Recognition*: Spartan Books.

Chapter Ten
Artificial Intelligence and Pattern Recognition

This final chapter of the book describes the very special approach to classification problems that is typical of the fields of artificial intelligence (AI) and pattern recognition (PR). AI is concerned with the automation of tasks and processes that are normally considered to be the exclusive province of humans. Generally speaking one might say that AI is an attempt to build (or program) an intelligent machine. Of course this definition avoids the all-important question of what we mean by 'intelligence' but it is clear enough for most purposes. The classification problem occurs within AI because of the need to make decisions based upon the available data. For example an 'intelligent' program that makes diagnoses based on the symptoms presented to it can clearly be thought of as a classifier which assigns a patient to one of a number of disease types. On the other hand there are plenty of AI problems and approaches that are equally clearly not easily converted into simple classification.

Pattern recognition is, as its name suggests, concerned with the automatic recognition of patterns of all sorts. The aims of PR are often summed up as 'computer vision' but this misses the fact that much of PR is concerned with the recognition or classification of patterns that are not directly related to images. An obvious non-visual example is speech recognition where the raw data is a signal from a microphone. Clearly a subject with the word 'recognition' in its title is going to be very interested in classification but in fact there are two distinct uses of the word 'recognition' within PR. Firstly there is 'supervised recognition' (often referred to as 'learning with a teacher') and this corresponds to the classification problem that we have considered in the earlier chapters. Secondly there is 'unsupervised recognition' (often referred to as 'learning without a teacher') and this corresponds to the area of statistics usually known as cluster analysis. Even so PR is not simply the engineering end of the statistical theory of classification. There are problems posed by PR that are quite unique and have led to special methods of classification, feature selection and implementation that are characteristic of the subject.

Artificial Intelligence and Pattern Recognition 175

It is appropriate to consider the AI and PR approach to classification in this final chapter because, as well as providing alternative methods to the statistical approach, they are also the only fields that consider more closely the nature of the measurements that we make and the way our results are presented. For example, so far it has always been assumed that a set of measurements, x, has been made and the classification problem commences from this point. However in PR it is often the case that we are presented with a number of groups of images and, while the differences between them are clear – one group might consist of letter As, the next Bs and so on – there are no obvious ways of determining what measurements should be made on them. In the same way it has been assumed that the assignment of a case to one of the possible groups was a sufficient solution to the classification problem but an explanation of *why* the case was so assigned is sometimes an absolute requirement. For example, a classifier that is good at medical diagnosis is unlikely to be accepted unless it is capable of interpretation by a doctor in terms other than raw discriminant scores. In some sense it is true to say that PR is forced to examine the 'front end' of the classification problem in that it is often concerned with the problem of what to measure and AI deals with the 'back end' in that it must explain the reasons for any assignments it makes. Much of this chapter is devoted to a general discussion of the AI and PR techniques that are relevant to classification. It is intended as a guide to help interested readers find their way around both subjects and make appropriate connections with classification theory.

The data explosion

One of the principle differences between the sort of classification problems we have looked at so far and the problems that are tackled within PR is simply the amount of data involved. In any of the examples in the previous chapters the number of variables was counted in tens but in PR the number of variables has to be thought of in terms of hundreds or thousands of measurements. For example, a small image composed of an array of only 10 by 10 brightness measurements poses a classification problem involving 100 variables! Finding the covariance matrix for 100 variables is time consuming enough, let alone finding its inverse. In practice images are generally composed of 1000 by 1000 brightness measurements and a direct application of the classification rules that have been developed in earlier chapters is clearly impossible. To make this data 'explosion' problem even more difficult there is usually a time constraint on PR problems that is so absolute that even a correct classification is of no use after a given time. For example, if a vision system is being used to guide a robot arm then it must recognise an object in a time that is small compared to the arm's movement. A missile detection and interception system that depended on a procedure that took longer to recognise a missile than the missile took to reach the target is an even more extreme example of the importance of speed of classification in PR!

The large amounts of data and the need to classify quickly have led to the development of simple but possibly suboptimal classification rules. In particular, PR classification rules have tended to use exclusively linear classifiers which can easily be implemented as simple but fast hardware. Also there is a tendency to prefer the simultaneous use of a number of simple classification rules, rather than a single complicated one, to allow for parallel computation. So a typical PR classification rule would be composed of a number of linear classifiers along with some method of making a final assignment. (This is discussed later in this chapter.)

In a field where too much data is the general problem, feature selection is clearly going to be very important and indeed, PR uses a wide range of feature selection techniques. However once again the amounts of data and the time restrictions demand that only simple selection procedures can be used. In many cases it is possible to take a great deal of time over the initial design of the features that will be used in classification but it is always important for the calculation of the features from the raw data to be quick.

Thus the classification methods that are typical of PR are simple but suboptimal classification rules and fast feature selection and computation – and it is worth examining both of these in turn.

Simple classification rules

As already explained the large amounts of data, even after feature selection, involved in PR have led to the development of simple but suboptimal classification rules. In particular there has been a great deal of work in trying to derive linear discriminant functions that have reasonable error rates irrespective of whether they are appropriate in the sense of being an approximation to the Bayes' rule. Much of this work is an attempt to avoid a consideration of the underlying distributions and hence tends to be based on concepts of the geometry of the situation.

For example, the so-called 'perceptron algorithm' attempts to find a line (or in general a hyperplane) that completely separates two groups. The algorithm starts off by placing the line arbitrarily in the sample space and then examining which side of the line each case is on. If a case is on the wrong side of the line then the position of the line is altered either to place the case on the correct side or simply to bring the case closer to being on the correct side of the line. (There are a number of possible ways of updating the line's position.) If this process is repeated and there is a line that divides the two groups then eventually all of the cases will lie on the correct side of the line (i.e. group 1 on one side and group 2 on the other). If however there is no line that completely separates the two groups then this procedure never settles down and the adjustment causes the line to oscillate between a number of positions. Clearly this procedure is entirely geometrical and the final dividing line between the two groups has no claim to a low error rate if it is used for the classification of subsequent cases. It is non-parametric in that no assumptions are made about the distributions of the groups and it is easy to compute in that the covariance matrix isn't needed but if the groups are not completely separate there is no unique dividing line between them. There are ways of forcing the procedure to settle down to a final line even if the groups are not separate but on the whole the perceptron procedure has little to recommend it over the linear discriminant function.

There are many other simple classification procedures in use in PR – many of them are modifications of the perceptron algorithm – but some are simply reduced versions of the linear discriminant function. For example if we assume that the covariance matrix of the sample is the identity $\mathbf{I}$, in other words all of the measured variables are uncorrelated, and have unit variance then the linear discriminant function becomes:

$$\boldsymbol{\mu}_i' \mathbf{I}^{-1} \mathbf{x} - \tfrac{1}{2} \boldsymbol{\mu}_i \mathbf{I}^{-1} \boldsymbol{\mu}_i$$

or

$$\boldsymbol{\mu}_i' \mathbf{x} - \tfrac{1}{2} \boldsymbol{\mu}_i' \boldsymbol{\mu}_i$$

which is proportional to:

$$\sqrt{(\boldsymbol{\mu}_i - \mathbf{x})'(\boldsymbol{\mu}_i - \mathbf{x})}$$

which is simply the distance of $\mathbf{x}$ from the mean $\boldsymbol{\mu}_i$. Thus if we assume that all the variables are uncorrelated and have unit variance then the linear discriminant classification rule is equivalent to a 'nearest means' classifier. That is, classify a new case to the group that has the closest mean. Of course we can still use the rule even if the assumptions about the covariance matrix are not true and then the nearest means classifier is a simple but suboptimal rule whose performance gets worse as the covariance matrix becomes more unlike the identity $\mathbf{I}$.

A slightly better version of the nearest means classifier is obtained if the covariance matrix is assumed to be diagonal but not to be the identity matrix. This is equivalent to assuming that the variables are uncorrelated within each group but their variances can take on any value. In this case the linear discriminant function is proportional to:

$$\sqrt{\sum_{j=1}^{n} \frac{(\mu_{ij} - x_j)^2}{s_j}}$$

which is nothing more than a distance from the mean $\mathbf{\mu}_i$ but weighted by the variance of each of the variables.

The idea of a nearest means classifier can be extended to produce classification rules that use the concept of a 'prototype'. If the measurement vector $\mathbf{v}_i$ can be thought of as typical of group i then a reasonable classification rule is to assign a new case $\mathbf{x}$ to the group with the closest typical case $\mathbf{v}_i$. In this sense the $\mathbf{v}_i$s are group prototypes used as standards against which to compare $\mathbf{x}$. The nearest mean rule obviously uses the group means as prototypes but there is nothing stopping us from using other measures of group location such as the group modes. If this nearest prototype rule is extended to include the case where every case in a sample is taken as a prototype then we have the nearest neighbour rule described in Chapter 9.

As already mentioned all of the above rules are linear but this doesn't mean that they are all easy to calculate. For example the nearest neighbour rule is very difficult to use (see Chapter 9). In practice only the simple nearest mean, or nearest prototype, rule is used very much and it is worth testing this sort of rule to see if an acceptable error rate can be achieved. It has to be admitted that linear rules are very attractive and it makes sense to ask if it is possible to find such rules that are in any sense optimal. The Bayes' rule has the lowest error rate of all rules no matter what their form and by analogy we can define a linear Bayes' rule as one that has the lowest error rate of all linear rules. In other words there may be better rules than the linear Bayes' rule but they are not linear and, hence they are not as simple. Unfortunately it turns out that these rules are not easy to derive. Even for the normal case with unequal covariance matrices it is necessary to use an iterative procedure [1]. For example, for normal distributions with unequal covariance matrices an iterative procedure has to be adopted to calculate the discriminant function.

There are a number of other approaches to constructing classification rules that are used within PR. However most of them are intuitive procedures that neither attempt to produce, nor claim to result in, the minimum error rate. It is particularly important to know under what conditions a particular rule is optimal or nearly so. For example the nearest means classifier is conceptually simple but it is only optimal for normal groups with uncorrelated variables all with unit variance and any deviation from these conditions results in a suboptimal rule. For general applications the linear discriminant function introduced in earlier chapters still has many advantages over the simpler PR rules.

Fast feature selection

Feature selection in PR nearly always means unconstrained feature selection. The variable selection problem arises less often because of the way that all of the variables in a PR problem are potentially valuable. For example, given a 10×10 image of brightness measurements, it is more reasonable to ask for a small number of linear combinations to use in classification than it is to ask which of the 100 measurements should be used. Since this is the case you might think that the standard method of feature selection used in PR would be canonical analysis (see Chapter 7) but this is not so because of the amount of work involved in finding the canonical vectors. Indeed canonical analysis is often ignored in books on PR in favour of the simpler method of principal components analysis. Canonical analysis seeks to find directions that best separate the groups whereas principal components analysis seeks directions that maximise the spread of the data irrespective of group structure. (In PR principal components analysis is often referred to as the Karhunen-Loeve expansion.) There are many good reasons for using the first m principal components [2] to represent the behaviour of a data set but they are not optimal if classification is the objective.

Even principal components analysis involves finding the eigenvectors and eigenvalues of the covariance matrix and for many PR problems this is simply too time consuming. For this reason a number of 'fixed' feature selection procedures have evolved (see References [1] and [3]) based on transformations such as the Fourier, Walsh and Harr transformations. The technical details of these transformations is too complicated to go into here but essentially they construct linear combinations of the data that tend to be less correlated than the raw data and maximise the spread of the data. For example the Fourier transformation decomposes the data into a number of periodic components. These components tend to have low correlations with one another and the low frequency components account for most of the variation within the sample. Thus the Fourier transform produces linear combinations which have properties that are similar to the principal components but without having to find eigenvalues and eigenvectors.

Once again, for general use these feature selection methods have little to offer over the methods described in Chapters 7 and 8 unless the number of variables involved in the problem makes it impossible to compute the covariance matrix or the canonical vectors.

180 Classification Algorithms

One of the most interesting results of the examination of classification rules based on large numbers of variables is the conclusion that unlike mulitiple regression, say, the performance of a classifier does not necessarily improve as new variables are added [4]. At first thought it seems reasonable to assume that classification accuracy could only improve or stay the same as extra variables are added to the classifier – after all an extra measurement might add some extra useful information in which case the error rate would decrease, or it would add no information and the error rate would stay the same. In practice for any give sample size used to design a classifier there is an optimum number of measurements – after this optimum the error rate starts to increase again. This is yet another reason for applying variable selection techniques to a classification problem.

The measurement problem

All applied statistical analysis starts with the process of measurement. Although *how* some quantity might be measured is sometimes considered, it is rare for there to be any consideration of *what* might be measured. From the point of view of statistics which quantities are to be measured is a question to be answered by the discipline using the statistical methods. For example what measurements and tests should be conducted on a patient is a matter for medicine not statistics. However within PR the problem of what to measure to achieve good classification results presents itself in a very clear form. If we are confronted by a collection of letter As and a collection of letter Bs then there is no doubt that they form two separate groups which can be successfully classified with an error rate at least as good as a human's performance. The trouble is *what* information should be gathered to use in an automatic classification rule? It is possible to use all of the brightness measurements that make up the image as a data vector x and attempt to find $P(G_i|x)$ from $P(x|G_i)$ in the usual way but this leads to a number of theoretical, let alone practical, problems. As already mentioned several times in earlier chapters simple classification rules arise from simple divisions of the sample space. Simple linear divisions of the sample space are a result of the distribution $P(x|G_i)$ being roughly elliptical and in general simple divisions result from $P(x|G_i)$ having a high degree of symmetry. Unfortunately it is not difficult to show that $P(x\,G_i)$ is very strange when x represents brightness values from an image. For example a letter A written slightly to one side of its usual position is still recognisably a letter A and in general shifting any image by an amount s in any direction doesn't alter it from the point of view of recognition. What this means for the distribution $P(x|G_i)$ is that:

$$P(x \mid G_i) = P(y \mid G_i)$$

if **y** is an image obtained from **x** by shifting it in a given direction. (The probabilities must be the same because the images are considered equally good representatives of their class.) This idea can be generalised to include other 'transformations' than simple shifts. If **T** is a transformation and we consider **x** and **Tx** to be the same then x is said to be invariant under the transformation. For example if **S** is shift in any direction then **Sx** and **x** are regarded as the same image and images are said to be shift invariant. Another example of an invariance can be found in speech recognition. A word does not change depending on the time at which it was said and so all speech is invariant under a time shift.

A consideration of such invariances tells us quite a lot about the structure of $P(x \mid G_i)$. For one thing it demonstrates that for images $P(x \mid G_i)$ has a very complicated symmetry that makes the probability of all shifted images the same. Invariances also highlight redundant information within the measurements that we make. For example as images are shift invariant there is little point in processing measurements that contain information about the location of the image. Following this observation it seems obvious that we should seek a transformation of the original variables that somehow removes this redundant information. That is, if **x** is invariant under **T**, then find a transformation R such that if:

$$\mathbf{R}(\mathbf{x}) = \mathbf{z}$$

then

$$\mathbf{R}(\mathbf{T}(\mathbf{x})) = \mathbf{z}$$

This simply means taking all the objects that we consider equivalent and converting them to a single standard prototype. It should be obvious that after this reduction $P(\mathbf{R}(\mathbf{x}) \mid G_i)$ contains the same information as $P(\mathbf{x} \mid G_i)$ but it is simpler.

In the case of shift invariant images it is easy to find a transformation **R** that satisfies the above equation. The power spectrum of an image doesn't change with the image's position and so can be used to remove redundant position information. (The power spectrum is the square of the Fourier transform of the image and indicates the 'power' of each frequency within the image.) Thus taking the Fourier transform of an image and then using the modulus of each frequency component not only allows us to ignore position shifts in the image it is likely to result in a simpler classification rule.

182 Classification Algorithms

(Notice that this is a different reason for using the Fourier transform to the one given in the previous section on fast feature selection – within PR the two uses of the Fourier transform are often confused.)

It would be convenient if all invariances were so easy to remove but in general they are much more troublesome. (However it is no accident that the periodic functions that are the basis of the Fourier transform are eigenfunctions of the translation operator but this doesn't lead to a useful general method.) What the identification of invariances has to offer general classification is much more an approach to selecting measurements rather than a complete and automatic theory. For example, suppose the classification problem in hand was to recognise cubic boxes and rectangular boxes. The most obvious approach would be to measure the sides of the boxes and calculate a linear discriminant function. However if you consider the fact that a cubic box is invariant under a change of scale then it is obvious that the difference between cubes and rectangles is contained in the ratio of the lengths of their sides not in the absolute magnitudes. This means that a simple linear discriminant calculated from the length measurements can never recognise the difference between a cube and a rectangle because no linear combination of measurements can ever produce a ratio. On the other hand a linear discriminant function using the ratio of the lengths does stand a chance of having a good classification performance.

Admittedly the example involving cubes and rectangles is contrived but invariance arguments can help to pinpoint measurements or combinations of measurements that are likely to produce a good classification rule. If an object is considered invariant when subject to a set of transformations then a measurement that will discriminate between it and other objects will be invariant under the same set of transformations. As a final practical comment it is worth pointing out that ratios of length measurements are often referred to as 'shape indices' and are generally useful for separating out the effects of absolute size as opposed to differences in shape. For example the differences between the three types of iris in Fisher's iris data can be explored by forming the ratios of sepal length to sepal width and petal length to petal width – giving a pair of shape indices for sepal shape and petal shape. If you attempt to discriminate using just these two shape indices then you will find that while group 1 is still well separated from groups 2 and 3 the difference between groups 2 and 3 decreases. This can be interpreted to mean that iris setosa is different in shape to iris versicolor and iris virginica which themselves differ in size rather more than shape.

The need to reason

If the major problem in PR is the large quantity of data to be processed then the problem within AI is the complexity of the data. The aim of AI is to mimic the reasoning processes that humans use to reach decisions and this doesn't necessarily involve vast quantities of information just the complex inter-relations between observations. The way that humans reach decisions and classify is to a large extent still a matter for conjecture but it does seem unlikely that computing covariance matrices and linear discriminant functions play a major part. Indeed it is not even very clear that probability, in its strict sense of the number of times something will happen in the long run, plays any direct part in human reasoning. Thus to mimic human behaviour AI is forced to consider alternative methods of decision making, classification and recognition. Although these alternative methods may be valid within AI this doesn't mean that they are going to be practically useful as alternatives to statistical classification. Even if humans do not use linear discriminant functions to classify, their performance is still judged by the error rate.

The real reason for being interested in 'human' methods of classification is not optimality but the prospect of generating rules that are natural and explicable. For example in clinical diagnosis there is a mistrust of a linear discriminant function that assigns a patient to a disease group because a linear combination of symptoms exceeds all others. Diagnosis is usually made in non-numerical terms that weighs and combines evidence in a very complex logical way. In other words diagnosis involves reasoning about the observed symptoms but not formally assigning scores and numeric weights. One could argue that this is irrelevant and our aim is to construct accurate classifiers no matter how they work but an accurate classifier that reaches its conclusions in an apparently magical way doesn't instill trust and there are many situations where it would not be used. In short there are cases where the presentation of a classification rule is as important as its performance and a comprehensible classifier is preferred as long as its error rate is reasonable.

The standard AI approach to classification and decision making is the 'expert system' [5]. An expert system is an attempt to store and use rules similar to the ones used by a human expert. However the type of rule used is of the very simple:

IF condition THEN conclusion

type. For example in diagnosing what is wrong with a car a mechanic may use a rule of the sort:

IF engine will not turn over AND battery OK
AND solenoid OK THEN starter motor faulty.

184   Classification Algorithms

What is surprising is that a large set of such simple rules really does seem capable of representing the knowledge of an expert. It also has the advantage of being easy to explain to a user how the system came to a particular conclusion. However the example given above doesn't include any allowance for uncertainty and it is here that the expert system approach and statistical classification methods overlap. There are two distinct forms of uncertainty that find their way into IF...THEN rules – first the user may not be sure of the observations in the IF part of the rule, second the conclusion may not always follow from the observations. Thus a program may ask the user how certain is the fact that the battery is good etc. and supply a final figure that estimates the probability that the starter motor is faulty. In the same way the probability of a conclusion following from the observations is obtained as subjective estimates from a human expert while the system is being constructed. In this sense expert systems are attempts to derive decision making and classification without making objective measurements. The difficulty is that it is not obvious how to combine such subjective 'probabilities' to arrive at a final estimate of the probability of the condition. The trouble is that the uncertainties of the observations are measures of belief or doubt rather than statements about relative frequencies. The most rigorous interpretation of probability is that it is a quantity that can be measured experimentally – i.e. it is a long-term relative frequency. Using probability to summarise degrees of belief takes probability theory into the realm of the unmeasurable. For example what does it mean to say that I hold that a mathematical theorem is true with a probability of 0.5? There is no way that this can correspond to a relative frequency of the theorem being true or false – it is either true or it is false, it certainly cannot fluctuate at random between the two. It is clear that in this case the probability sums up my internal mental state concerning the truth of the theorem and as such it cannot be measured over and above my statement of its value. However my assessment of what I believe can be taken as a statement of what betting odds I would accept in a wager concerning the theorem and it is possible to develop a number of theories of probability based on the behaviour of a group of coherent gamblers [6]. In practice however, even if these problems of interpretation are ignored there are serious difficulties with applying probability to the reasoning or decision making process. We have met the main difficulties many times in the previous chapters and they are no less serious in AI approaches to classification – insufficient data and too many parameters.

Consider first the simpler problem of working out the unreliability of a conclusion drawn from *uncertain observations*. For example, suppose that if two symptoms are observed then a particular disease is always present, that is:

IF A and B THEN C

where A and B are symptoms and C is the disease. If the first symptom is observed with probability P(A) and the second with probability P(B) then the reliability of the conclusion that the patient has disease C is simply P(A and B), which (see Chapter 2) is given by:

$$P(A \text{ and } B) = P(A \mid B)P(B) = P(B \mid A)P(A)$$

Thus to go from P(A) to P(A and B) it is necessary to know P(B|A) but P(B) is the only other probability that we know. It is usual in such problems to assume that A and B are independent and therefore:

$$P(B \mid A) = P(B)$$

and

$$P(A \text{ and } B) = P(A)P(B)$$

In other words, if we assume that our observations are independent then the uncertainties are combined to give an overall uncertainty by multiplication. Unfortunately it is clear from the rule 'IF A and B THEN C' that A and B are dependent in that if the disease C actually occurs then the symptoms A and B will tend to occur together rather more than P(A)P(B) would suggest. This means that P(A)P(B) overestimates the uncertainty of our final conclusion. For example if P(A)=0.5 and P(B)=0.5 then we can conclude that the patient has C with a probability of 0.25 if we assume that A and B are independent. Multiplying even larger probabilities together soon results in a very small number and so an expert system that uses this independence assumption would tend to claim very low reliability for conclusions based on very certain data.

The proper solution to this problem is to investigate the dependencies between the data but of course this requires a very large sample. The usual solution is to abandon probabilities and multiplication and treat quantities like P(A) as estimates of certainty that can be combined by minimisation. That is the certainty of the conclusion C based on observation A with certainty 0.75 and B with certainty 0.5 is min(0.75,0.5) or 0.5. This approach derives from the theory of 'fuzzy sets' [5] but it can be seen as an attempt to account for the dependencies in the data by approximating P(A)P(B) by min(P(A),P(B)). As P(A and B) tends to be larger than P(A)P(B) and min(P(A),P(B)) ⩾ P(A)P(B) combining probabilities using 'min' results in estimates of uncertainty that are more acceptable (although not necessarily

186 Classification Algorithms

more accurate) even when used with a large number of observations.

The same problem occurs when there is an uncertainty about the *conclusion* to draw from the data. For example the rule:

IF A and B THEN C with probability 0.75

has the intuitive meaning that if symptoms A and B are observed then disease C is suggested with probability 0.75. There is no problem in interpreting this probability – it implies that in 75% of the cases where A and B are observed disease C is present. However there is the same problem in combining evidence to produce a final probability. For example if the expert system has the two rules:

IF A THEN C with probability 0.5

and

IF B THEN C with probability 0.6

and A and B are *both* observed what is the probability that the patient has disease C? Using Bayes' theorem we have:

$$P(C \mid A \text{ and } B) = \frac{P(A \text{ and } B \mid C)P(C)}{P(A \text{ and } B)}$$

If A and B are independent then:

$$P(C \mid A \text{ and } B) = \frac{P(A \mid C)P(B \mid C)P(C)}{P(A)P(B)}$$

$$= P(C \mid A)P(C \mid B)$$

In other words if the observations are independent then once again the appropriate rule to combine probabilities is multiplication. Of course it is unlikely that the symptoms will be independent precisely because they tend to occur together in the disease C! Most expert systems do combine evidence by multiplication or by some method that ignores the need to take dependencies into account. The result is that the estimates of certainty that most of them produce have to be treated with some caution. The most obvious way of avoiding the problem altogether is simply to use composite rules such as:

IF A and B and C and D ... THEN conclusion with probability P

if it is suspected that A, B, C, D ... are dependent, but this is not the way that most human experts draw conclusions and so this too has its disadvantages.

It is of very little use to be told that a conclusion has been reached on the basis of a single piece of complex evidence unless that evidence can be broken down and the contribution of each piece to the final conclusion made clear.

In short, expert systems provide a valuable way of structuring knowledge about how a decision or classification should be made but they are not a replacement for traditional probability-based classification methods. They are particularly worth considering when the conclusions follow from the evidence with a high degree of certainty.

Presenting results

The failure of the expert system to provide any advantage over traditional classification methods in the estimation of probabilities of class membership is not a reason for abandoning the responsibility to present classification rules as clearly as possible. There is no reason why the classification rules described in earlier chapters could not be presented as part of a program that asks the user questions and is capable of explaining the reason for the conclusion. For example canonical analysis (Chapter 7) can be used to find meaningful names for the linear combinations that separate the groups and these can then be used to give reasons for a classification. The contribution of each measurement within a linear discriminant to the final score can also be reported to indicate which measurements were important in the classification. For categorical variables or a mixture of categorical and continuous variables the problems of taking into account and making clear the effects of any dependencies is very difficult and this often forces an assumption of independence. (For an excellent example using categorical variables see Reference [7].)

Currently there are very few examples of classification methods being used within programs capable of gathering data and explaining the reasons for classification. One reason for this is that currently each situation demands a tailor-made solution that involves both statistical analysis to construct a good classifier and software development to implement it. The expert system approach avoids the statistical analysis by using simple rules and asking a human expert to provide subjective estimates of the probabilities involved. In this sense it only tackles half of the problem!

References

1. Fukunaga, K. (1972) *Introduction to Statistical Pattern Recognition*: Academic Press.
2. Chatfield, C. and Collins, A.J. (1980) *Introduction to Multivariate Analysis*: Chapman and Hall.
3. Andrews, H.C. (1972) *Introduction to Mathematical Techniques in Pattern Recognition*: Wiley.
4. Chen, C.H. (1973) *Statistical Pattern Recogntion*: Hayden.
5. James, M. (1984) *Artificial Intelligence in BASIC*: Newnes.
6. Hacking, I. (1965) *Logic of Statistical Inference*: Cambridge University Press.
7. Spiegelhalter, D.J. and Knill-Jones, R.P. (1984) 'Statistical and knowledge-based approaches to clinical decision-support systems', *Journal of the Royal Statistical Society*, **147**, 35–77.

Appendix One
Matrix Theory for Statistics

In this appendix some of the ideas and results of matrix theory that are important within statistics are described. For a fuller treatment see Searle[1].

Vectors and matrices

A matrix is a table of values arranged into rows and columns. A familiar example is the correlation matrix where each entry is the correlation between a pair of variables. The entries in a matrix are usually called elements and a particular element is specified by giving the row and column it occupies. Thus if R is a correlation matrix consisting of n rows and n columns then r_{12} is the element in the first row and second column – that is the correlation between variable 1 and variable 2. A general element of a matrix is often indicated by the use of variable subscripts. For example R is the entire correlation matrix but r_{ij} is a single element of the matrix in the ith row and jth column. A matrix can have any number of rows and columns and the number of rows doesn't have to equal the number of columns. For example a general 3 by 2 matrix (notice that anything to do with the rows is always quoted first) would be:

$$\begin{bmatrix} a_{11} & a_{12} \\ a_{21} & a_{22} \\ a_{31} & a_{32} \end{bmatrix}$$

A matrix with different numbers of rows and columns is called a rectangular matrix and a matrix with the same number of rows and columns is called a square matrix.

A matrix with only a single column is known as a vector. In statistics vectors are often used to represent the results of a number of measurements. For example a measurement of two quantities, height and weight say, can be represented as a vector with two elements:

190   Classification Algorithms

$$\begin{bmatrix} \text{height} \\ \text{weight} \end{bmatrix}$$

Because the elements are written down the page this is sometimes referred to as a column vector. In general the vector **x** represents the results of measuring n individual variables, where n is the number of rows in the vector.

Addition, subtraction and scalar multiplication

Matrices only become useful when rules for combining them are defined. In the same way as ordinary numbers would be lacking something without the rules of arithmetic, matrices need rules for addition, subtraction, multiplication and division.

The addition of two matrices is achieved simply by adding corresponding elements. That is if **A** and **B** are a pair of matrices then the matrix **C** obtained by adding **A** and **B** is

$$C = A + B$$

and has elements c_{ij} given by

$$c_{ij} = a_{ij} + b_{ij}$$

Subtraction can be defined in the same way. That is if

$$C = A - B$$

then

$$c_{ij} = a_{ij} - b_{ij}$$

Notice that both addition and subtraction assume that the matrices **A** and **B** have the same number of rows and columns. Although matrix addition and subtraction can always be performed on matrices of the same size it may not always make sense to do so. For example it is difficult to give any meaning to the result of adding together a pair of correlation matrices.

Multiplication and divison of matrices are sufficiently involved to require sections to themselves but multiplication or division of a matrix by an ordinary number (a scalar) is quite easy. If

$$C = wA$$

where w is a number then:

$$c_{ij} = wa_{ij}$$

In other words each element of **C** is equal to the corresponding element of **A** multiplied by w. Division by a scalar is achieved by simply multiplying by $1/w$. Using these two ideas it is easy to see that if **T** is a vector of totals then:

$$\frac{1}{m}T$$

is a vector of means if m is the number of cases.

Matrix multiplication

The rule for matrix multiplication often seems a little complicated when you first meet it but after practice it becomes very natural. The best way of introducing the rule is to first describe how to multiply a row by a column. Multiplying a row by a column is simply a matter of multiplying each pair of elements in turn and adding up the result. For example the row:

$$[1 \quad 2 \quad 3]$$

multiplied by the column

$$\begin{bmatrix} 4 \\ 5 \\ 6 \end{bmatrix}$$

is

$$[1 \quad 2 \quad 3] \begin{bmatrix} 4 \\ 5 \\ 6 \end{bmatrix} = 1 \times 4 + 2 \times 5 + 3 \times 6 = 32$$

In other words the first element of the row times the first element of the column plus the second element of the row times the second element of the column and so on.

If **C** is the product of two matrices **A** and **B**, that is:

$$C = AB$$

then the elements of **C** are given by multiplying the corresponding row of **A** by the corresponding column of **B**. That is:

$$c_{ij} = \text{(row i of } \mathbf{A}\text{) multiplied by (column j of } \mathbf{B}\text{)}$$

This can be written algebraically as:

$$c_{ij} = \sum_k a_{ik} b_{kj}$$

For example if:

$$\mathbf{A} = \begin{bmatrix} 1 & 2 \\ 3 & 4 \end{bmatrix} \quad \text{and} \quad \mathbf{B} = \begin{bmatrix} 5 & 6 \\ 7 & 8 \end{bmatrix}$$

then

$$\mathbf{C} = \mathbf{AB} = \begin{bmatrix} 1 & 2 \\ 3 & 4 \end{bmatrix}\begin{bmatrix} 5 & 6 \\ 7 & 8 \end{bmatrix} = \begin{bmatrix} 1 \times 5 + 2 \times 7 & 1 \times 6 + 2 \times 8 \\ 3 \times 5 + 4 \times 7 & 3 \times 6 + 4 \times 8 \end{bmatrix}$$

$$= \begin{bmatrix} 19 & 22 \\ 43 & 50 \end{bmatrix}$$

For it to be possible to multiply two matrices together there have to be as many elements in the rows of the first matrix as elements in the columns of the second. It is important to notice that for matrices it is not true that in general **AB**=**BA**. That is, the order of multiplication is important.

The identity and diagonal matrices

The identity matrix **I** plays the same role in matrix multiplication as the number 1 does in ordinary multiplication. That is for any matrix **A** (of the appropriate size so that the multiplications can be performed):

$$\mathbf{IA} = \mathbf{AI} = \mathbf{A}$$

The elements of the identity matrix have a very simple form in that all the off-diagonal elements are 0 and the diagonal elements are 1. For example the 3×3 identity matrix is:

$$\begin{bmatrix} 1 & 0 & 0 \\ 0 & 1 & 0 \\ 0 & 0 & 1 \end{bmatrix}$$

In general a matrix with all its off-diagonal elements zero is known as a diagonal matrix. If **D** is a diagonal matrix then

$$d_{ij} = 0 \quad \text{if } i \neq j$$

and

$$d_{ij} = d_i \quad \text{if } i = j$$

for example if **D** is 3×3

$$\begin{bmatrix} d_1 & 0 & 0 \\ 0 & d_2 & 0 \\ 0 & 0 & d_3 \end{bmatrix}$$

You might like to verify by example the following facts. Multiplying a matrix by a diagonal matrix on the left, that is

$$\mathbf{C} = \mathbf{DA}$$

multiplies each element in the ith row of **A** by d_i. Similarly multiplying a matrix by a diagonal matrix on the right, that is

$$\mathbf{C} = \mathbf{AD}$$

multiplies each element in the ith column of **A** by d_i.

Matrix division - the matrix inverse

Rather than introduce a new operation called matrix division it is simpler to extend the fact that division by a constant is the same as multiplying by one over the constant to matrices. In particular the result from standard arithmetic

$$\frac{1}{c} c = 1$$

suggests trying to find a matrix **B** that satisfies the equation

$$\mathbf{BA} = \mathbf{I}$$

The matrix **B** is called the inverse of **A** and is usually written as

$$A^{-1}$$

and has the following properties

$$A^{-1}A = I$$

and

$$AA^{-1} = I$$

It is also true that

$$(A^{-1})^{-1} = A$$
$$(AB)^{-1} = B^{-1}A^{-1}$$

and

$$(cA)^{-1} = \frac{1}{c}A^{-1}$$

where c is a constant.

Methods of finding the inverse of a given matrix involve a great deal of arithmetic and are beyond the scope of this simple introduction. What is important at this stage is not so much the ability to calculate a matrix inverse (computers are ideal for this!) but to understand the fundamental definition of the inverse

$$A^{-1}A = I$$

One of the main uses of the matrix inverse is solving equations. For example suppose we know the values of the elements of a vector **y** and a matrix **A** and need to know **x** where:

$$y = Ax$$

then it is easy to see that:

$$x = A^{-1}y$$

In other words solving **y**=**Ax** for **x** is just a matter of finding the inverse of **A**.

Transformations

Matrices have many applications in statistics but perhaps one of the most important and most elementary is the transformation of one set of variables to another. If we have a set of n measurements represented by a vector **x** then these can be converted into a related set of measurements **y** by use of the matrix **A**:

$$y = Ax$$

At this abstract level it is difficult to see why this changing of **x** into **y** might be useful. Each element of the new vector **y** is obtained by multiplying a row of **A** by the single column **x** and so you should be able to see that each new variable y_i is a linear combination of all of the old variables that constitute **x**. That is:

$$y_i = \sum_k a_{ik} x_k$$

For many statistical purposes the fact that **y** is a linear combination of the variables in **x** means that **y** contains the same information as **x**. This being the case we are free to choose **A** to give the variables that constitute **y** useful and simple properties. For example in Principal Components Analysis (PCA), a type of factor analysis, we try to find **A** such that y_1 is a new variable with the largest variance of any linear combination of the variables in **x**, y_2 has the largest variance subject to being uncorrelated with y_1, and y_3 has the largest variance subject to being uncorrelated with y_1 and y_2, and so on. There are many reasons why principal components are important but one of the most useful is that if you want to select a smaller number of variables to represent the data then you cannot do much better than choosing the first few principal components. For example a good idea of how the data is arranged can be obtained by examining a scatter plot of the first two principal components y_1 and y_2.

A simpler example of a useful statistical transformation is:

$$z = C^{-1}(x - \mu)$$

where **C** is a diagonal matrix of standard deviations. That is

$c_{ij} = 0$ if $i \neq j$
$c = s_i$ (the standard deviation of the ith variable) if $i = j$

and **μ** is a column vector of means. This is a standardising transformation in that each new variable in **z** has mean zero and standard deviation one.

Quadratic forms and the transpose

The most important distribution in statistics is the normal distribution and its multivariate generalisation, the multivariate normal. Part of the definition of the multivariate normal distribution involves a special sort of matrix product known as a quadratic form. A general quadratic form can be written:

$$x'Ax$$

where the dash next to the first **x** indicates a new operation – transposition. Transposition changes a column vector into a row vector, that is

$$\begin{bmatrix} 1 \\ 2 \\ 3 \end{bmatrix}' = \begin{bmatrix} 1 & 2 & 3 \end{bmatrix}$$

In general the transpose of a matrix **A** is obtained by replacing its first row by its first column, its second row by its second column and so on. For example:

$$\begin{bmatrix} 1 & 2 & 3 \\ 4 & 5 & 6 \\ 7 & 8 & 9 \end{bmatrix}' = \begin{bmatrix} 1 & 4 & 7 \\ 2 & 5 & 8 \\ 3 & 6 & 9 \end{bmatrix}$$

It is worth mentioning that a matrix **A** for which $A'=A$ is known as a symmetric matrix (because $A'=A$ implies $a_{ij}=a_{ji}$). For example the correlation or covariance matrices are both symmetric. It is also worth stating that:

$$(AB)' = B'A'$$

Returning to the definition of a quadratic form you should now be able to see that:

$$x'Ax$$

evaluates to a single number because **Ax** is a new column vector, **y** say, and **x'y** is simply the row and column product introduced in connection with matrix multiplication and this evaluates to a single number. Writing out the matrix expression for a quadratic form in full gives:

$$\sum_i \sum_j x_i a_{ij} x_j$$

which can be seen as a quadratic equation in the variables that constitute **x**. For example if $\mathbf{x}' = (x_1, x_2)$ then:

$$\mathbf{x}'\mathbf{A}\mathbf{x} = a_{11}x_1x_1 + a_{12}x_1x_2 + a_{21}x_2x_1 + a_{22}x_2x_2$$

In general the quadratic form **x'Ax** can be evaluated as the sum of all the terms like

$$a_{ij} x_i x_j$$

for every element a_{ij} in the matrix.

The geometry of quadratic forms

If we know the matrix of a quadratic form then we can try to solve the equation:

$$\mathbf{x}'\mathbf{A}\mathbf{x} = c$$

for **x** where c is a known constant. What is interesting about this problem is that there is more than one solution to the equation and the entire set of vectors that satisfy the equation map out a surface, known as a quadratic surface. For all of the quadratic forms that occur in statistics the quadratic surface is even more special in that it is a closed ellipsoid. For example if S is a convariance matrix the solutions to

$$\mathbf{x}'\mathbf{S}\mathbf{x} = c$$

map out the surface of an ellipsoid. This is of course the result described in Chapters 3 and 4 concerning the probability contours of the multivariate normal distribution. The equation for the multivariate normal is:

$$\frac{1}{(2\pi)^{n/2}|\Sigma|^{1/2}} \exp[-\tfrac{1}{2}(\mathbf{x}-\boldsymbol{\mu})'\Sigma^{-1}(\mathbf{x}-\boldsymbol{\mu})]$$

and you can see that the exponential term is a quadratic form:

$$-\tfrac{1}{2}(\mathbf{x}-\boldsymbol{\mu})'\Sigma^{-1}(\mathbf{x}-\boldsymbol{\mu})$$

Keeping the probability constant corresponds to setting the exponential term equal to a constant and this generates values of $(\mathbf{x}-\boldsymbol{\mu})$ that lie on the surface of an ellipsoid. Hence the ellipsoidal shape of the surfaces of equal probability of the multivariate normal distribution is a consequence of the quadratic form used in its definition.

Transformations and quadratic forms

It is interesting to ask what happens to the matrix of a given quadratic form if we use a matrix to change **x** into a new vector **y**. That is if $\mathbf{y}=\mathbf{Bx}$ what is $\mathbf{x'Ax}$ expressed in terms of **y**? This is quite easy to answer:

$$\mathbf{x'Ax} = (\mathbf{B}^{-1}\mathbf{y})'\mathbf{ABy}$$
$$= \mathbf{y'B'}^{-1}\mathbf{ABy}$$

or putting this another way

if
$$\mathbf{x} = \mathbf{Ty}$$
$$\mathbf{x'Ax} = \mathbf{y'Qy}$$
where
$$\mathbf{Q} = \mathbf{T'AT}$$

Eigenvectors and eigenvalues

The subject of eigenvectors and eigenvalues is perhaps the most advanced part of matrix algebra that finds application within statistics, however as long as it is understood in terms of its relationship to quadratic forms it is relatively simple. The so called eigen problem is to find a vector **x** such that

$$\mathbf{Ax}=\lambda\mathbf{x}$$

where λ is a constant. In general **Ax** is a new vector **y** which will not be simply related to **x** and so the eigen problem is to find a special vector **x** such that **Ax** is a vector **y** that is simply a multiple of the original vector **x**. Such a vector **x** is called an eigenvector and the constant λ is called an eigenvalue. Of course there is always the possiblity that there are no vectors xthat satisfy the requirement. For the matrices used in statistics we have the rather remarkable result that not only do eigenvectors exist but there exists a complete set of n eigenvectors and their corresponding eigenvalues. If each of the eigenvectors is written as a column of an n by n matrix, **E** say, and the eigenvalues are written as the diagonal elements of a matrix **D**, we can write:

$$\mathbf{AE}=\mathbf{ED}$$

It is also possible to show that **E** is remarkable in that $\mathbf{E}^{-1}=\mathbf{E}'$ (such matrices are called orthogonal). Using this it is easy to show that:

$$\mathbf{E}'\mathbf{A}\mathbf{E}=\mathbf{D}$$

In other words **E** can be used to diagonalise the matrix **A**.

There are many uses of eigenvectors and eigenvalues in statistics but the most important results from the fact that if **E** is an eigenvector matrix derived from the covariance matrix **S** then the new variables **y**=**Ex** have a covariance matrix given by $\mathbf{E}'\mathbf{S}\mathbf{E}=\mathbf{D}$. That is the transformation **y**=**Ex** gives a set of uncorrelated variables. In fact this is nothing more than the principal components analysis described earlier.

A second important reason for being interested in eigenvectors and eigenvalues lies in their relationship to the quadratic form contained within the multivariate normal distribution. As already described the quadratic form:

$$-\tfrac{1}{2}(\mathbf{x} - \boldsymbol{\mu})\boldsymbol{\Sigma}^{-1}(\mathbf{x} - \boldsymbol{\mu})$$

describes elliptical surfaces (when set equal to a constant). It can be shown that the eigenvectors of Σ lie in the same directions as the semi-axes of the ellipsoids and the eigenvalues are proportional to the length of the corresponding semi-axes. In this sense a knowledge of the eigenvalues can tell you how elliptical the distribution is. It can also be seen as another way of deriving the principal component result in that the eigenvector corresponding to the largest eigenvalue is in the direction of maximum spread and so on.

Determinants and volumes

It is possible to define the determinant of a matrix without reference to eigenvalues but for statistical applications the determinant has a direct interpretation in terms of the eigenvalues. The determinant of a matrix **A** is denoted by $|\mathbf{A}|$ and it is equal to the product of the eigenvalues of **A**. If **A** is a covariance matrix then you should be able to see that $|\mathbf{A}|$ is proportional to the volume of the ellipsoid of spread that it describes. The reason is simply that each of the eigenvalues of the covariance matrix is proportional to the length of one of the semi-axes of the ellipsoid and multiplying them together gives something that is proportional to the volume of the ellipsoid. Determinants often crop up in multivariate statistics as a general measure of spread or dispersion.

Conclusion

Matrix theory is an extremely rich and fascinating area of applied mathematics. There is usually more than one way to derive or look at a result and this can at first be confusing. In multivariate statistics matrix theory is very important and if this appendix has given you an interest in the subject then any further time you spend studying it will be amply repaid in understanding the practical methods of multivariate statistics.

References

1. Searle, S. R. (1966), *Matrix Algebra for the Biological Sciences*: Wiley.

Appendix Two
A Data Generator

The following program will generate samples of data from specified normal distributions and store results in a disk file suitable for use with any of the other programs given in this book. The use of the program is straightforward in that it prompts for any information – means, covariances etc. – that it requires. It is capable of generating data from any number of groups with equal or different covariance matrices but it is important to notice that the data is a sample from a normal population with the specified parameters. That is the generated data may not have the specified means or covariances but will be a representative (random) sample from a population with the specified parameters. The only real problem facing the user is the task of specifying a covariance matrix. Not all symmetric matrices are possible covariance matrices and so it is possible to input values for the elements of the covariance matrix that will cause the program to fail.

```
  10 GOSUB 1000:REM GET PARAMETERS
  20 GOSUB 2000:REM GET MEANS/COVARIANCES
  30 GOSUB 7000:REM DECOMPOSE S
  40 GOSUB 9000:REM GENERATE DATA
  50 STOP
1000 PRINT "DATA GENERATOR"
1010 PRINT
1020 PRINT "FILE NAME ";
1030 INPUT F$
1040 GOSUB 8000:REM OPEN OUTPUT FILE
1050 PRINT "NUMBER OF VARIABLES=";
1060 INPUT N
1070 PRINT "NUMBER OF GROUPS=";
1080 INPUT G
1090 DIM M(G)
1095 M=0
1100 FOR I=1 TO G
1110 PRINT "NUMBER IN GROUP ";I;"=";
1120 INPUT M(I)
1125 M=M+M(I)
```

```
1130 NEXT I
1140 PRINT "EQUAL COVARIANCES (Y/N)";
1150 INPUT A$
1160 IF A$<>"Y" AND A$<>"N" THEN GOTO 1140
1170 DIM A(N,G),V(N,G*N),S(N,N),D(N),X(N)
1180 RETURN

2000 PRINT
2010 FOR K=1 TO G
2015 PRINT
2020 PRINT "MEANS FOR GROUP ";K
2030 FOR I=1 TO N
2040 PRINT "MEAN OF VARIABLE ";I;"=";
2050 INPUT A(I,K)
2060 NEXT I
2070 NEXT K
2080 PRINT
2090 PRINT
2100 IF A$="Y" THEN PRINT "COMMON ";
2110 PRINT "COVARIANCES"
2120 IF A$="Y" THEN GOSUB 3000:
     REM COMMON COVARIANCE
2130 IF A$="N" THEN GOSUB 4000:REM UNEQUAL
2140 RETURN

3000 FOR I=1 TO N
3010 FOR J=1 TO I
3020 PRINT "S(";I;",";J;")=";
3030 INPUT V(I,J)
3040 V(J,I)=V(I,J)
3050 NEXT J
3060 NEXT I
3070 FOR K=2 TO G
3080 FOR I=1 TO N
3090 FOR J=1 TO N
3100 V(I,J+N*(K-1))=V(I,J)
3110 NEXT J
3120 NEXT I
3130 NEXT K
3140 RETURN

4000 PRINT
4010 FOR K=1 TO G
4015 PRINT
4020 PRINT "COVARIANCE FOR GROUP ";K
4030 FOR I=1 TO N
4040 FOR J=1 TO I
4050 PRINT "S(";I;",";J;")=";
4060 INPUT V(I,J+N*(K-1))
4070 V(J,I+N*(K-1))=V(I,J+N*(K-1))
4080 NEXT J
4090 NEXT I
4100 NEXT K
```

Appendix Two: A Data Generator

```
4110 RETURN

5000 R=RND-6
5010 FOR L=1 TO 11
5020 R=R+RND
5030 NEXT L
5040 RETURN

6000 S(1,1)=SQR(S(1,1))
6010 FOR J=2 TO N
6020 S(1,J)=S(1,J)/S(1,1)
6030 NEXT J
6040 FOR I=2 TO N
6050 FOR K=1 TO I-1
6060 S(I,I)=S(I,I)-S(K,I)*S(K,I)
6070 NEXT K
6080 S(I,I)=SQR(S(I,I))
6085 IF I+1>N THEN GOTO 6150
6090 FOR J=I+1 TO N
6100 FOR K=1 TO I-1
6110 S(I,J)=S(I,J)-S(K,I)*S(K,J)
6120 NEXT K
6130 S(I,J)=S(I,J)/S(I,I)
6140 NEXT J
6150 NEXT I
6160 RETURN

7000 FOR L=1 TO G
7010 FOR I=1 TO N
7020 FOR J=1 TO N
7030 S(I,J)=V(I,J+N*(L-1))
7040 NEXT J
7050 NEXT I
7060 GOSUB 6000
7070 FOR I=1 TO N
7080 FOR J=1 TO N
7090 V(I,J+N*(L-1))=S(I,J)
7100 NEXT J
7110 NEXT I
7120 NEXT L
7130 RETURN

8000 OPEN "O",#1,F$
8010 RETURN

8100 PRINT#1,R
8110 RETURN

8200 CLOSE #1
8210 RETURN

9000 R=N:GOSUB 8100
9001 R=M:GOSUB 8100
```

```
9002 FOR K=1 TO G
9004 PRINT
9005 PRINT "GROUP ";K
9010 FOR J=1 TO M(K)
9015 PRINT "CASE ";J
9020 GOSUB 9500:REM GENERATE X
9030 FOR I=1 TO N
9040 PRINT "VARIABLE ";I;" =";X(I
9045 R=X(I):GOSUB 8100
9050 NEXT I
9070 NEXT J
9080 PRINT
9090 NEXT K
9100 GOSUB 8200
9110 RETURN

9500 FOR I=1 TO N
9510 GOSUB 5000
9520 D(I)=R
9530 NEXT I
9560 FOR I=1 TO N
9570 X(I)=A(I,K)
9580 FOR L=1 TO I
9590 X(I)=X(I)+D(L)*V(L,I+N*(K-1)
9600 NEXT L
9610 NEXT I
9620 RETURN
```

The method used by this program is based upon the fact that if Z is multivariate normal with mean zero and covariance matrix equal to the identity I then:

$$X = TZ + M$$

is multivariate normal with mean M and covariance matrix S given by:

$$S = T'T$$

Subroutines 1000, 2000, 3000 and 4000 are all responsible for reading in the parameters of the problem. Subroutine 5000 generates a normally distributed random variable with mean zero and unit variance by adding together a number of uniformly distributed random numbers. You may have to change the RND(0) statement in lines 5000 and 5020 to whatever function corresponds to the random number generator in the version of BASIC that you are using. Subroutine 6000 factors the matrix S into the product $T'T$ (T is stored back into the array S). Subroutine 7000 uses 6000 to perform this factorisation on each group covariance matrix stored in V even

Appendix Two: A Data Generator 205

if they are all identical – this is inefficient but simple. Subroutines 8000, 8100 and 8200 all deal with the file handling and hence they may have to be changed to work on another version of BASIC. Subroutine 8000 opens a file F$ for ouput, 8100 writes the contents of R to the file and 8200 closes the file. Finally subroutine 9000 writes the correct number of cases for each group to the file using subroutine 9500 to apply the transformation given above to the random variables generated by subroutine 5000.

Software availability

All of the programs in this book are available as part of the general and multivariate statistics package, SAM (Statistical Analysis for Microcomputers). As well as discriminant analysis, the package contains general descriptive statistics, non-parametric statistics, factor analysis, cluster analysis, regression, etc. It is available for a wide range of microcomputers and in many formats. For more information contact:

International Software (UK)
PO Box 160, Welwyn Garden City
Hertfordshire

Telephone: (07073) 26633

Appendix Three
Fisher's Iris Data

Iris Setosa

Sepal Length	Sepal Width	Petal Length	Petal Width
5.1	3.5	1.4	0.2
4.9	3.0	1.4	0.2
4.7	3.2	1.3	0.2
4.6	3.1	1.5	0.2
5.0	3.6	1.4	0.2
5.4	3.9	1.7	0.4
4.6	3.4	1.4	0.3
5.0	3.4	1.5	0.2
4.4	2.9	1.4	0.2
4.9	3.1	1.5	0.1
5.4	3.7	1.5	0.2
4.8	3.4	1.6	0.2
4.8	3.0	1.4	0.1
4.3	3.0	1.1	0.1
5.8	4.0	1.2	0.2
5.7	4.4	1.5	0.4
5.4	3.9	1.3	0.4
5.1	3.5	1.4	0.3
5.7	3.8	1.7	0.3
5.1	3.8	1.5	0.3
5.4	3.4	1.7	0.2
5.1	3.7	1.5	0.4
4.6	3.6	1.0	0.2
5.1	3.3	1.7	0.5
4.8	3.4	1.9	0.2
5.0	3.0	1.6	0.2
5.0	3.4	1.6	0.4
5.2	3.5	1.5	0.2
5.2	3.4	1.4	0.2
4.7	3.2	1.6	0.2
4.8	3.1	1.6	0.2

Sepal Length	Sepal Width	Petal Length	Petal Width
5.4	3.4	1.5	0.4
5.2	4.1	1.5	0.1
5.5	4.2	1.4	0.2
4.9	3.1	1.5	0.2
5.0	3.2	1.2	0.2
5.5	3.5	1.3	0.2
4.9	3.6	1.4	0.1
4.4	3.0	1.3	0.2
5.1	3.4	1.5	0.2
5.0	3.5	1.3	0.3
4.5	2.3	1.3	0.3
4.4	3.2	1.3	0.2
5.0	3.5	1.6	0.6
5.1	3.8	1.9	0.4
4.8	3.0	1.4	0.3
5.1	3.8	1.6	0.2
4.6	3.2	1.4	0.2
5.3	3.7	1.5	0.2
5.0	3.3	1.4	0.2

Iris Versicolor

Sepal Length	Sepal Width	Petal Length	Petal Width
7.0	3.2	4.7	1.4
6.4	3.2	4.5	1.5
6.9	3.1	4.9	1.5
5.5	2.3	4.0	1.3
6.5	2.8	4.6	1.5
5.7	2.8	4.5	1.3
6.3	3.3	4.7	1.6
4.9	2.4	3.3	1.0
6.6	2.9	4.6	1.3
5.2	2.7	3.9	1.4
5.0	2.0	3.5	1.0
5.9	3.0	4.2	1.5
6.0	2.2	4.0	1.0
6.1	2.9	4.7	1.4
5.6	2.9	3.6	1.3
6.7	3.1	4.5	1.4
4.6	3.0	4.5	1.5
5.8	2.7	4.1	1.0
6.2	2.2	4.5	1.5
5.6	2.5	3.9	1.1
5.9	3.2	4.8	1.8
6.1	2.8	4.0	1.3
6.3	2.5	4.9	1.5

6.1	2.8	4.7	1.2
6.4	2.9	4.3	1.3
6.6	3.0	4.9	1.4
6.8	2.8	4.8	1.4
6.7	3.0	5.0	1.7
6.0	2.9	4.5	1.5
5.7	2.6	3.5	1.0
5.5	2.4	3.8	1.1
5.5	2.4	3.7	1.0
5.8	2.7	3.9	1.2
6.0	2.7	5.1	1.6
5.4	3.0	4.5	1.5
6.0	3.4	4.5	1.6
6.7	3.1	4.7	1.5
6.3	2.3	4.4	1.3
5.6	3.0	4.1	1.3
5.5	2.5	4.0	1.3
5.5	2.6	4.4	1.2
6.1	3.0	4.6	1.4
5.8	2.6	4.0	1.2
5.0	2.3	3.3	1.0
5.6	2.7	4.2	1.3
5.7	3.0	4.2	1.2
5.7	2.9	4.2	1.3
6.2	2.9	4.3	1.3
5.1	2.5	3.0	1.1
5.7	2.8	4.1	1.3

Iris Virginica

Sepal Length	Sepal Width	Petal Length	Petal Width
6.3	3.3	6.0	2.5
5.8	2.7	5.1	1.9
7.1	3.0	5.9	2.1
6.3	2.9	5.6	1.8
6.5	3.0	5.8	2.2
7.6	3.0	6.6	2.1
4.9	2.5	4.5	1.7
7.3	2.9	6.3	1.8
6.7	2.5	5.8	1.8
7.2	3.6	6.1	2.5
6.5	3.2	5.1	2.0
6.4	2.7	5.3	1.9
6.8	3.0	5.5	2.1
5.7	2.5	5.0	2.0
5.8	2.8	5.1	2.4
6.4	3.2	5.3	2.3

6.5	3.0	5.5	1.8
7.7	3.8	6.7	2.2
7.7	2.6	6.9	2.3
6.0	2.2	5.0	1.5
6.9	3.2	5.7	2.3
5.6	2.8	4.9	2.0
7.7	2.8	6.7	2.0
6.3	2.7	4.9	1.8
6.7	3.3	5.7	2.1
7.2	3.2	6.0	1.8
6.2	2.8	4.8	1.8
6.1	3.0	4.9	1.8
6.4	2.8	5.6	2.1
7.2	3.0	5.8	1.6
7.4	2.8	6.1	1.9
7.9	3.8	6.4	2.0
6.4	2.8	5.6	2.2
6.3	2.8	5.1	1.5
6.1	2.6	5.6	1.4
7.7	3.0	6.1	2.3
6.3	3.4	5.6	2.4
6.4	3.1	5.5	1.8
6.0	3.0	4.8	1.8
6.9	3.1	5.4	2.1
6.7	3.1	5.6	2.4
6.9	3.1	5.1	2.3
5.8	2.7	5.1	1.9
6.8	3.2	5.9	2.3
6.7	3.3	5.7	2.5
6.7	3.0	5.2	2.3
6.3	2.5	5.0	1.9
6.5	3.0	5.2	2.0
6.2	3.4	5.4	2.3
5.0	3.0	5.1	1.8

Index

AI, 174, 182
ANOVA 4

Bayes' rule, 9
bias, 58, 76
binary variables, 158
bivariate normal, 16

canonical analysis, 96
categorical variables, 149
classification table, 152
cluster analysis, 3
confusion matrices, 82
contingency table, 150
correlation, 16
cost, 63
covariance matrix, 19, 38

data entry, 30
discriminant analysis, 2
discriminant function, 21, 25, 29
division of the sample space, 12

eigenvalue, 100
eigenvector, 100
error rates, 75
expert system, 182

feature selection, 74, 127, 179
fixed error rate, 63

histogram method, 162

iris data, 52, 112, 145, 171, 206

kernal method, 162

linear Bayes' rule, 178
linear discriminant function, 25, 56, 61
linear discriminant program, 33
logistic model, 157

MANOVA, 4, 118
measurement, 180
minimax error, 63
missing values, 72
multivariate normal, 15

nearest means, 177
nearest neighbour, 166, 178
nearest prototype, 178
non-parametric methods, 149, 161
normal form of Bayes' rule, 20

outliers, 71

perceptron, 177
probabilities of classification, 68
probability, 8

quadratic discriminant function, 21, 61
quadratic discriminant program, 43

reject option, 70

sampling models, 155
semi-Bayesian estimates, 67
stepwise discrimination, 127
structural models, 154
sweep operators, 40, 142

TEC, 8

two group case, 28

Wilks' lambda, 118, 129